Barbara Hamm

Let's Discover Computers!

Ready-to-Use Computer Discovery Lessons & Activities for Grades K-3

THE CENTER FOR APPLIED RESEARCH IN EDUCATION
West Nyack, New York 10995

Dedication

This book is dedicated to Ryan, Bridget, and all children who enjoy hearing a good story—even if they learn something from it.

Library of Congress Cataloging-in-Publication Data

Hamm, Barbara R.
Let's Discover Computers! / Barbara Hamm.
p. cm.
ISBN 0-87628-271-0 (paper). —ISBN 0-87628-520-5 (spiral)
1. Computers—Juvenile literature. I. Title.
QA76.23.H35 1997
372.3`4044—dc21 97-7188
CIP

Printed in the United States of America

10 9 8 7 6 5 4 3 2 1

ISBN 0-87628-271-0 (Paper) ISBN 0-87628-520-5 (Spiral)

Illustrations by Barbara Hamm

THE CENTER FOR APPLIED RESEARCH IN EDUCATION
West Nyack, NY 10994
A Simon & Schuster Company

On the World Wide Web at http://www.phdirect.com

Prentice Hall International (UK) Limited, *London*
Prentice Hall of Australia Pty. Limited, *Sydney*
Prentice Hall Canada, Inc., *Toronto*
Prentice Hall Hispanoamericana, S.A., *Mexico*
Prentice Hall of India Private Limited, *New Delhi*
Prentice Hall of Japan, Inc., *Tokyo*
Simon & Schuster Asia Pte. Ltd., *Singapore*
Editora Prentice Hall do Brasil, Ltda., *Rio de Janeiro*

About This Resource

Let's Discover Computers! is intended primarily to teach computer understanding in a concise, straightforward manner, using techniques children like — storytelling, games, and activities. It covers the basic literacy topic, plus correct and responsible care in using a computer.

The use of the storytelling style will help you teach a difficult concept to very young children. The short units of instruction, the numerous illustrations, the abundant review questions, and the games and activities form a complete learning experience — easy for you to use and enjoyable for your students. Students are able to retain information through the short learning modules. Retention and reinforcement are further enhanced by the variety of end-of-story questions, games, and activities. The lessons are brief to allow adequate time for hands-on computer experiences using software already available in the classroom.

Many different software titles may be used with each lesson; there is no specific list of titles needed. Use whatever programs you have in your classroom. (**Note:** Your hardware may differ somewhat, but you can adapt the lessons for use with the hardware and software available to you.)

The stories, games, activities, and work sheets in *Let's Discover Computers!* are designed for use with K - 3 students. The object is for students to gain knowledge about computer basics. They do not need prior knowledge of computers, and this resource is not specific to any particular brand of computer. The materials are flexible and may be modified to fit your particular schedule and instructional needs.

Each lesson begins with a page to you, the teacher, and offers an outline designed to help you know at a glance the emphasis for each story. The lesson plan also offers objectives, new words, and suggested guided activities. A glossary at the end of the book gives short, factual definitions of words in each lesson, and includes the number of the lesson in which the word is found. The questions at the end of each story are short and intended to quickly review the objectives of the lesson. The activities are designed to be fun yet educational. The students may request enjoyable games again and again, and they can play them as many times as your schedule allows.

The collection of thirty-eight stories in *Let's Discover Computers!* was selected for the usual forty-week school year. Students may come to class one day a week, or your school may teach computer classes in an eight-to-ten-week semester block. In either case, the number provides enough material for your curriculum. You can cover a story, ask the follow-up questions, do an off-computer activity, and then use related software for closure.

In Ryan's journey through Computer Land, Ryan represents all boys and girls in the class, and the parts of the computer are personified. Ryan asks questions to learn how the computer works and what he must do to be successful in computer class. Ms. Barbara, the teacher, helps Ryan have fun using the computer. Ryan has questions that all children have about computers, and they are answered in a friendly, nonthreatening manner. The computer parts have such problems as not feeling appreciated, running away, getting sick, and having contests to see who is the best. Each story has a problem to be solved and an outcome, following the childrens' literature format, while teaching a computer concept. The stories are not specific to either IBM or Apple computers, but are meant to give general knowledge about chips, disks, and other computer parts and how they work. Illustrations are simple, but interesting enough to hold a student's attention while the lesson is being taught. (Lessons are geared to the use of overhead transparencies.) The off-computer activities at the end of each story include board games and worksheets that reinforce the story lesson.

Students in primary grades have very short attention spans, and you'll find that the combination of stories, questions, off-computer activities, and software activities in *Let's Discover Computers!* will fill a normal forty-five-minute class period very well.

Barbara Hamm

About the Author

Barbara Hamm is a teacher, wife, mother, and grandmother. The boy in the stories named Ryan is actually named after her grandson, Ryan. She has been teaching in both public and parochial schools for over twenty years. Half of her years in teaching have been devoted to elementary school computer education. Her professional credentials include a life certificate in education, a Master's Degree in Secondary Education-Technology Core, and Librarian and Instructional Design Certification. She has been nominated for Who's Who Among America's Teachers, 1994, and received the MO-CAPE Educator of Achievement Award, 1996, and the Emerson Electric Excellence in Teaching Award.

When Barbara was given the responsibility for teaching computer education at Incarnate Word Elementary School in Chesterfield, Missouri, she used her years of teaching experience and advanced education to develop the computer curriculum that she uses at her school. In developing the curriculum for the primary grades, she found that a void exists in computer literacy materials. The more she searched, the more she realized that someone needed to develop materials to educate primary grade students about computers. The idea emerged that storytelling might be the best way to maintain student interest while teaching computer basics.

Ms. Barbara in the stories is named after herself. She feels that Ryan, Ms. Barbara, and all of the computer parts will teach young students as well as their parents computer basics. These stories have been tested by Barbara in her own classroom and have been field tested to maintain student interest while expanding their computer knowledge and understanding.

Acknowledgments

Special thanks to Connie Kallback and Evan Holstrom for their expertise in reviewing and shaping this project. Their keen eyes, insight, and guidance made it a reality.

Thanks, also, to my husband, Edward Hamm; my daughter, Gina Tierney; my son-in-law, Dan Tierney; my mother, Virginia Swiercz; and all family members who give me moral support, enthusiasm, and devotion in everything I do.

To my students, who make teaching an enjoyable and memorable experience, I offer my thanks.

Contents

---

[1] (**Note:** The "To the Teacher" page at the beginning of each lesson offers you the following outline: I. Objectives; II. Instructional Input and Learning Activities; III. Check for Understanding; IV. Guided Practice; V. Independent Practice and Application Using the Computer.

Section 1

Meeting the Computer

LESSON 1-1 RYAN MEETS THE COMPUTER

To the Teacher

Ryan is in a new school. He passes by the computer room door and is drawn in by voices. The voices are the computer parts talking. The computer parts give a general introduction of themselves and say that computer class is going to be fun.

New words in this lesson:	monitor	computer	mouse
	software	electricity	CPU
	disk drive	keyboard	microwave

I. Objectives

- Recognize that computers are everywhere.
- Realize that computers need electricity and software to operate.
- Understand that humans and computers need to work together.

II. Instructional Input and Learning Activities

- Make overhead transparencies for each page of the story.
- Place the transparency on the stage of the overhead projector and cover the portion of the page you are not using.
- Read the story to the children.

III. Check for Understanding

Use the review questions at the end of the story to test for story comprehension. Cover the questions as you read the last page of the story. Answers are in parentheses.

IV. Guided Practice

Distribute the "Find the Hidden Computers" work sheet. This activity helps students understand that computers are everywhere. Duplicate the work sheet for students or make an overhead transparency. Students are instructed to circle the pictures of objects that use computers in the playroom. The answer sheet follows the work sheet.

V. Independent Practice and Application Using the Computer

Play a software game that reinforces the lesson. Any game may be repeated. You may review words that need further reinforcement in the New Words segment of any lesson plan. The Glossary at the end of the book will also help with frequently used terms.

LESSON 1-1 RYAN MEETS THE COMPUTER

Ryan was walking down the hall of his new school. He was going to his classroom when he heard loud voices. He looked around but he didn't see anyone.

"What is going on?" he said.

The voices got louder and louder. He wanted to know what they were saying. The voices were coming from the computer room. He had never been in this room before.

When he opened the door he didn't see anyone.

"Wow! Is anyone here?" he asked.

"We're here," the voices said.

"Who are you? Where are you?" Ryan asked.

"Right under your nose," said a bright, happy voice.

Ryan looked down and saw a big smile. The big smile was on something that looked like his television at home, but it wasn't a television.

"Hi," said the smile. "I haven't seen you here before."

Ryan took a step backward. "Who are you?" he asked.

The smile said, "My name is Monty — Monty Monitor. I look like a television, but I'm really part of a computer."

"What is a computer?" asked Ryan.

Just then a very loud voice said, "A computer is a special machine that can do many things like play games, do arithmetic, practice spelling, and teach."

"Enough already," a squeaky voice interrupted.

"Who are you?"

"I'm Mo — Mo Mouse — and this is Kiki Keyboard. You've been talking to Computer Brain, CPU for short. He knows everything. Well, he thinks he knows everything, but he really needs someone like you or he can't do a thing.

You will press Kiki's keys or point, click, and drag with me to do hundreds of different things like playing games, or drawing pictures."

"He also needs electricity and software," said Monty.

Ryan said, “I know what electricity is. It makes my television and train set work. But what is software?”

“Software — why talk about that when you can talk about me?” said CPU. “People are always using computers — even if they don’t know it.”

"There are computers in your dad's car, your mom's microwave oven, and your watch. They don't all look the same, but they are computers. I am the most important part."

"No, you are not," said Monty.

Dizzy Disk Drive spoke up. "We all have to work together. We need software, too."

Ryan picked up a disk with a label that said, "Learn About Animals."

"This looks like fun," Ryan said.

The Parts all said, "We need you as part of our team. Let's play games, do arithmetic, and have fun."

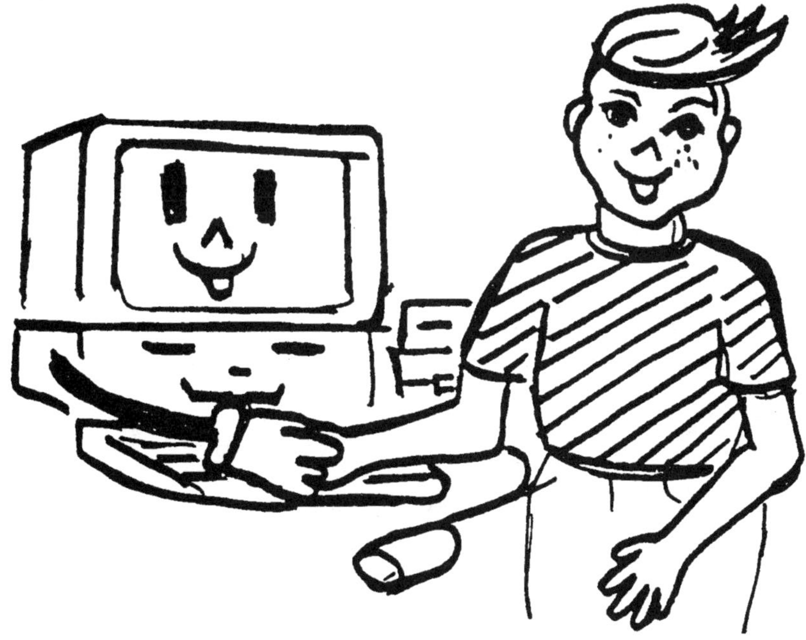

"I'm looking forward to being in computer class and learning how we all work together to help me learn and have fun," said Ryan. "See you tomorrow."

Lesson 1-1 Questions

1. Who had the smiling face? (Monty Monitor)
2. Why do we need Monty Monitor? (to see what the computer is doing)
3. What does Monty Monitor look like? (a television set)
4. Who thought he knew everything? (CPU — Computer Brain)
5. What can a computer do? (play games, do arithmetic, practice spelling, and teach)
6. Where are computers? (everywhere)
7. What does a computer need? (electricity and software)
8. What does Ryan use electricity for at home? (his television and train set)
9. Who spins the disks (software)? (Dizzy Disk Drive)
10. How will Ryan and you use Kiki Keyboard and Mo Mouse? (press the keys on Kiki and point, click, and drag with Mo Mouse)

Name ________________________________

1-1 Find the Hidden Computers

I-1 Find the Hidden Computers (Answers)

LESSON 1-2 RYAN MEETS THE RULES

To the Teacher

Ryan is going to computer class but can't go in until "Rules" tells Ryan what will be expected of him. The "Rules" are (1) following directions, (2) listening to the teacher, and (3) having fun.

New words in this lesson: There are no new words.

I. Objectives

- List the rules needed to make using computers fun.
- Recognize that teachers help students learn how to use computers.

II. Instructional Input and Learning Activities

- Make overhead transparencies for each page of the story.
- Place the transparency on the stage of the overhead projector and cover the portion of the page you are not using.
- Read the story to the children.

III. Check for Understanding

Use the review questions at the end of the story to test for story comprehension. Cover the questions as you read the last page of the story. Answers are in parentheses.

IV. Guided Practice

The "Rules Says" game is played with Simon Says rules. This game teaches computer room rules. Emphasize safe and respectful handling of computers.

Materials - list of rules you want students to know and follow

Example: Rules Says touch your monitor. (Students should touch monitor.)
Rules Says light touch on keyboard. (Students should lightly touch keyboard.)
Run to the teacher's desk. (Students should not move.)

If the students follow "Rules Says," they stay as participants in the game. If they do the wrong thing (the directions are not preceded by the words "Rules Says") they take a seat out of the game area. The last youngsters still following "Rules Says" are the winners.

V. Independent Practice and Application Using the Computer

Play a software game that reinforces the lesson.

LESSON 1-2 RYAN MEETS THE RULES

Ryan was ready to start school. He knew he was going to learn how to read, write, and do arithmetic. He also knew he was going to learn how to use a computer, and how to have fun using a computer.

Ryan walked down the hall to the computer room. He was just about to go in when right in front of him was a big sign that said “RULES.”

Rules said, “You can’t come in until you and I get to know each other.”

Ryan said, “What is there to know?”

“There are many things,” said Rules.

“Like what?” asked Ryan.

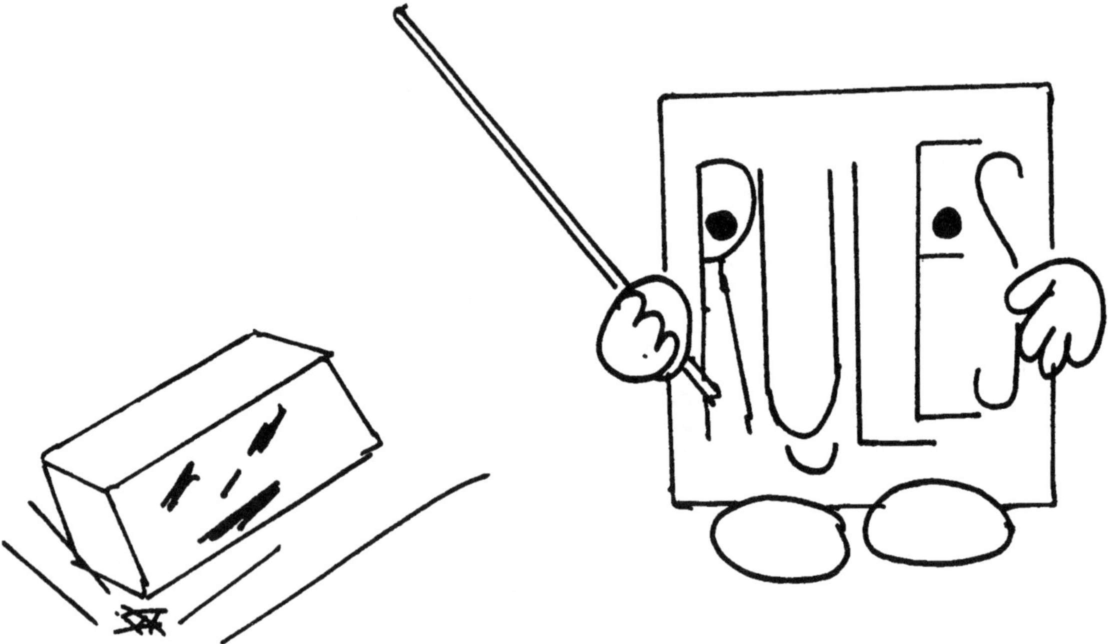

Rules took out a big pointer so he could point to each rule. He said, “Rule Number One: Always walk in the computer room. No silly business.”

“That sounds like an OK rule,” said Ryan. “I know there are many computers and I have to be careful so they do not fall and get hurt — and so they don't fall on me and hurt me.”

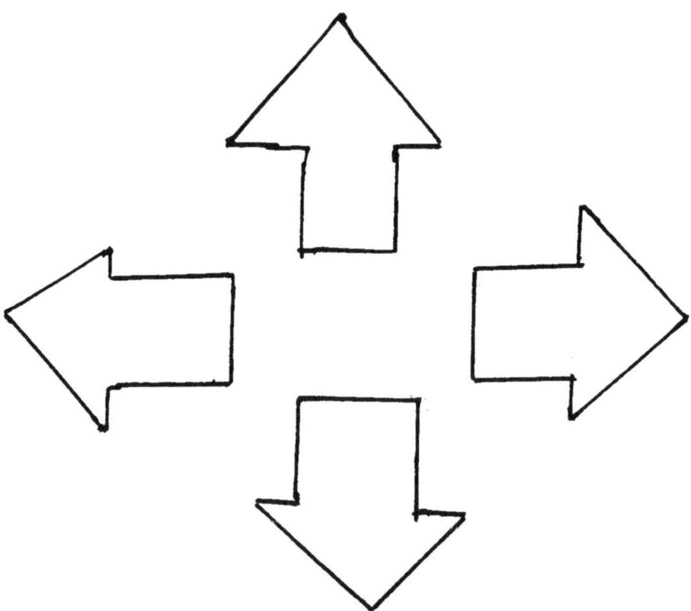

“Very good,” said Rules. “Rule Number Two: Follow Directions and listen carefully to everything the teacher says.”

“Easy, I can do that,” said Ryan.

"Rule Number Three: Have fun," said Rules.

"Is that all I have to do? Piece of cake," said Ryan. "It was a pleasure meeting you. I'm ready."

"Not so fast," said Rules. "Sometimes little boys and girls say they know the rules and then they forget."

"I won't," said Ryan.

"Let me tell you a story," said Rules.

"Good," said Ryan. "I like stories."

Once upon a time there was a little computer. He wanted to have many friends and he put a sign on himself. The sign said, "Have fun."

First a little turtle came. He had muddy feet. He tried to have fun, but the keys became covered in mud, and he went away.

Then a rabbit came along. He read the sign. He couldn't see the keys. He jumped up and down on every key, but nothing happened, so he went away.

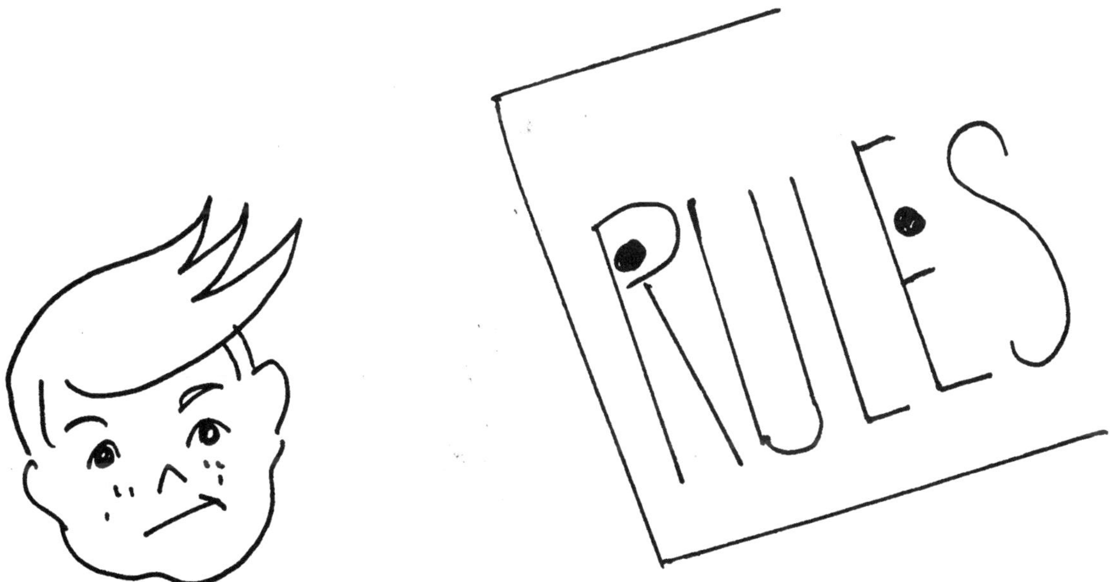

"What is the point of this story?" asked Ryan. "Those animals weren't very nice to that computer."

"That is the point," said Rules. "You must take care of your computer if you want to have fun."

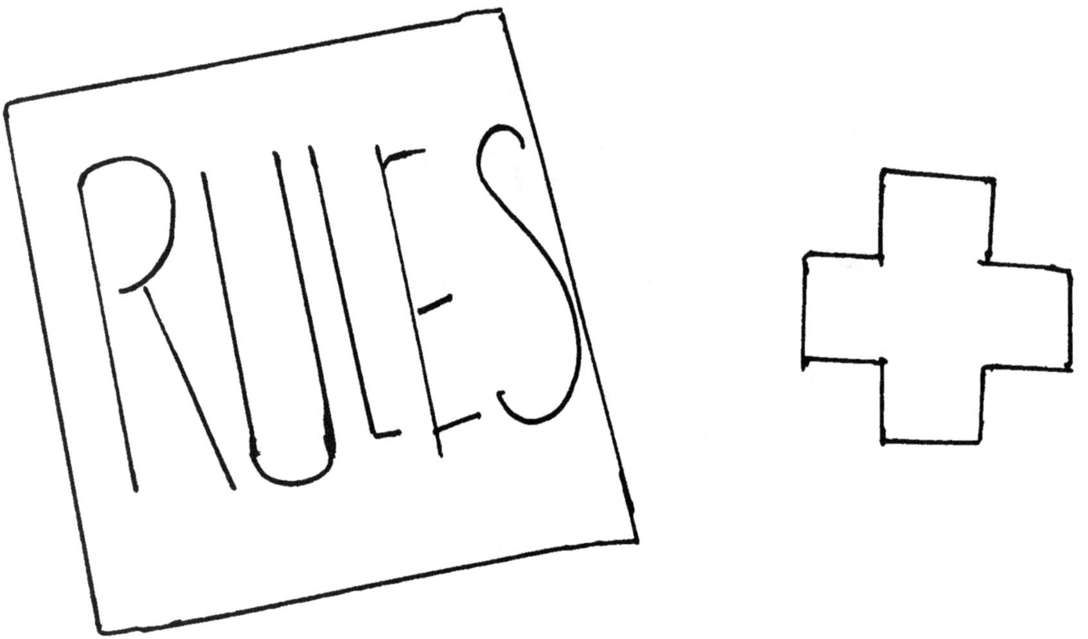

"It isn't enough to have a sign," said Ryan. "You need someone to help you."

"That is right," said Rules. "The most important rule is to always listen to your teacher and do what the teacher tells you. The teacher will teach you about special keys, like Delete and Return. Your teacher will teach you not to touch your computer while the red light is on. Your teacher is very important."

"I know," said Ryan. "My teacher will help me have fun."
"Very good," said Rules. "It is time for you to come in and have fun."
And Ryan followed the RULES.

Lesson 1-2 Questions

1. Why do we need rules? (to know what to do and how to do it)
2. Why should we walk in the computer room? (safety for the computer and you)
3. Why do we follow directions? (to keep things working correctly)
4. Who forgets rules? (We all do.)
5. Why are the rules printed on paper and hung up in the room? (to remind us of the rules)
6. What did the sign on the little computer in the story say? (have fun)
7. What would mud and dirt do to computer keys? (keep us from seeing the letters on the keys; slow the keys down or make them not work at all)
8. What would hard hitting or pushing on the keys do? (break them)

9./10. What are the two most important rules? (1. Listen to your teacher. 2. Use your computer with respect.)

I-2 Rules

Walk

Listen

Follow Directions

HANDS

Clean

Light Touch

On Own Computer

GOLDEN RULE

Be Good to Each Other

LESSON 1-3 LOOK AT ME

To the Teacher

Computer is looking at himself in four mirrors. He is surprised to see his reflections are different in each mirror. In one mirror he is tall and slender — a tower case. In another the disk drives and CPU are in a single case, side by side. In a third, the CPU is alone, with the disk drives on the side, and in the fourth, he is very small with the monitor, disk drives, keyboard, and mouse all together. He is small enough to be carried around like a notebook. Even though the outside cases are different the insides still work the same. The story explains early computers and the need for different styles of computer cases. Even though computers can look different, just as people can look different, we are all the same on the inside. We can learn and have fun with computers.

New words in this lesson: tower notebook chips

I. Objectives

- Identify the different styles of computer cases.
- Understand that even though the cases look different on the outside, they still work basically the same way.
- Realize that computers have changed through the years and new, smaller, and better computers are yet to come. Perceive that change is good.

II. Instructional Input and Learning Activities

- Make overhead transparencies for each page of the story.
- Place the transparency on the stage of the overhead projector and cover the portion of the page you are not using.
- Read the story to the children.

III. Check for Understanding

Use the review questions at the end of the story to test for story comprehension. Cover the questions as you read the last page of the story. Answers are in parentheses.

IV. Guided Practice

"Concentrate-O" teaches students to concentrate and develop memory skills. Divide students into teams and show a picture on the overhead projector for a short time (20 seconds). The students list the items they can remember. The team with the most remembered items is the winner. Pictures may be transparency copies of textbook pictures, prints, old masters, or advertisements; they should have many details or activities in them so children will have a long list.

V. Independent Practice and Application Using the Computer

Play a software game that reinforces the lesson.

LESSON 1-3 LOOK AT ME

One day Computer was walking by four mirrors. He enjoyed looking at himself. He stopped to admire himself every moment he could. Today he was surprised because none of the mirrors looked exactly like him.

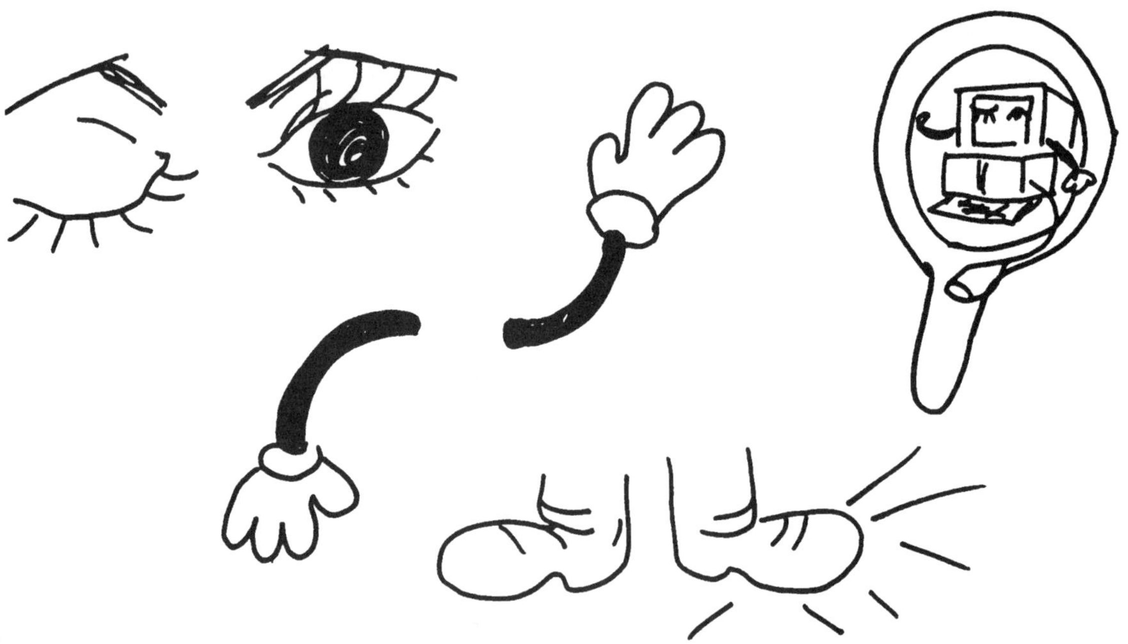

He waved his arms, tapped his foot, blinked, and watched the mirrors to see if the computers would wave, tap, and blink also. They sure did. That really was Computer in the mirror!

In one mirror Computer was tall and slender on top of Dizzy Disk Drive. He looked like a princess-and-dragon tower.

In the second mirror he was a big rectangular-shaped box, side by side with Dizzy Disk Drive.

In the third mirror Computer and Dizzy Disk Drive were separated into two different pieces.

In the fourth mirror Computer looked like a notebook, folding and opening. All the parts were squeezed together. You could barely see Dizzy Disk Drive and Mo Mouse.

"Could that be me?" he asked. "Is this a dream? I look very different but I still feel the same."

"I have changed through the years. I was as big as a room and very hot a long time ago. Now, I have chips and I can be very small. I can be carried like a notebook. I am a "cool dude," Computer bragged.

Some people like to take computers wherever they go. Some people have computers sitting on a table or desk in their home, school, office, library, or store.

Computer smiled. "I am still me. People need computers. Computers are fun. Computers work for people. Computers are everywhere."

Computer turned around and around as he admired himself. "What I look like is not important. I can be short or tall, fat or small. I still am GREAT."

Computers can look different; that is what makes them so special. Your computer can be a tower, or a side-by-side connected to Dizzy Disk Drive, or separate parts, or a compact go-anywhere computer, and the rules are still the same.

Computers do what YOU tell them to do. Computers are here to help you learn.

Computers can look different, just as you can look different. Don't worry about the outside. Learn that we are all here to work together and have fun.

Look at me, and look at you. We are different, but we are all the same. WE are people. WE want to have fun. WE want to learn about COMPUTERS.

Lesson 1-3 Questions

1. Do all computers look alike? (no)
2. Are all computers the same size? (no)
3. What is a computer with a tall, slender case called? (tower)
4. Do all computers stay in one place to work? (no)
5. What do the traveling computers look like? (notebooks)
6. Are the basic rules the same for all computers? (yes)
7. Do computers do what they want to do? (No, humans tell them what to do.)
8. What invention has made computers become smaller? (chips)
9. Where are computers? (everywhere)
10. Why do we have computers? (to save us work, have fun, save time and energy, learn)

LESSON 1-4 CAN DO

To the Teacher

Ryan and CPU (better known as Computer Brain) have a contest to see who can do the most. CPU is surprised to know that even though he does thousands of jobs, he still only follows directions and needs Ryan. That means they are both winners, because neither one would like to be without the other.

New words in this lesson:	hard drive	librarian
	supermarket checker	memory
		program

I. Objectives

- List the advantages of computers.
- Understand that computers do jobs to make life easier.

II. Instructional Input and Learning Activities

- Make overhead transparencies for each page of the story.
- Place the transparency on the stage of the overhead projector and cover the portion of the page you are not using.
- Read the story to the children.

III. Check for Understanding

Use the review questions at the end of the story to test for story comprehension. Cover the questions as you read the last page of the story. Answers are in parentheses.

IV. Guided Practice

The "Who Can Do It?" work sheet compares tasks that can be done by a computer with those that a human can do. The student determines who would do the job better. Duplicate the work sheet for students or make an overhead transparency. Have the students place a check in the "Ryan" column to indicate those tasks that can be done better by humans, and in the "CPU" column to indicate tasks that can be done better by computers. The answer sheet follows the work sheet.

V. Independent Practice and Application Using the Computer

Play a software game that reinforces the lesson.

LESSON 1-4 CAN DO

One day Computer Brain, better known as CPU, was sitting around feeling pretty happy with himself. All the other parts of the computer were looking at him and shaking their heads.

"He sure is bragging," they all said. "What can we do to make him stop thinking he is better than a human?"

Ryan heard the computer parts talking and said, "We can make a list of the things I can do and the things CPU can do."

"That sounds like a good idea," said all the parts. "Let's make a list."

It didn't take long for CPU to be ready with his bragging list. After all, he really did think he could do more than any human.

CPU said, "Good. I'll go first. I can add hundreds of numbers in a few seconds. Can you?"

Ryan said, "No."

Computer Brain, CPU, thought it would be easy to win the contest. He said, "I can print my name 500 times in less than a minute. Can you?"

"No," said Ryan.

CPU said, "I can correct your spelling mistakes in the letters you write."

"That is very helpful," said Ryan.

CPU said, “I don’t make mistakes.”

“That is true, too,” said Ryan. “But. . .”

“But what?” said CPU. “I’m better than you.”

Ryan said, “No. No you are not. All computers do is follow directions. You do what humans tell you to do.”

CPU looked surprised. No one had talked to him like this before.

“It is true you are very fast, never get tired or bored, and you don’t make mistakes, but. . .”

“But,” said CPU.

“But you need programs to do everything. Sometimes programs are already on your hard drive, but anything new for you to do has to be added to your memory,” said Ryan. “I can think for myself. I like to eat good food. I have an imagination. I can laugh at a good joke. I can move around. You can’t do that,” said Ryan.

"Well, who wins the contest?" asked the parts.

"We both do," said Ryan.

"CPU does the jobs that are boring. I don't like to do the same thing over and over again, and Computer Brain doesn't mind. And he can do them VERY FAST."

"He can do many different kinds of jobs, like librarian, supermarket checker, automatic bank teller, game player, clock, and so on, and make those easier and faster for humans. He can do all these things, but first of all a human has to tell him how to do them."

CPU said, "You know, you wouldn't want NOT to have me around. I do make life a lot easier for you and a lot more fun, especially with my games."

CPU looked at the parts. "Everyone needs me. I am everywhere. I am in your television, your car, your watch, your. . ."

"Okay, okay. We all see that you are as good as you think you are. But you are also only as good as the human who helps you," said the parts.

Computer Brain and Ryan shook hands. They were both winners. Neither one wanted to be without the other. Computers are everywhere. Computers will always do what people tell them to do. Computers are here to help you.

Lesson 1-4 Questions

1. What is another name for computer Brain? (CPU)
2. What is the only thing computers can do? (follow directions)
3. Do computers get tired of doing the same thing over and over again? (no)
4. Do computers work fast? (yes)
5. Does a computer make mistakes? (no)
6. Can a computer think for itself? (no)
7. Are all the programs you will ever want on the hard drive of the computer? (no)
8. Can computers do what they want and take over the world? (no)
9. Where are computers? (everywhere)
10. Who is helped by computers? (everyone)

Name ______________________________

1-4 Who Can Do It?

Put a check ✔

Ryan	Computer Brain	
		I can draw.
		I can count. •1 •2 •3
		I can eat.
		I can add. $1 + 1 = 2$
		I can swim.
		I can read words.
		I can think for myself.
		I can only follow directions.
		I can write my name 5000 times in one minute. Name Name Name Name
		I can remember everything.
		I can think of a new idea.
		I never forget anything.
		I never make a mistake.
		I don't get tired.
		I am a machine.
		I feel happy.

Who Can Do It? (Answers)

Put a check ✓

Ryan	Computer Brain	
✓	✓	I can draw.
✓	✓	I can count. •1 •2 •3
✓		I can eat.
✓	✓	I can add.
✓		I can swim.
✓	✓	I can read words.
✓		I can think for myself.
	✓	I can only follow directions.
	✓	I can write my name 5000 times in one minute. Name Name Name Name
	✓	I can remember everything.
✓		I can think of a new idea.
	✓	I never forget anything.
	✓	I never make a mistake.
	✓	I don't get tired.
	✓	I am a machine.
✓		I feel happy.

LESSON 1-5 CURSOR–WHERE AM I?

To the Teacher

Students learn that computers are not magic; they are machines. They need electricity, and will wait forever until you are ready. Cursor is introduced as a helper to let students know where they are. Students and Cursor make up a team working together through Kiki Keyboard and Mo Mouse.

New words in this lesson: cursor highlighted maze

I. Objective

- Describe the many different appearances of the cursor.

II. Instructional Input and Learning Activities

- Make overhead transparencies for each page of the story.
- Place the transparency on the stage of the overhead projector and cover the portion of the page you are not using.
- Read the story to the children.

III. Check for Understanding

Use the review questions at the end of the story to test for story comprehension. Cover the questions as you read the last page of the story. Answers are in parentheses.

IV. Guided Practice

The "Mo Mouse Meets Kiki Keyboard" maze is used to emphasize to the students that the keyboard and mouse are connected, and that they are interchangeable.

Materials - maze work sheet, pencil or crayon

Duplicate the maze work sheet for each student. Instruct them to use a pencil or crayon to draw a line from the picture of Mo Mouse at the top to the picture of Kiki Keyboard at the bottom of the maze. (They must not cross any lines.) The answer sheet follows the work sheet.

V. Independent Practice and Application Using the Computer

Play a software game that reinforces the lesson.

LESSON 1-5 CURSOR – WHERE AM I?

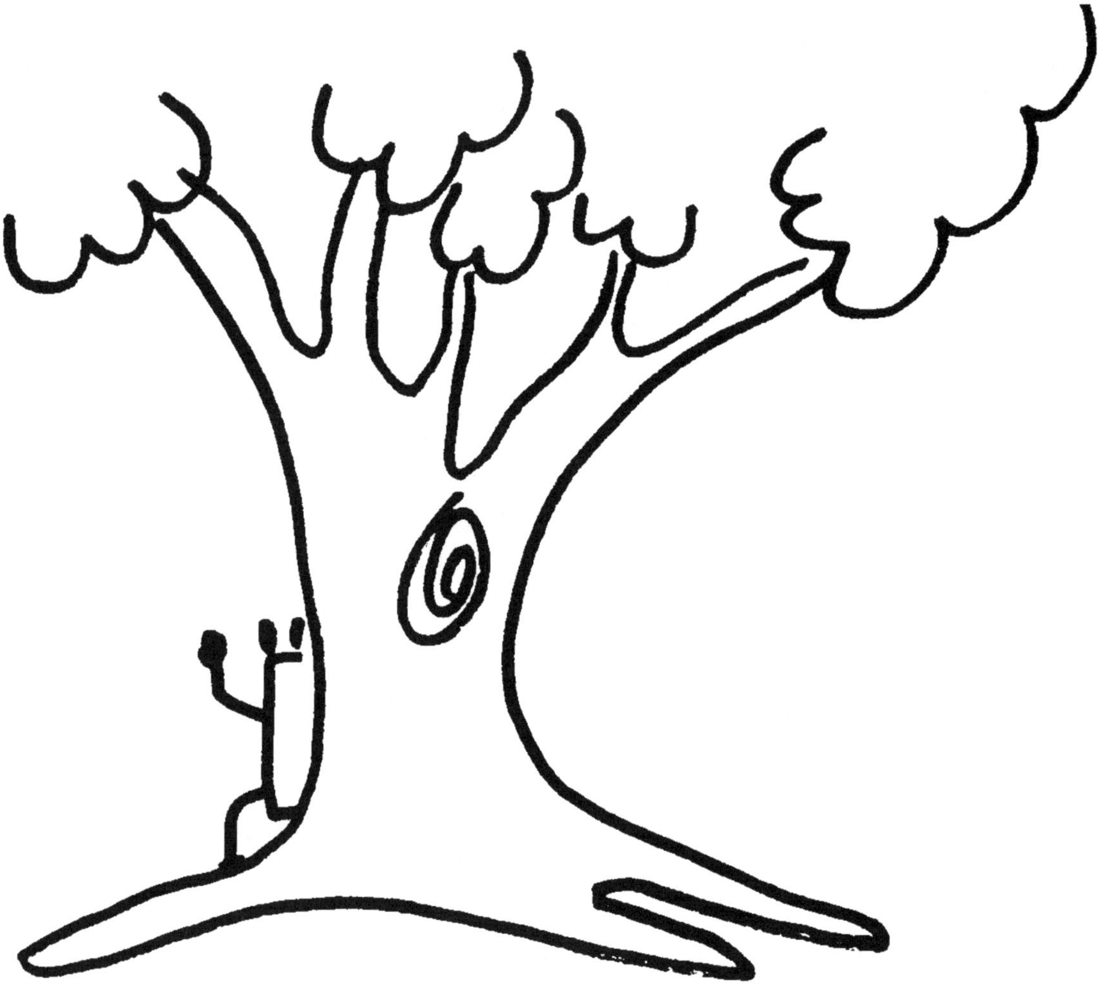

Do you like playing hide and seek? Cursor does. It is fun to trick people so they think you have disappeared. Everyone wants to hide. When you are It, you want to be able to find the others quickly.

In Computer Land you are always It. The computer will never be looking for you.

You will press the keys on Kiki Keyboard.

You will point, click, and drag Mo Mouse. You will look at Monty Monitor's face and find where you are with Cursor.

Cursor can change how he looks depending on the job he is doing. You must find him because that is where you are. Look for a blinking square or a highlighted box.

Of course, you know where you are; you are sitting in a chair in front of your computer. But you also want to know where you are in your computer game. It's like playing Hide and Seek, or finding your way through a maze.

You can't be magic and get really tiny and walk around in the screen of your monitor like Cursor because computers are not magic. They are machines. Machines need electricity, not fairy dust. Computers need Cursor to blink on and off and say, "Here you are."

Computer will wait forever. Take your time. Find yourself with Cursor.

Cursor is connected to you — not by strings or a leash, but through Kiki Keyboard and Mo Mouse.

Cursor doesn't leave a trail or footprints. He is like a map that leads you to a treasure—the treasure of having fun and learning new interesting things.

Make friends with Cursor. Let Mo Mouse and Kiki Keyboard help you find your way through the maze, and you'll know where you are.

Lesson 1-5 Questions

1. Why do you need to know where you are? (so you can have fun)
2. Who is It in Computer Land? (boys and girls who use computers)
3. How does Cursor move? (every key on the keyboard)
4. What are computers? (machines)
5. What do computers need in order to work? (electricity)
6. How long will a computer wait for you to answer? (forever)
7. What does the Cursor look like on Monty Monitor's face? (blinking square or highlighted box)
8. How do you control the Cursor? (keyboard or mouse)
9. Does Cursor always look the same? (no, he can be a highlighted word or picture.)
10. Can he look like anything else? (Yes, he changes shape on different computer systems or programs.)

Name ____

1-5 Mo Mouse Meets Kiki Keyboard

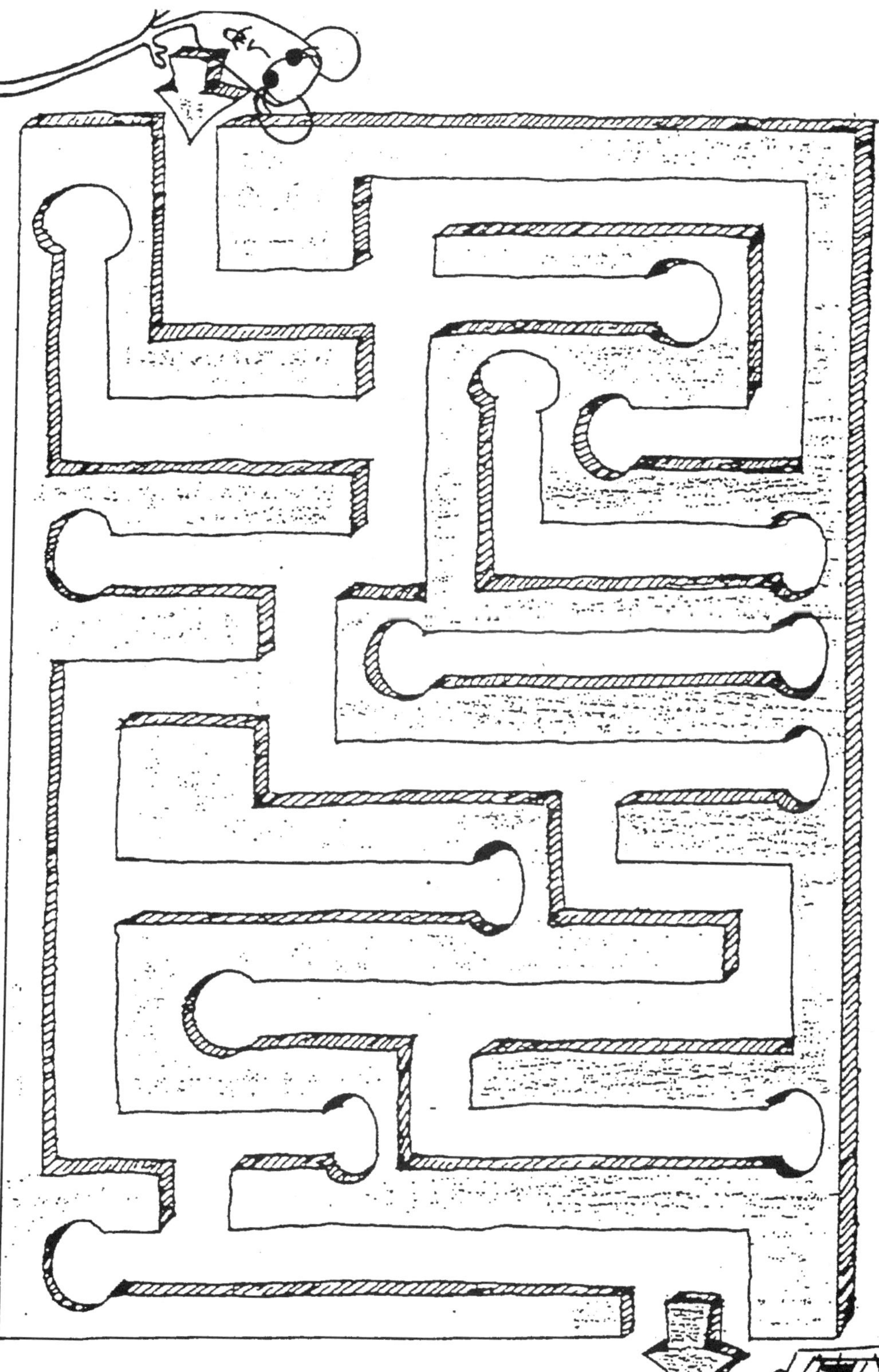

Mo Mouse Meets Kiki Keyboard (Answers)

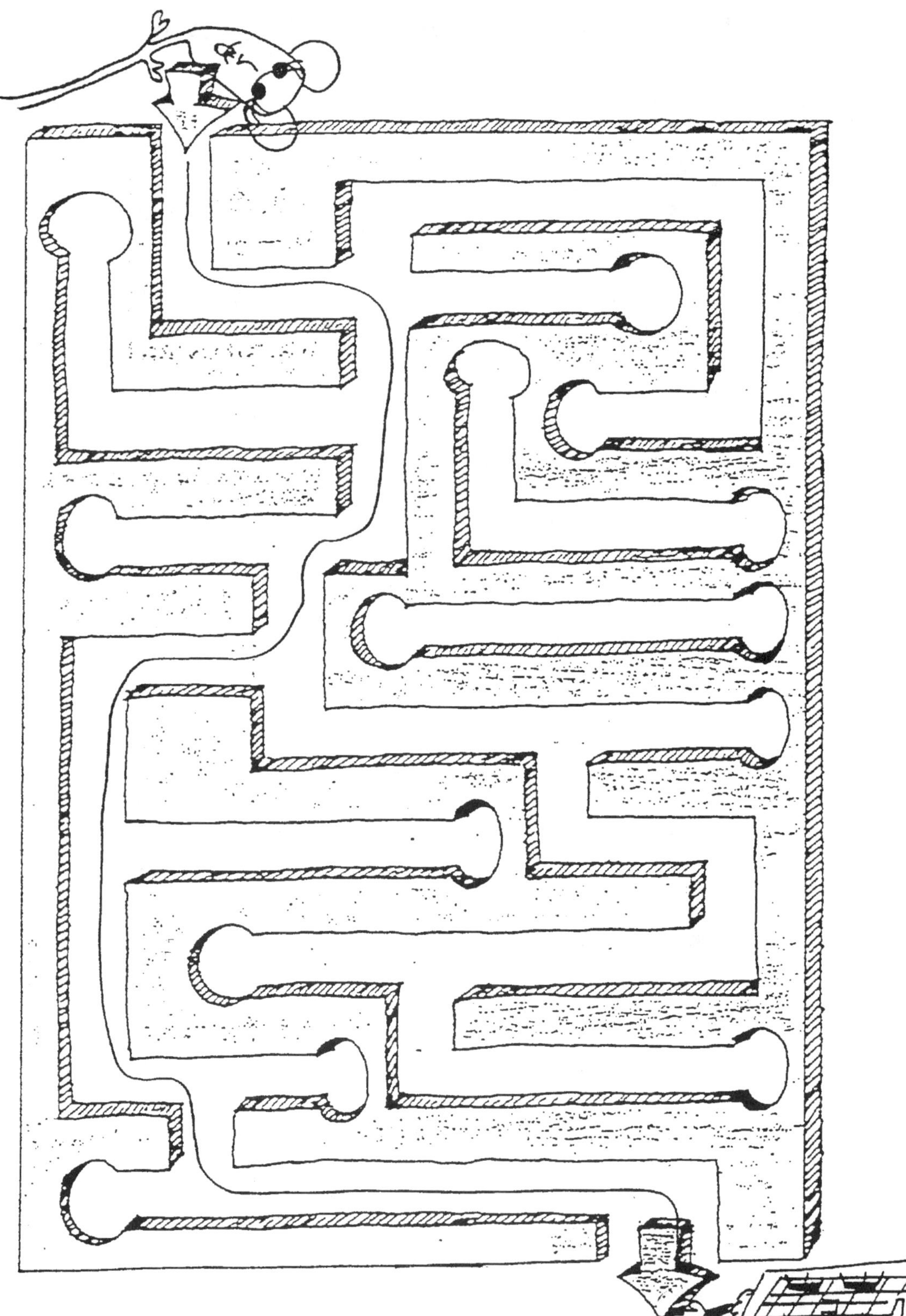

LESSON 1-6 RED LIGHT

To the Teacher

Early history of computers is taught. Lights have important jobs. CPU learns that Red Light will help everyone know when Dizzy Disk Drive and Susie Software are loading information into CPU and it is not safe to use Kiki Keyboard and Mo Mouse. Mister Policeman helps the parts learn that Red Light means stop and wait while the computer is working.

New words in this lesson: vacuum tubes printer transistors

I. Objective

- Identify warning lights on computers and compare them to traffic lights.

II. Instructional Input and Learning Activities

- Make overhead transparencies for each page of the story.
- Place the transparency on the stage of the overhead projector and cover the portion of the page you are not using.
- Read the story to the children.

III. Check for Understanding

Use the review questions at the end of the story to test for story comprehension. Cover the questions as you read the last page of the story. Answers are in parentheses.

IV. Guided Practice

The "Red Light" board game teaches waiting or stopping when the lights of the computer are lit; they show that the computer is working with information.

Materials - game board, one die, flipping coin, markers

Duplicate the game board, glue it together, and laminate it. Cut a cardboard circle for each game board. One side should be green, the other red. Game markers can be pictures of the parts of computers available in the classroom. Divide the class into groups of three or four. Roll the die to see who goes first. Put markers on Start. Players in turn flip the red/green coin. The red side equals no turn. The green side equals roll the die and move that number of places. If you land on a square with a direction, do what it says. First one to "End" is the winner.

V. Independent Practice and Application Using the Computer

Play a software game that reinforces the lesson.

LESSON 1-6 RED LIGHT

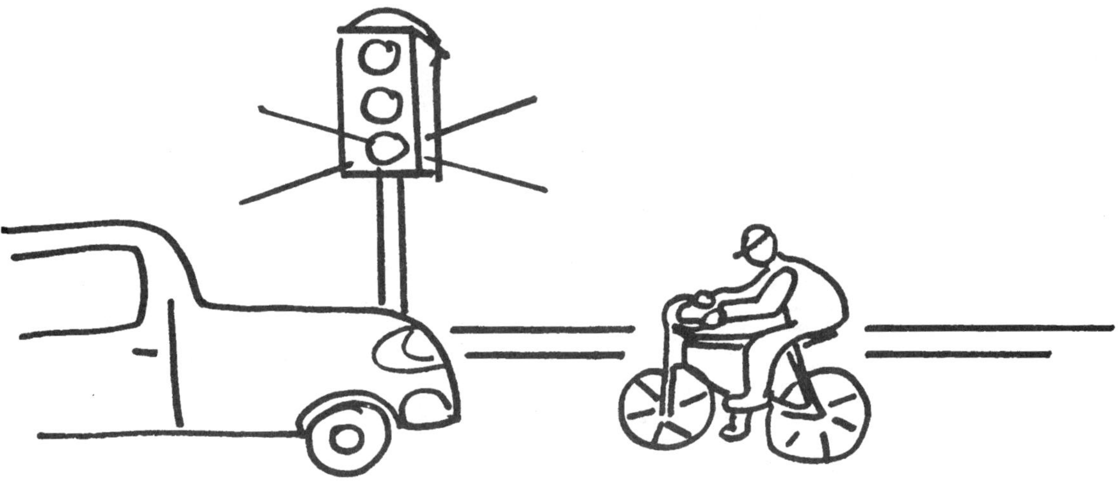

Red light, green light — what a fun game! You can move only when the light is green.

Red light, green light, yellow light. Your dad or mom can drive your car only when the light is green. You can walk or ride your bicycle across a street only when the light is green.

You have white lights when you want to read a book or see in the dark. Lights are important.

CPU, Computer Brain, had many lights called vacuum tubes in the early days. They were hot and burned out so often that soon he wanted them replaced so he wouldn't have to stop thinking. He wanted to work faster and cooler, and to get even smaller. CPU at that time was as big as a room. People who worked with CPU were always looking for burned-out lights, and falling over wires.

CPU said, "I'm tired of lights. I don't want them anymore."

Soon, instead of lights, CPU had things called transistors and chips inside him. He got smaller and smaller until he could fit on your table or in your hand. He also got cooler and cooler. He likes to have air conditioned rooms around him because he knows he is a "cool dude."

CPU liked Monty Monitor. He was fast at showing what CPU was thinking.
CPU liked Mo Mouse. She could point and click fast.
CPU liked Kiki Keyboard. She could type fast.

Peter Printer was a little slower because he had to wait until CPU was finished before he could do his job, but that was OK, because when CPU was finished, he just wanted to admire his work.

But . . . CPU had a problem with Dizzy Disk Drive and Susie Software. They weren't as fast. In fact they made CPU wait, and wait, and wait.

Finally, one day CPU said, "Is there anyway I can know when you two are finished and I can do my work? I have to guess. I have to sit and wait. I don't know when you are ready for me to use the information that Susie has on her disk. I don't know when it is added to my thinking power. I don't want to start too soon."

"Well, what should we do?" The parts all started arguing. Just then Mister Policeman came around the corner. "What is going on here?" he asked.

"We have a problem knowing when to GO AHEAD," said Mo.

Mister Policeman said, "Go is easy. Go is when the light is green, or when there isn't a red light."

"We don't have any lights," said Monty. "Maybe you should," said Mister Policeman. "A red light would say stop and wait, and a green light would say go." "I don't like lights," said CPU.

"I do," said Dizzy. "I can wear a red light, and when I am spinning Susie I will turn my red light on. When I am finished, I will turn it off and you will know it is safe to start working. Kiki and Mo will be able to see my light, and they won't do anything until they see that my light is off."

"I like it," said Mo and Kiki.

CPU said, "Lights that go on and say DON'T DO ANYTHING — STOP — can be good. I like it, too."

"That way you boys and girls won't get into any trouble," said Mister Policeman. "Just remember RED LIGHT — STOP — DON'T DO ANYTHING — WAIT — and you won't have any problems."

Lesson 1-6 Questions

1. Why doesn't Computer Brain have vacuum tubes anymore? (They are hot and they burn out quickly.)
2. How big was CPU in the "old days"? (as big as a room)
3. What replaced vacuum tubes? (transistors and chips)
4. CPU doesn't work alone. What part lets you see what you are doing? (Monty Monitor)
5. What part lets you type your name? (Kiki Keyboard)
6. What does Mo Mouse do? (points and clicks)
7. When does Peter Printer work? (after CPU finishes)
8. What does the glowing light mean? (stop and wait)
9. Where is the glowing light? (Dizzy Disk Drive)
10. Why do you wait? (to avoid damage to disks and programs)

Name ______________________________

1-6 Red Light

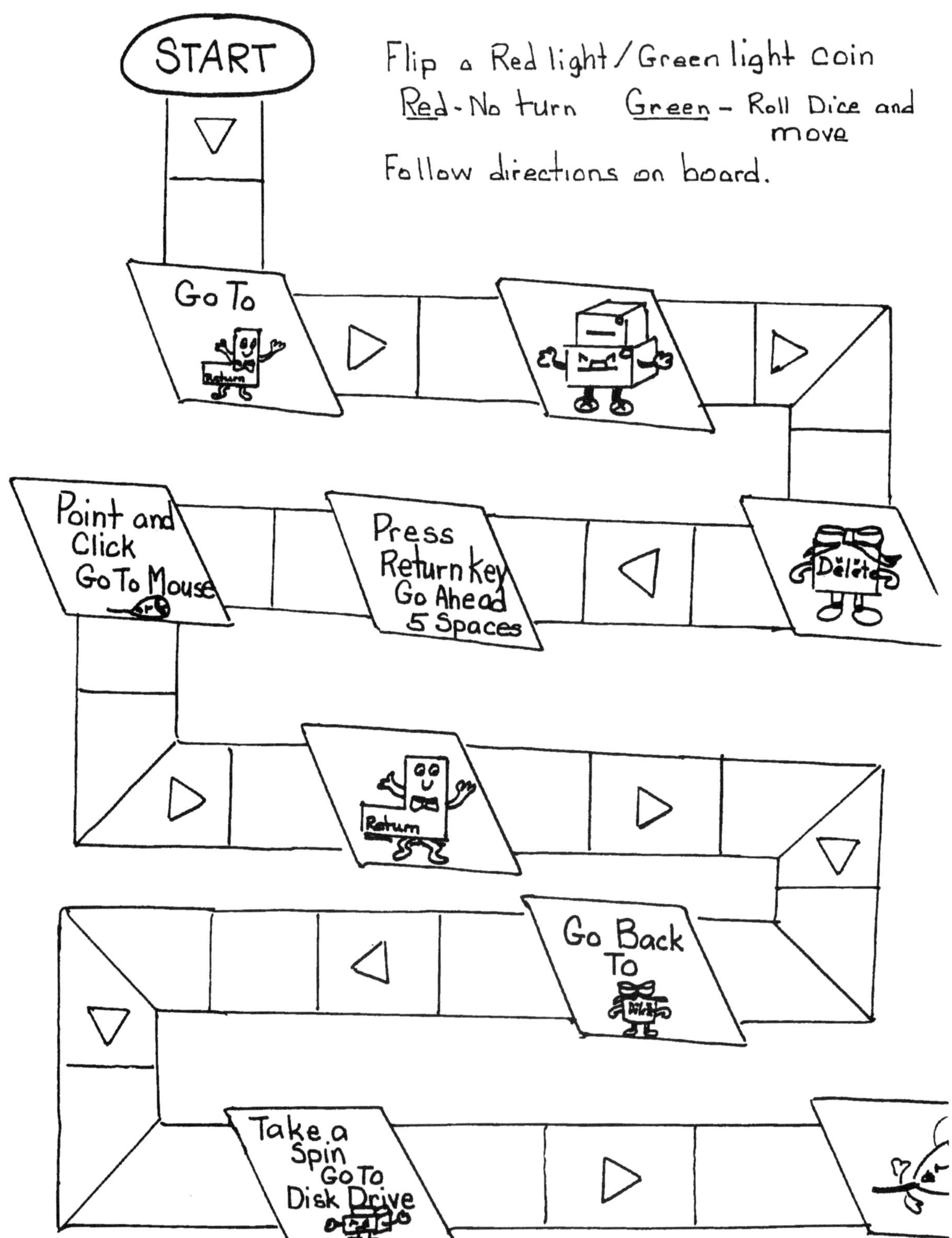

Name ____

1-6 Red Light (Continued)

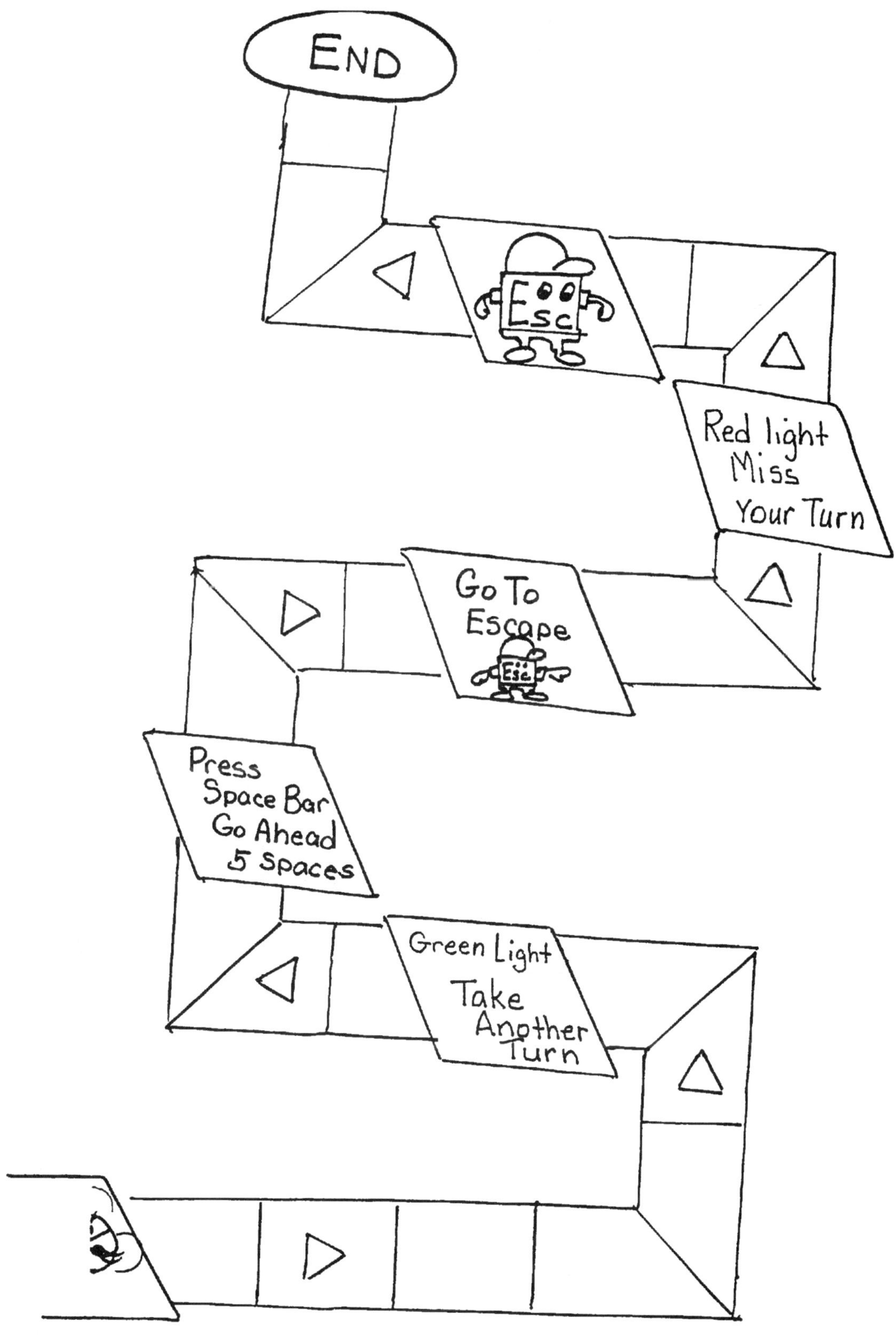

LESSON 1-7 ICONS - WINDOWS - PICTURES

To the Teacher

Ryan learns that pictures are important in helping you know what to do. You don't always need a word. Sometimes a picture can mean the same thing.

New words in this lesson: icons windows

I. Objectives

- Recognize that pictures are used in place of words.
- Understand that computers will wait until you are ready.
- Appreciate that computers don't care if you make mistakes.

II. Instructional Input and Learning Activities

- Make overhead transparencies for each page of the story.
- Place the transparency on the stage of the overhead projector and cover the portion of the page you are not using.
- Read the story to the children.

III. Check for Understanding

Use the review questions at the end of the story to test for story comprehension. Cover the questions as you read the last page of the story. Answers are in parentheses.

IV. Guided Practice

Color the squares on the "Find the Computer" work sheet. This activity acquaints the students with the different parts of a computer. Duplicate the work sheet for the students. Instruct students to color the squares to reveal the picture of a computer. A color code is included at the top of the work sheet. Students use markers or crayons to complete the picture. Review the names of the parts of the computer and their purpose as the students color the squares. The answer sheet follows the work sheet.

V. Independent Practice and Application Using the Computer

Play a software game that reinforces the lesson.

LESSON 1-7 ICONS - WINDOWS - PICTURES

Ryan was going to be learning to use computers. He was a little worried. Why was he worried? He couldn't read. He had just started school and the boys and girls were just learning the alphabet. How could he do computer things when he couldn't read words?

On the first day of computer class, Ryan walked in very slowly. He met his new teacher, Ms. Barbara. She showed all the boys and girls how to come in and take their seats.

She showed them the different parts of the computer. She said they were going to have fun, and that all they had to do was follow directions.

Ryan knew he could follow directions. He followed directions for brushing his teeth and feeding his dog. But now he had to read, and he knew he could not do that.

Ms. Barbara stood in front of the room. She had some cards in her hand. Ryan felt afraid. He was going to have to read words. She turned over the first card. There wasn't a word on it — just a picture.

Ms. Barbara said, "I know you boys and girls haven't learned to read yet and you are all wondering how you will be able to talk to your computer. We will talk with pictures." She pointed to the monitor. "Your monitor looks like your television. It will show you the pictures."

Ryan looked at his monitor, and yes, it had pictures on it.

"You will use your keyboard," Ms. Barbara said, as she held up a picture of a keyboard, "or your mouse." The picture of the mouse really didn't look like a mouse, but if that was what Ms. Barbara called it he would call it a mouse, too.

Ryan was very happy. He wouldn't have to know words right away. He would just need to find a picture. He could do that.

Ms. Barbara taught the boys and girls how to use the arrow keys to point to the pictures on the monitor. She taught them how to point and click with the mouse. It was fun.

"Pictures make computer work easy," said Ryan.

"Yes," said Ms. Barbara. "After we learn about the pictures, we will learn the words. There are not a lot of words to learn. You will have fun."

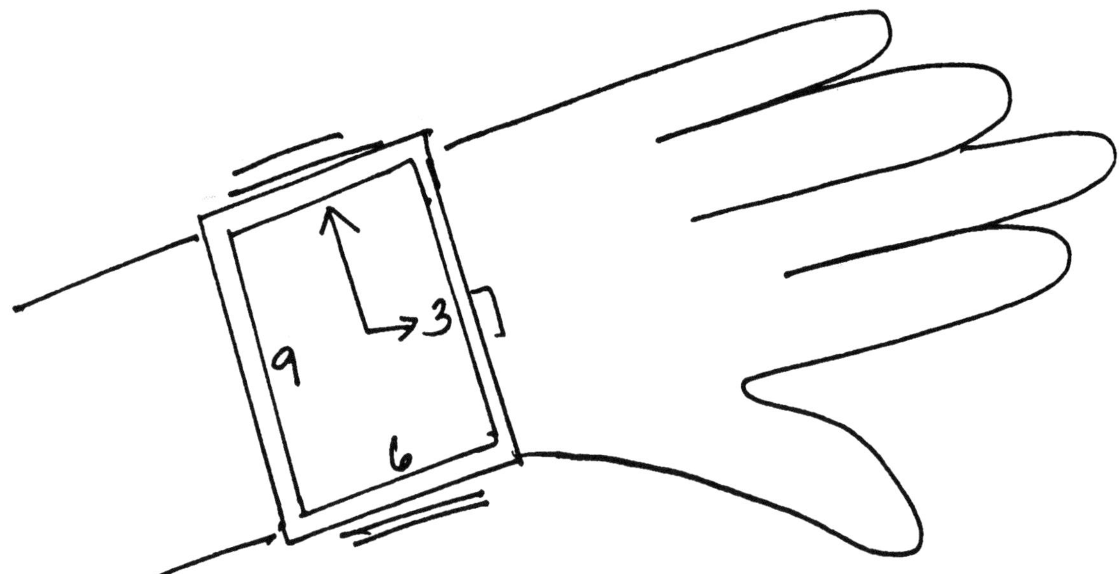

Ryan was ready, but he still worried. What if he took too much time? Would the pictures disappear?

Ms. Barbara answered that question, too.

"Don't worry about taking too much time to find an answer," Ms. Barbara said. "Your computer will wait forever. The pictures will not change until you are ready. The computer doesn't care if you make a mistake. You can always start over."

All of Ryan's questions were answered. He didn't have to read right away. He could take his time.

He could even make mistakes without worrying that the computer would laugh at him. Computers were going to be fun!

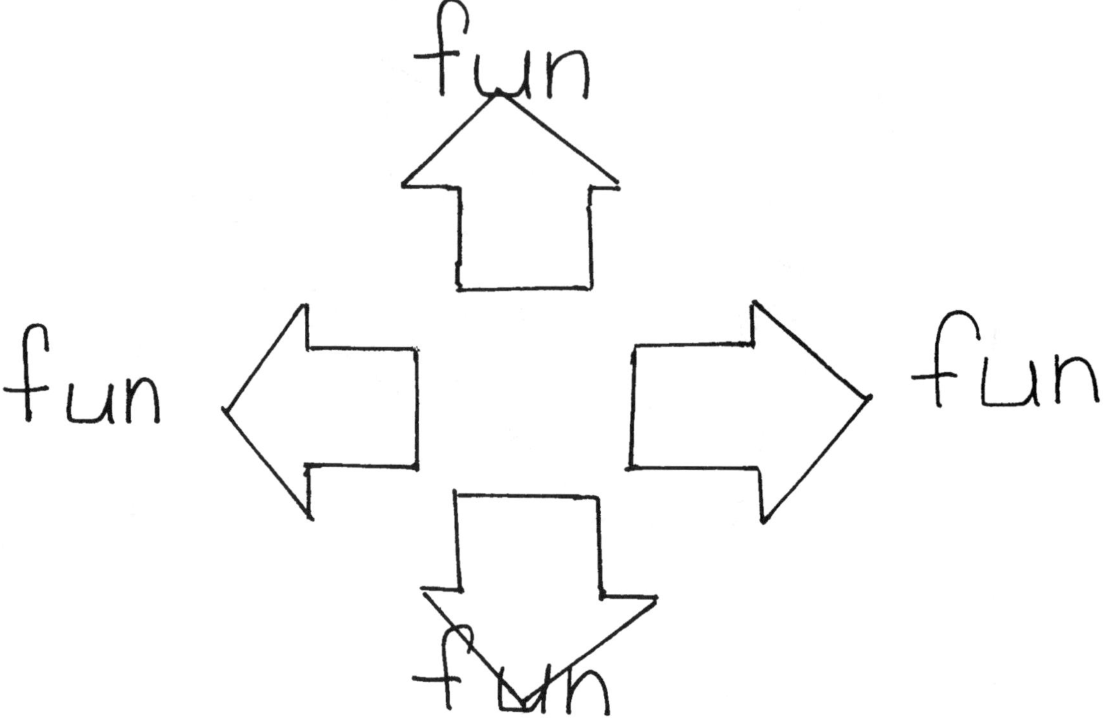

He was really ready now — ready to follow directions and have fun!

Lesson 1-7 Questions

1. What are the most important things boys and girls should do in computer class? (follow directions)
2. What does your monitor look like? (a television set)
3. What does the monitor do? (shows you what your computer is doing)
4. Why does a computer have arrow keys? (to move the cursor around the screen of the monitor)
5. How long will the computer wait for you to do something? (forever)
6. Does the computer care if you make a mistake? (no)
7. Can you start over if you want to? (yes)
8. How do we talk to the computer? (keyboard and mouse)
9. How do you pick a picture with your mouse? (point and click)
10. How do you pick a picture with your keyboard? (use arrow keys to the picture and press the return key)

Name ______________________________

1-7 Find the Computer

1 = Red 3 = Yellow 5 = Blue 7 = Brown
2 = Orange 4 = Green 6 = Purple 8 = Black

8	8	8	8	8	8	8	8	8	8	8	8	8	8	8	8
8	6	6	6	6	6	6	6	6	6	6	6	6	6	6	8
8	6	1	1	1	1	1	1	1	1	6	6	6	6	6	8
8	6	1	7	7	7	7	7	7	1	6	6	6	6	6	8
8	6	1	7	7 8	7	7 8	7	7	1	6	6	6	6	6	8
8	6	1	7	7	7 8	7 8	7	7	1	6	6	6	6	6	8
8	6	1	7	7	7	7	7	7	1	6	6	6	6	6	8
8	6	1	7	7	7	7	7	7	1	4	4	4	6	6	8
8	6	1	1	1	1	1	1	1	1	4	4	4	6	6	8
8	6	6	2	2	2	2	2	2	6	4	4 4	4	6	6	8
8	6	6	2	2	2	2	2	2	6	4	4	4	6	6	8
8	6	6	3	3	3	3	3	3	3	6 3	6	6	6	6	8
8	6	6	3 6	3	3	3	3	3	3	3	6	6	6	6	8
8	6	6	6	6	6	6	6	6	6	6	6	6 5	5	5	8
8	6	6	6	6	6	6	6	6	6	6	6	5	5	5 6	8
8	6	6	6	6	6	6	6	6	6	6	6	6	6	6	8
8	8	8	8	8	8	8	8	8	8	8	8	8	8	8	8

Find the Computer (Answers)

1 = Red		3 = Yellow		5 = Blue		7 = Brown	
2 = Orange		4 = Green		6 = Purple		8 = Black	

8	8	8	8	8	8	8	8	8	8	8	8	8	8	8	8
8	6	6	6	6	6	6	6	6	6	6	6	6	6	6	8
8	6	1	1	1	1	1	1	1	1	6	6	6	6	6	8
8	6	1	7	7	7	7	7	7	1	6	6	6	6	6	8
8	6	1	7	7 8	7	7 8	7	7	1	6	6	6	6	6	8
8	6	1	7	7	7 8	8 7	7	7	1	6	6	6	6	6	8
8	6	1	7	7	7	7	7	7	1	6	6	6	6	6	8
8	6	1	7	7	7	7	7	7	1	4	4	4	6	6	8
8	6	1	1	1	1	1	1	1	1	4	4	4	6	6	8
8	6	6	2	2	2	2	2	2	6	4	4 4	4	6	6	8
8	6	6	2	2	2	2	2	2	6	4	4	4	6	6	8
8	6	6	3	3	3	3	3	3	3	3 6	6	6	6	6	8
8	6	6	6 3	3	3	3	3	3	3	3	6	6	6	6	8
8	6	6	6	6	6	6	6	6	6	6	6	6 5	5	5	8
8	6	6	6	6	6	6	6	6	6	6	6	5	5	5 6	8
8	6	6	6	6	6	6	6	6	6	6	6	6	6	6	8
8	8	8	8	8	8	8	8	8	8	8	8	8	8	8	8

LESSON 1-8 I WANT TO START OVER

To the Teacher

Ryan presses the Arrow and Return keys too fast and picks the wrong number from the menu. He learns that if you make a mistake, you can start over and that the computer doesn't care if you make mistakes. He learns about the main menu and its importance. He also learns to raise his hand to get help from his teacher.

New words in this lesson: escape key space bar splash screen

I. Objective

- Understand the importance of menus.

II. Instructional Input and Learning Activities

- Make overhead transparencies for each page of the story.
- Place the transparency on the stage of the overhead projector and cover the portion of the page you are not using.
- Read the story to the children.

III. Check for Understanding

Use the review questions at the end of the story to test for story comprehension. Cover the questions as you read the last page of the story. Answers are in parentheses.

IV. Guided Practice

The "Computer Escape-O" game is played like Old Maid. This game reviews the ways of stopping a program or going back to the menu to do something new.

Materials - Deck of "Escape-O" cards (two of each, but only one Escape card—total of forty-seven cards)

Duplicate and laminate the deck of cards at the end of this lesson for each group of four or five students. Shuffle and deal cards to students. Students make matching pairs and lay them on the table in front of themselves. After matches have been made, each student gives a card to the player on his or her left. The object of the game is to make as many matches as you can and not be caught with the Escape card.

V. Independent Practice and Application Using the Computer

Play a software game that reinforces the lesson.

LESSON 1-8 I WANT TO START OVER

Ryan had come to the computer room to play his favorite game. He walked into the room and sat down. When he looked at Monty Monitor, he didn't see the name of his favorite game. He saw something new.

"Oh my," said Ryan. "I don't know how to play this game."

Ms. Barbara saw that Ryan and the other children were surprised to see a new software program waiting for them. She said, "Hello boys and girls. Today we are going to learn to play a new game."

Ryan and the other children knew Ms. Barbara was there to help them learn and have fun with the computers. Everyone sat up and listened while Ms. Barbara gave the directions.

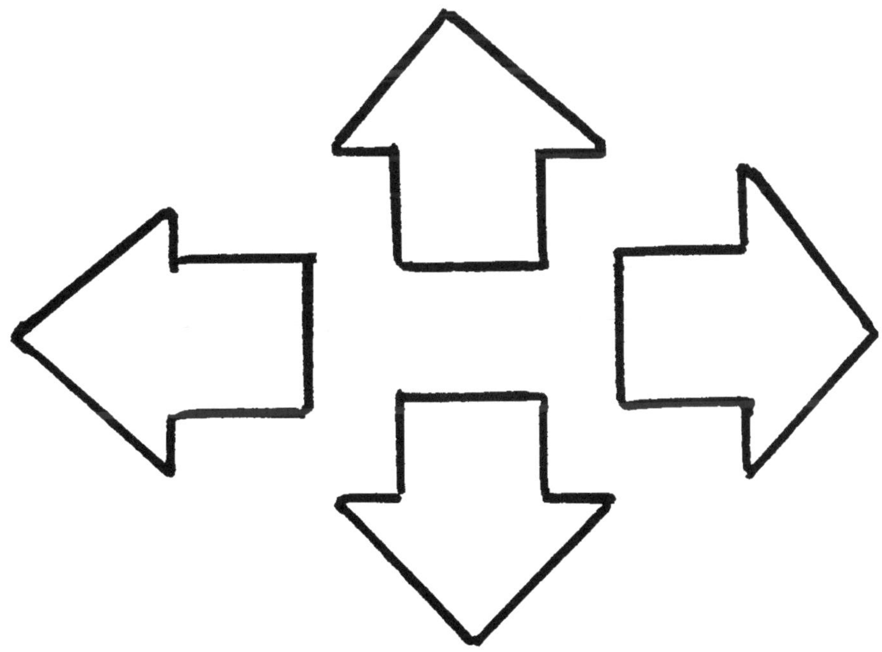

Everyone has to follow directions. Boys and girls have to follow directions and so do computers. Computers do only what you tell them to do.

Ryan wanted to press the keys right away, but he knew if he did he might do something he shouldn't, so he put his hands on the table top.

Ms. Barbara showed the name of the software on the Splash Screen, which is like the title of a book. Then she pressed the Return Key and told everyone else to do the same thing.

Everyone pressed the Return Key and the Main Menu showed on Monty Monitor's face. There were five different choices.

Ryan was very excited. He had never played a game with so many parts. He had a hard time reading all the words because he was just learning how to read. He did know his numbers. One, Two, Three, Four, Five. That seemed easy enough. All Ms. Barbara had to say was pick a number. He could do that.

Ms. Barbara said, "Pick Number One by using your arrow keys, or point and click with your mouse.

Ryan was so excited. He knew Number One. He started pressing the arrow key, and then it happened. He pressed the arrow key one time too many, and he landed on Number Two and pressed the Return Key.

Ryan looked at Monty Monitor's face. The other students had a dancing bear on their screen. He had a box with big words that he couldn't read. What was he going to do?

He did the only thing he could do. He raised his hand and said, "Ms. Barbara, I am not looking at the same thing everyone else is. What should I do?"

Ms. Barbara knew that boys and girls will sometimes make mistakes. She said, "Boys and girls, whenever you make a mistake, raise your hand and I will help you. You can press the Escape Key. You can point and click your mouse on the Main Menu picture. You can start over."

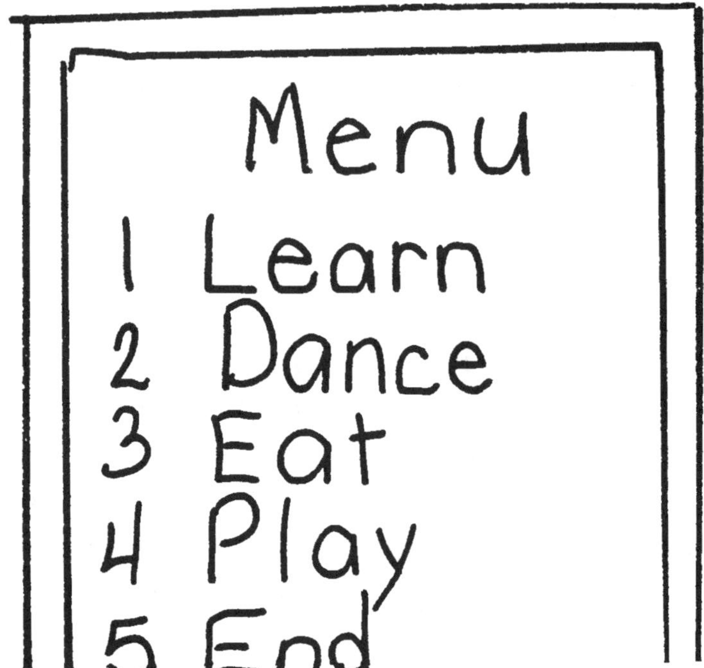

Soon Ryan was back at the Main Menu.

"Remember," said Ms. Barbara, "if you want to start over, you must press your Escape Key, or point and click your mouse on the picture of the Main Menu. The computer doesn't care if you make a mistake. It can't remember mistakes. You must wait for the red light to go off, and just start over."

Ryan was very happy to have Ms. Barbara there to help him. He knew if he followed directions and treated his computer gently he would not have to worry. Ms. Barbara knows all about boys and girls, and all about computers, too.

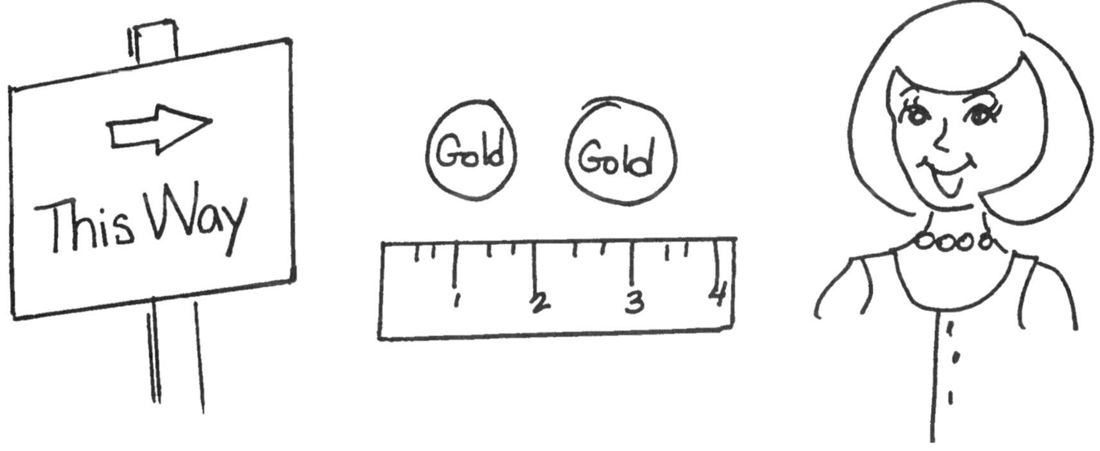

"I will remember. Follow directions, and treat the computer the way you would like to be treated. If you have problems, ask your teacher. And if you want to start over, just return to the Main Menu," said Ryan. "It is easy and fun to use the computer. Let's play."

Lesson 1-8 Questions

1. Who has to follow directions? (everyone)
2. Do computers have to follow directions? (yes)
3. What is a splash screen? (It is like the title page of a book for software.)
4. What keys do you use to choose from the menu screen? (arrows and return key)
5. What should you do if you have a problem with your computer? (raise your hand and get help from your teacher)
6. Is the computer mad if you make a mistake? (no)
7. What key do you use to start a program over? (escape key)
8. How many times do you press the escape key? (two times)
9. What happens when you press the escape key twice? (The computer returns to the main menu.)
10. How should you treat your computer? (respectfully — the Golden Rule)

Name ____

1-8 Computer Escape-O

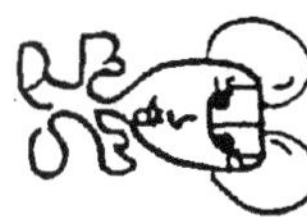

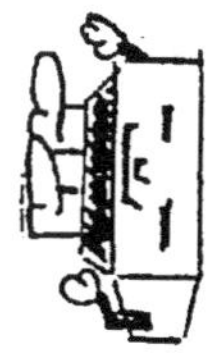

Name ____

1-8 Computer Escape-O (Continued)

Name ____

1-8 Computer Escape-O (Continued)

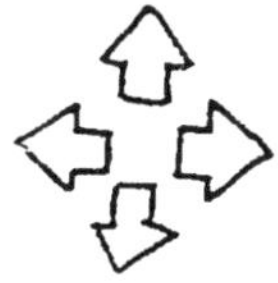

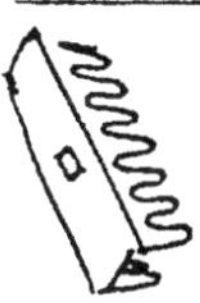

Name ____

1-8 Computer Escape-O (Continued)

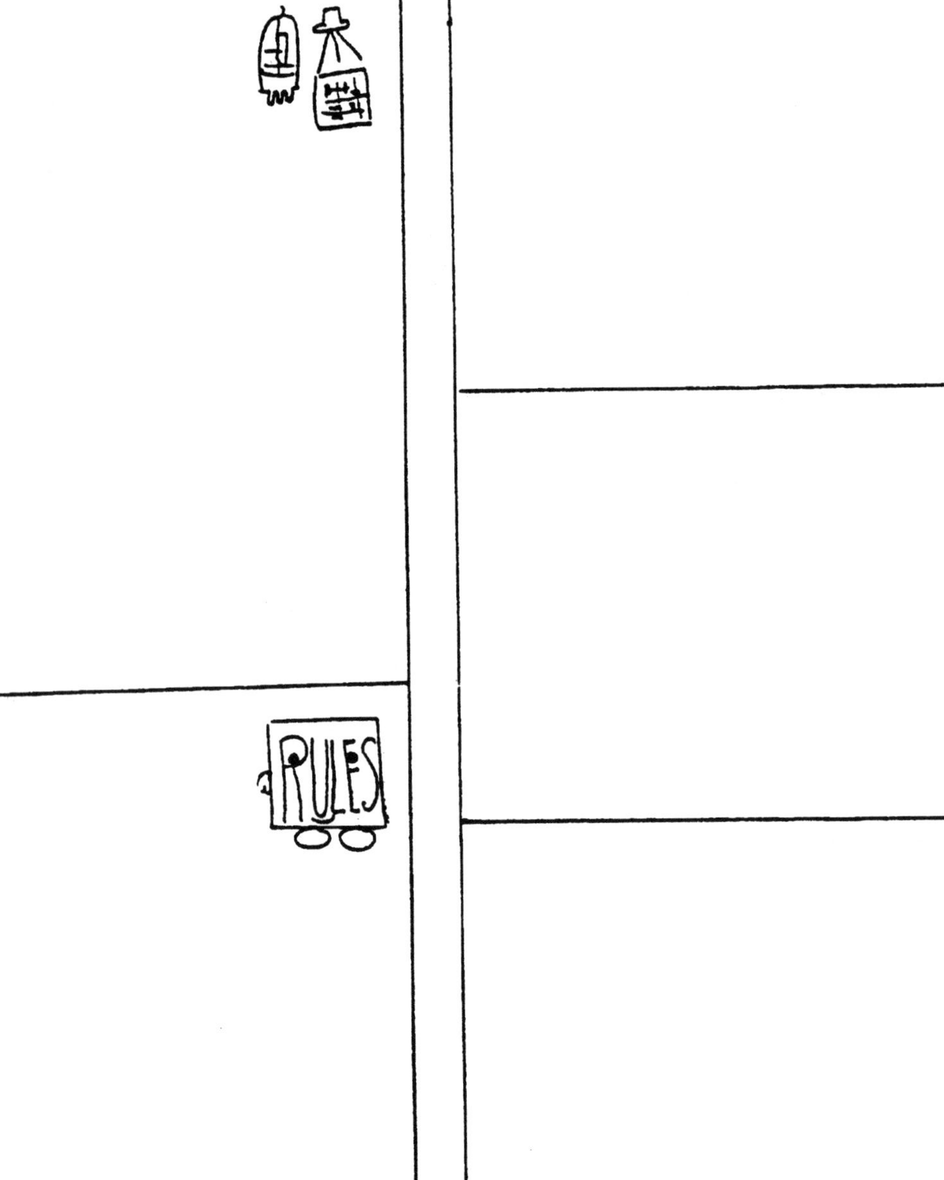

Name ____

1-8 Computer Escape-O (Continued)

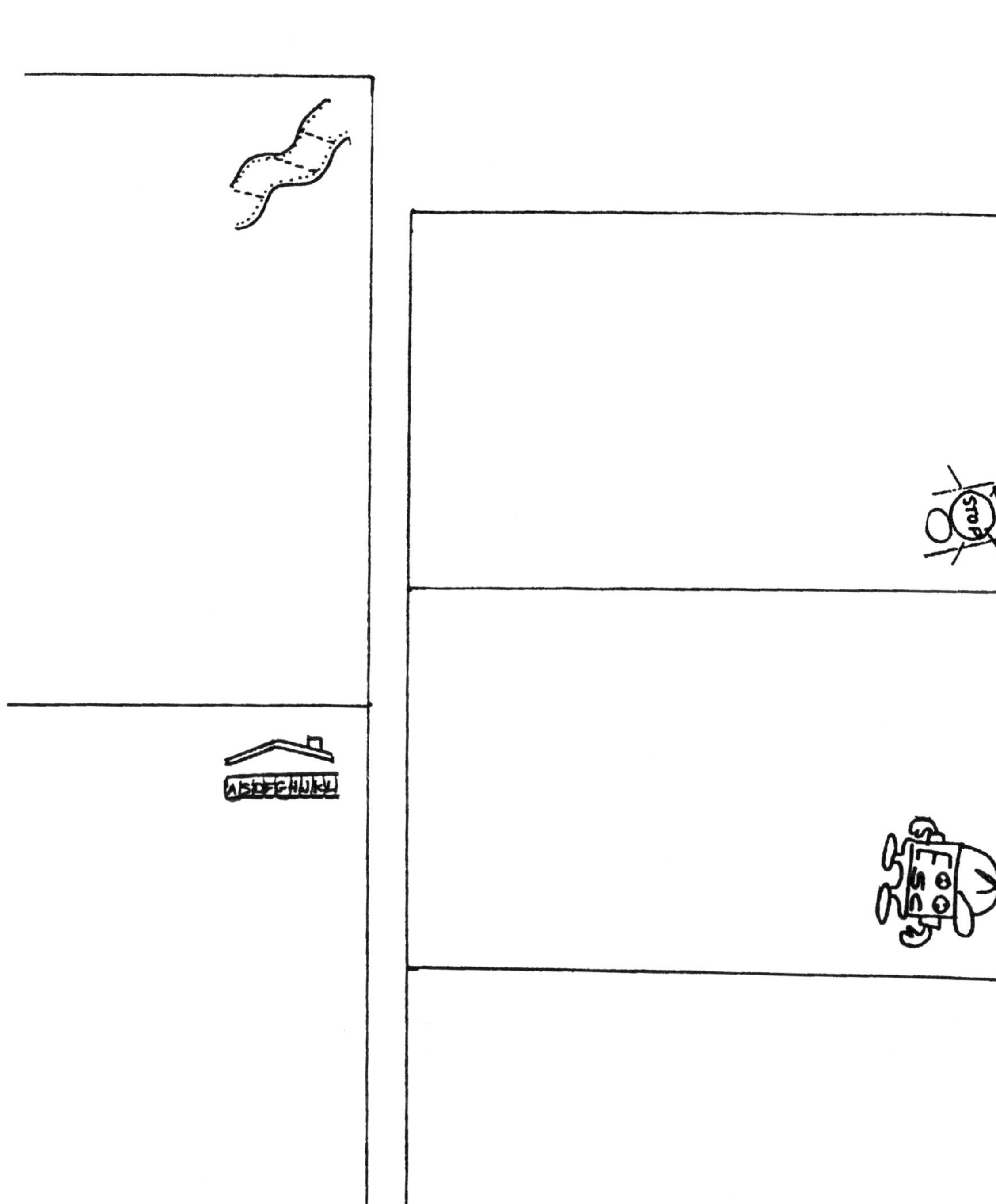

LESSON 1-9 RUN, RUN AS FAST AS YOU CAN

To the Teacher

CPU is missing and all the other computer parts are wondering what has happened to him. CPU has run away because he is tired of working. The computer parts think he is mad at them for not paying more attention to him. They remember that CPU said he was tired of working. They know that he has relatives everywhere and have to think hard to find him. CPU is with his cousin Digital Clock, because he always liked the way Digital Clock ran. CPU says, "Running is fun; working is hard." Digital Clock tells CPU that it is all in how you look at it. Running and working are the same. CPU decides to go back if the computer parts will say "run" instead of "work."

New words in this lesson: digital binary

I. Objective

- Understand that the terms "work" and "run" both mean that the computer is operating.

II. Instructional Input and Learning Activities

- Make overhead transparencies for each page of the story.
- Place the transparency on the stage of the overhead projector and cover the portion of the page you are not using.
- Read the story to the children.

III. Check for Understanding

Use the review questions at the end of the story to test for story comprehension. Cover the questions as you read the last page of the story. Answers are in parentheses.

IV. Guided Practice

The "Binary Bump" game teaches Binary as one - yes, and zero - no. Mark the keyboard with your "bumped" (reference point letter) keys. Keyboard manufacturers designate two keys as reference points for the right- and left-hand home-row letters. The bump may be a raised dot or line at the bottom of the key, although the bumped keys on your keyboard may be on different letters from those shown on the work sheet. (*Note also:* While your keyboard may not look exactly like the Apple keyboard work sheet, the letter and number keys will be the same for the students' use.) Fill in all the letters and make a transparency of the picture of your keyboard with the "bumped" keys shown. Use a plastic marker to keep track of guessed movement. Answer "one" or "zero" to student questions.

Example: Pick the letter "R" secretly. Students rotate asking questions, which may be answered "yes" (one) or "no" (zero).

1. Is the starting point the "D" key? 1 - yes
2. Is the letter in the same row? 0 - no
3. Is it below the "D" key? 0 - no
4. Is it in the row above the "D" key? 1 - yes
5. Is it the "E" key? 0 - no
6. Is it the "R" key? 1 - yes

The player who guesses the letter is the next person to pick a secret letter and answer questions by using "one" and "zero."

V. *Independent Practice and Application Using the Computer*

Play a software game that reinforces the lesson.

LESSON 1-9 RUN, RUN AS FAST AS YOU CAN

In Computer Land everyone is a hard worker. But who wants to work all day?

Computer Brain, CPU, said "I am tired of everyone telling me to work. I think I will run away. Work, work, work is not fun."

So the next morning when it was time to work, no one could work. Why couldn't they work? CPU had run away.

Monty Monitor looked like a light bulb.

Peter Printer looked like a blank piece of paper.

Mo Mouse pointed, clicked, and dragged, but no magic arrow slid across Monty's face.

Kiki Keyboard's letters just jumped up and down, but with no one between them and Monty Monitor, no letters showed on Monty's face. No letters would show on Peter Printer's paper.

Dizzy Disk Drive spun Susie around and around but no one paid attention and she just got dizzy, really dizzy.

"Something is wrong. Someone is missing," they all said together.

"I feel very disconnected," said Dizzy.
"So do I," said all the others. "Where is CPU?"
Right in the middle of Peter, Mo, Kiki, Monty, and Dizzy was a big space.

"I should have noticed it right away," said Monty. "I usually sit right on top of CPU. I knew something felt strange."

Everyone looked around.

Maybe CPU is sick and home in bed. Maybe someone took him away. Maybe he is lost. Each of the parts tried to give a reason for CPU not being where he should be — where everyone expected him to be.

"I bet CPU is mad at us for not paying more attention to him," said Peter. "Sometimes I feel left out because not everyone makes papers to take with them, and I wait a long time for someone to write a letter."

"Maybe you are right. CPU didn't ask to make a hard copy — a paper note — for us, did he, Peter?" asked Dizzy.

"No, I'm worried. We can't do anything without him," said Peter.

"I remember CPU had to go get repaired when his on/off switch wasn't working," said Kiki Keyboard.

"He was feeling fine. Except that he was saying all he did was work, work, work," said Monty.

"That must be it. CPU is tired of working and has run away," said Mo Mouse.

"Where will we look for him, and how will we get him to come back?" asked Peter.

"I know he has relatives everywhere. It will be hard to find him," said Monty. "What else did he say all the time?"

"He said he'd like to run away," said Kiki.

"Where could he run away to?" asked Peter.

"He always said he liked the way his cousin Digital Clock ran. He might be visiting him," said Monty.

The parts of the computer called Digital Clock. Sure enough, CPU was watching Digital Clock run.

"Running is fun. Working is not fun," said CPU.

Digital Clock said, "Running and working are the same thing."

"Running and working are the same thing?" asked CPU.

"I can say I am running, or I can say I am working. I am still telling time," said Digital Clock.

"Are you having fun?" asked CPU.

Digital Clock said, "Yes, I run all the time. You have to wait for someone to press the Return Key or Enter Key to run."

"Work," said CPU. "Work."

"It is all in how you look at it. You say it is work. I say it is fun — run. Fun — Run. Run — Fun. Why don't you think of it that way, too?" asked Digital Clock.

"That is a good idea," said CPU.

Digital Clock said, "Your friends, Monty, Dizzy, Peter, Kiki, and Mo want you to come back. What shall I tell them?"

CPU thought for a minute and said, "Tell them I will come back if I don't have to work. I will come back if they say Run instead of Work. That sounds like more fun."

Today in Computer Land all the parts of the computer are working — no, running — together and having fun.

When Return Key or Enter Key is pressed, the red light goes on and everyone stops and waits for CPU to run, because he is having fun and so will you.

Lesson 1-9 Questions

1. Why didn't the computer parts work? (CPU had run away.)
2. What did Monty look like? (a blank television or a light bulb)
3. Why does Peter Printer feel left out? (No one needs paper copies of everything CPU does.)
4. Where are computers? (everywhere)
5. Where did CPU go? (to see his cousin Digital Clock)
6. Are running and working the same thing in Computer Land? (yes)
7. Why is running better then working? (It isn't; they are the same.)
8. What happens when the red light is on? (All the parts wait for it to stop.)
9. Why do you stop for the light? (Disk drives are spinning and inputting information into the computer.)
10. Could the other parts work without CPU? (no)

Name ______________________________

1-9 Binary Bump

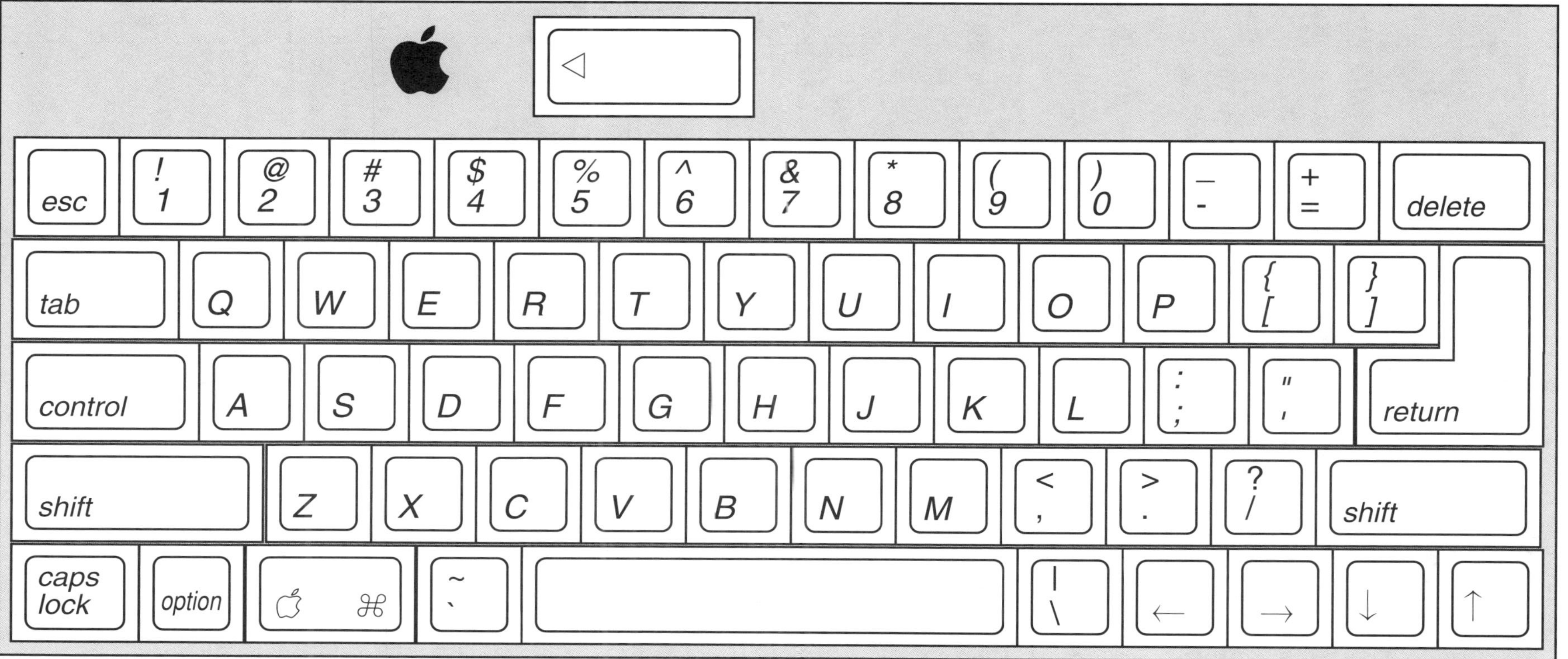

LESSON 1-10 INPUT, PROCESS, OUTPUT

To the Teacher

CPU is very proud of himself and is bragging to all the other computer parts. Ryan wants to have a little fun with CPU. Ryan tells CPU that he can do only three things. CPU lists the thousands and thousands of jobs that he does. The other parts are really interested because CPU is so upset. Ryan says the three things are inputting, processing, and outputting. Ryan lists the computer parts that input. Ryan then lists the computer parts that output. Now CPU realizes how smart he really is, because the three things that he does can make rockets go to the moon and allow people to play games or write letters. All the computer parts agree that CPU is great and should be allowed to brag about himself.

New words in this lesson: input process output hard copy

I. Objective

- Define input, process, and output.

II. Instructional Input and Learning Activities

- Make overhead transparencies for each page of the story.
- Place the transparency on the stage of the overhead projector and cover the portion of the page you are not using.
- Read the story to the children.

III. Check for Understanding

Use the review questions at the end of the story to test for story comprehension. Cover the questions as you read the last page of the story. Answers are in parentheses.

IV. Guided Practice

The "Input, Process, Output" work sheet develops the sequential-order thinking process. Duplicate the work sheet for students. Instruct students to place the numbers 1, 2, and 3 in front of the pictures to show the process of making a finished product. The answer sheet follows the work sheet.

V. Independent Practice and Application Using the Computer

Play a software game that reinforces the lesson.

LESSON 1-10 INPUT, PROCESS, OUTPUT

Computer Brain, better known as CPU, was always very proud of himself. After all, he knew computers were everywhere. He knew that he could do the boring jobs that people didn't want to do and that he could do everything very fast. He liked himself.

Ryan saw CPU. He knew that Computer Brain liked to brag. Today, he thought he would have a little fun.

Ryan said, "Computer Brain, you think you are so good and can do everything and you are everywhere, but you can do only three things."

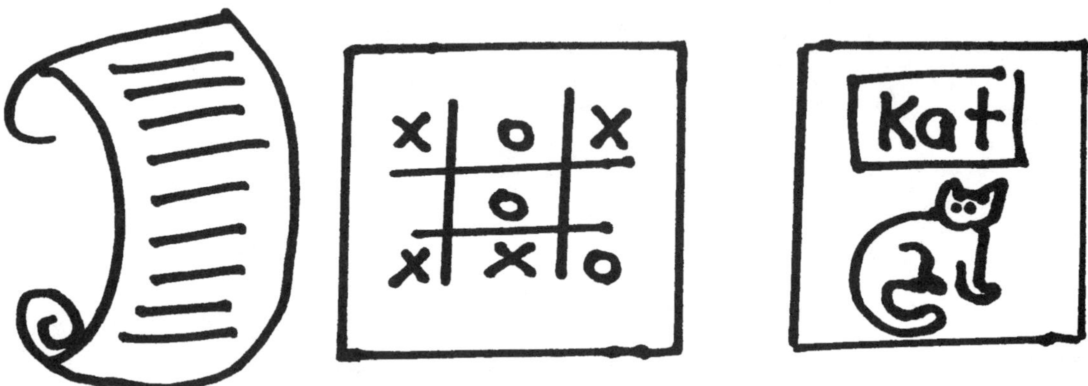

"What are you talking about — only three things? I can add really big numbers. I can remember really long lists. I can do really boring things over and over. I can play games. I can correct your spelling mistakes. That is more than THREE THINGS," said CPU. He felt really insulted.

Ryan said, "Those are all jobs you do, and very well, too. But you really can do only three things."

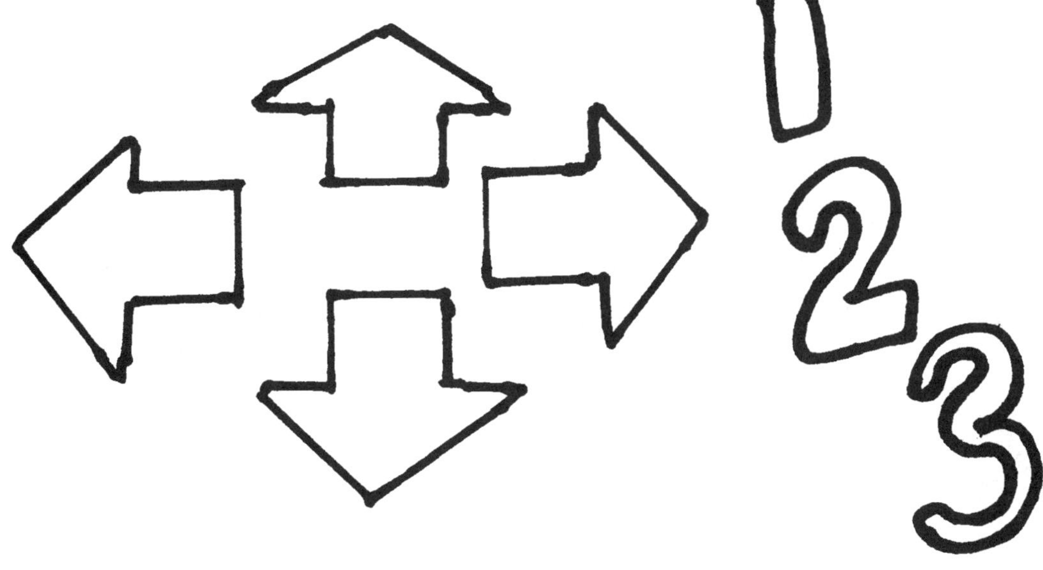

CPU was getting angry. He was ready to list more and more things when Ryan spoke.

"I don't want to hurt your feelings. You follow my directions. You can do all the things you said. But you really do only three things."

Ryan stood up tall and said, "You do three things. Input, Process, Output."

"What?" said all the parts. Their eyes were wide and really interested now.

"I give you directions. You put them into your memory. Then you mix them with other information, or you change the information, and you give me the answer. Input, Process, Output."

"Do you mean every job is the same?" asked the other parts.

"Yes," said Ryan. "I use Kiki Keyboard or Mo Mouse to give CPU the directions I want him to follow. Dizzy Disk Drive and Susie Software work with CPU to mix the job and CPU's memory together, and then like magic my answer is on Monty Monitor's face or Peter Printer can make a hard copy.

Three Things. Computer Brain really is smart, but he does only three things. He can make rockets go to the moon.

He can add hundreds of numbers in seconds.

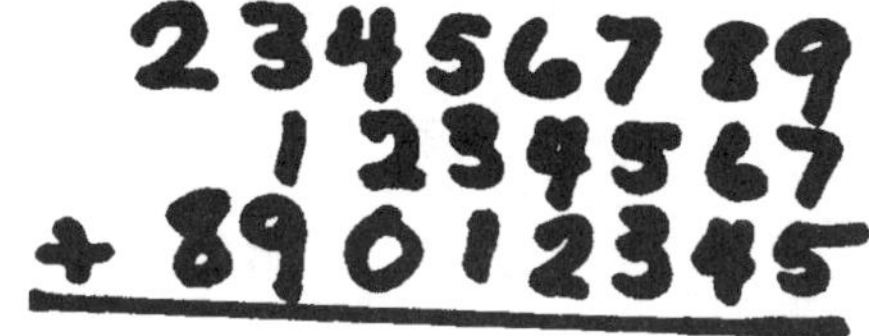

He can play a game.

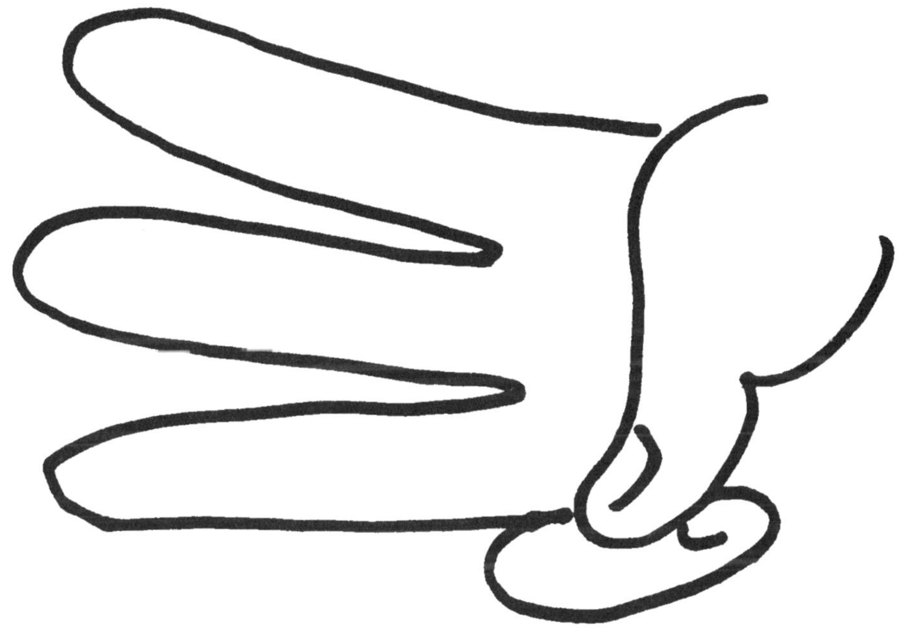

CPU said, “See I told you. I am good. I am GREAT. I do only three things, and I can do everything. I can be everywhere. I can help people all over the world. Who else can say that?”

Everyone had to agree. Computer Brain really is Great. And he does only three things:

INPUT PROCESS OUTPUT

Great, really great!

Lesson 1-10 Questions

1. Where are computers? (everywhere)
2. What kinds of jobs do computers do? (boring jobs, big number jobs, big stories, games)
3. How many things can CPU do? (three)
4. What are the three things? (input, process, output)
5. Is every job the same? (yes)
6. Does CPU follow directions? (yes)
7. Who gives CPU directions? (you,with the help of Kiki Keyboard and Mo Mouse)
8. Who does the processing — mixing? (CPU)
9. Who does the output — answer? (Monty Monitor, Peter Printer, Dizzy Disk Drive)
10. What is Peter Printer's paper called? (hard copy)

Name ______________________________

1-10 Input, Process, Output

1. Input
2. Process
3. Output

Put the pictures in order.

I-10 Input, Process, Output (Answers)

1) Input
2) Process
3) Output

Put the pictures in order.

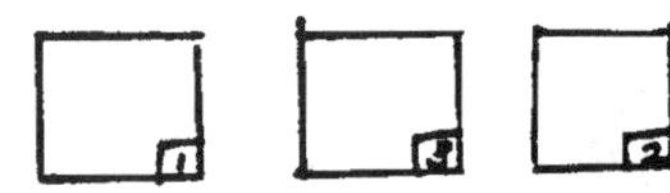

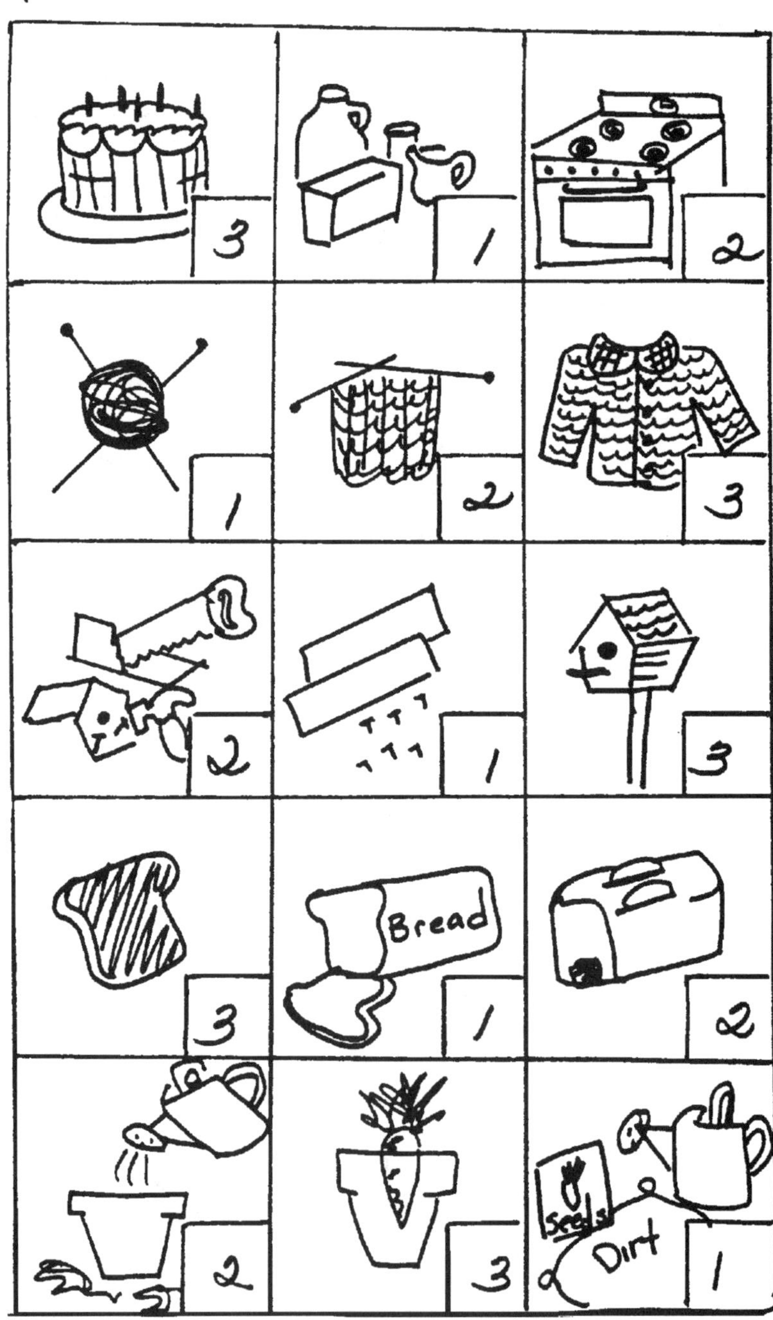

LESSON 1-11 ELECTRICITY

To the Teacher

One day in Computer Land, all the computer parts tried to power up, but nothing happened. Larry Lamp came to explain the reason. CPU didn't think a lamp could know what was wrong with him. Larry told him that they both had the same problem; they needed electricity and a storm had caused a tree to fall on the electric wires. No electricity could continue through the line and enter the school. Soon Larry feels tingly. The electricity is back and there is power to light up and play.

New words in this lesson: There are no new words.

I. Objective

- Recognize that computers need electricity to operate.

II. Instructional Input and Learning Activities

- Make overhead transparencies for each page of the story.
- Place the transparency on the stage of the overhead projector and cover the portion of the page you are not using.
- Read the story to the children.

III. Check for Understanding

Use the review questions at the end of the story to test for story comprehension. Cover the questions as you read the last page of the story. Answers are in parentheses.

IV. Guided Practice

The "Does It Need Electricity?" work sheet helps students understand that some things need the power of electricity to operate. Duplicate the work sheet for students. Instruct students to draw a circle around the pictures of objects that need electricity to operate. Students should be encouraged to bring to class pictures of objects that operate on electricity. The answer sheet follows the work sheet.

V. Independent Practice and Application Using the Computer

Play a software game that reinforces the lesson.

LESSON 1-11 ELECTRICITY

It was dark. It was very dark. CPU tried to POWER UP — to turn on. Nothing happened.

Monty Monitor tried to light his face. Nothing happened.

Dizzy Disk Drive tried to spin Susie Software. Nothing happened.

"What is wrong? I've flipped my switch on and off, off and on and — nothing happened. I don't understand! Why can't I tell Dizzy to spin Susie? Why can't Monty's face light up? Why? Why? Why?"

"We'd better call for help," said Dizzy.

"Help, help," said Monty.

"Help, help, help," said Susie.

"Who is calling?" asked Larry Lamp. Larry usually sits by CPU so that it isn't dark. But even Larry wasn't making it light. "I said, who is calling?"

"We are all calling," said CPU.

"What is the problem?" asked Larry.

"I tried to POWER UP; I flipped my switch; I tried to turn on, and nothing happened," said CPU.

"What should happen?" asked Larry.

CPU said "Dizzy Disk Drive should spin Susie Software and the name of a program should light up on Monty Monitor's face."

"And?" asked Larry.

"And nothing happened," said CPU.

"Nothing," said Larry. "I think I know what the problem is. It is also bothering me."

"You — you are a light. You are not a computer," said CPU.
"That is true, but we both need the same thing," said Larry.
"What is it?" asked Dizzy.

"It is electricity," said Larry.
"Electricity," they all said together.

"Yes, electricity comes to you through your wire and plug, and I have a wire and plug too," said Larry. "We both use electricity to work. Last night there was a storm and a tree fell on the wires that bring the electricity in here. They are fixing the wires right now. Electricity can be dangerous, but it is also very helpful. It makes lights, televisions, and computers work."

"I feel kind of tingly," said Larry. "The electricity is back. Try your switch now."

CPU flipped his switch. Dizzy started spinning Susie Software and Monty Monitor's face lit up and said, "Let's Play the Power Game."

Everyone said, "Hurray!"

It is no longer dark. CPU has POWERED UP, and now something is going to happen. We need power — electric power — to light up, and to play."

Lesson 1-11 Questions

1. What does "power up" mean in computer language? (turn on the computer)
2. How do you "power up?" (use switches on the CPU case)
3. Who came to answer the call for help? (Larry Lamp)
4. Did CPU think Larry Lamp could help? (no)
5. Did they both need the same thing? (yes)
6. What was it? (electricity)
7. Why wasn't there electricity? (A storm had made a tree fall on the outside wires to the school.)
8. How do you get electricity? (through wires and plugs)
9. Can any of the computer parts work without electricity? (no)
10. What needs electricity? (anything with a wire and a plug)

Name ______________________________

1-11 Does it Need Electricity?

Does it get plugged in to work?

I-11 Does it Need Electricity? (Answers)

LESSON 1-12 ON/OFF SWITCH

To the Teacher

Everyone in Computer Land is asleep. The computer parts are eager to start computing, but nothing is happening. CPU starts yawning and everyone starts feeling different. Everyone wants to know what is happening. They know that the electricity is on because Larry Lamp is on. Snappy Switch is the reason. CPU stays asleep until Snappy changes from her "0" side to her "1" side. The good and bad points about electricity are taught by Snappy who takes her job very seriously. Dizzy and Susie get ready for CPU before Snappy flips her switch. Snappy tells the computer parts to be sure they want to quit before her switch is turned off, because once the electricity is turned off, you can't go back.

New words in this lesson: switch

I. Objectives

- Understand that switches control electricity.
- Recognize the "1" for on and "0" for off switch.
- Realize that computers lose information when the electricity is turned off.

II. Instructional Input and Learning Activities

- Make overhead transparencies for each page of the story.
- Place the transparency on the stage of the overhead projector and cover the portion of the page you are not using.
- Read the story to the children.

III. Check for Understanding

Use the review questions at the end of the story to test for story comprehension. Cover the questions as you read the last page of the story. Answers are in parentheses.

IV. Guided Practice

The "What Is Inside?" work sheet is designed to help students understand what things look like on the inside. Duplicate the work sheet for students. Instruct students to draw a line from an external picture of an object to the internal picture of the same object. The answer sheet follows the work sheet.

V. Independent Practice and Application Using the Computer

Play a software game that reinforces the lesson.

LESSON 1-12 ON/OFF SWITCH

One day in Computer Land the keys were waiting for something to happen. It was a day like any other day. Computer Brain, better known as CPU, was asleep. If CPU was asleep, everyone else was asleep also.

Peter Printer was asleep because he did not have anything to put on paper.

Dizzy Disk Drive and Susie Software were asleep because no one had asked for a special program to spin in Dizzy and give the information to CPU.

Mo Mouse was asleep and not doing her pointing.

Monty Monitor's face was dark. He was asleep. If CPU didn't have anything to show anyone, there was no need for Monty to be bright and shiny.

"Dizzy, Susie, how about spinning and playing a game?" called Return Key.

"We would love to, but we can't." said Dizzy.

"You can't! What do you mean?" asked Return Key.

"Something is wrong," said Dizzy. "I don't feel that I can spin Susie at all."

"And I don't feel right, either," said Monty.

Just then CPU began to yawn and stretch. Everyone looked at him. They started feeling different. Monty Monitor's face was bright. Dizzy was spinning Susie. Peter Printer woke up and his ready light glowed like a bright candle.

"What happened?" asked Return Key. "Weren't you feeling well, CPU? Why was everything so dark and — and. . . ? "

"And OFF," said CPU. "You were all waiting for something to happen. It is like any other day. I stay asleep until something important happens."

"Until what happens?" asked Return Key. He was very excited and impatient. He wanted to know why nothing happened when Dizzy tried to spin Susie, and why Monty's face was dark.

"It is because of me," a small voice interrupted.

"Who are you?" everyone asked together.

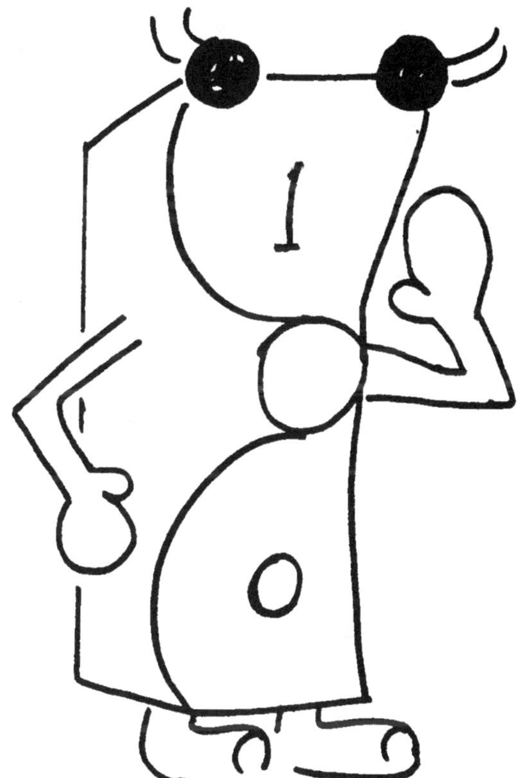

"I am the on/off switch," said the voice. The owner of the voice looked like a seesaw on a playground. She had a one and a zero on the sides of her small body. "My name is Snappy Switch."

“Snappy,” said Return Key. “What do you do that you can wake Computer Brain when all of the rest of us tried and he wouldn’t get up?”

“Well,” said Snappy. “I flip from my ‘0’ — off — side to my ‘1’ — on — side, and the electricity wakes everyone up.”

Everyone waited for Snappy to say something else, but she didn’t.

“Is that all?” asked everyone.

“That is all I do. If my “1” side is flipped, electricity can run to CPU and wake him up. If my “0” side is flipped, electricity cannot run to CPU and he shuts off and goes to sleep,” said Snappy.

"Wow! I've heard about electricity. It makes the lights bright," said Peter Printer. "It can also be dangerous if it is not handled correctly."

"Right," said Snappy. "That is why I take my job very seriously. I can wake up CPU, but he has to be ready with Susie Software and Dizzy Disk Drive; otherwise Monty will show a blank face and we have to start all over again."

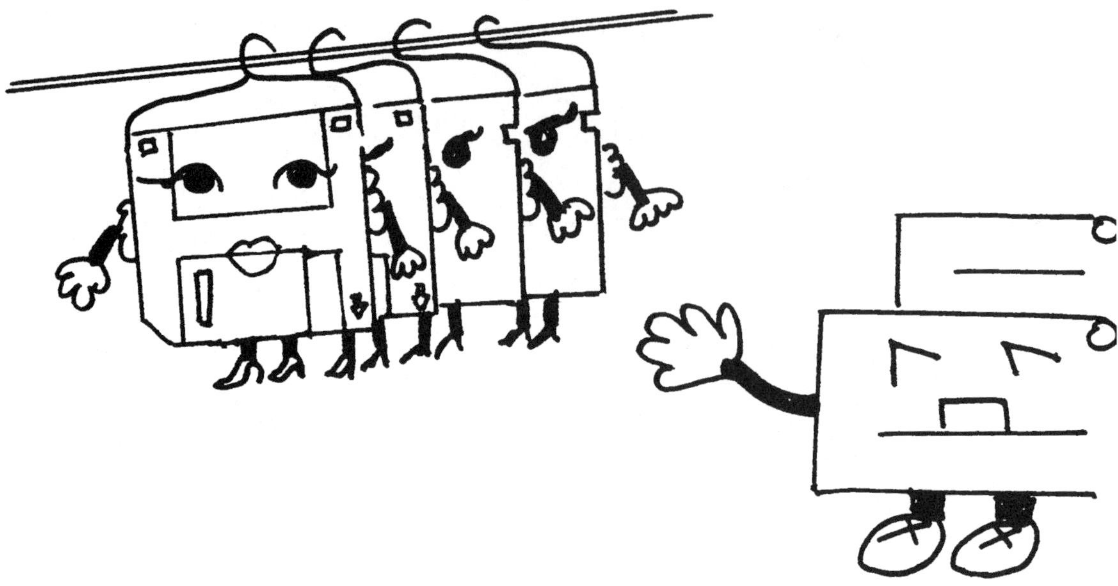

Dizzy and Susie said they would be happy to get ready first. After all, it takes time to pick out what you want to do and you shouldn't waste CPU's time. He is very important and can do so many different things.

"One last thing," said Snappy. "Be sure you want to stop when I flip my switch to '0', or you will lose everything you are doing. You can't go back to the same place once the electricity is gone — so think."

Menu

End

Quit

Susie said, "Don't forget — you always should go back to Main Menu before you stop. Go back to Main Menu, take out Susie Software, then quit, then switch."

Lesson 1-12 Questions

1. Why was everyone asleep? (because CPU was asleep)
2. What does CPU do to get his electricity flowing? (turns on with the power switch)
3. What does the computer switch look like? (There is a "1" on the "on" side of the switch and a "0" on the "off" side.)
4. Which side lets the electricity flow? (the "1" side)
5. Should you keep switching on and off between programs? (no)
6. Who has to be ready before switching on? (Dizzy Disk Drive and Susie Software)
7. What happens if Snappy Switch switches off in the middle of your program? (You lose everything.)
8. What should you do first if you want to stop? (return to Main Menu)
9. Should you take out your software before you turn off your computer? (yes)
10. Is electricity dangerous? (yes)

Name ______________________________

1-12 What Is Inside?

1-12 What is Inside? (Answers)

1-20
2-15
3-18
4-19
5-13
6-17
7-16
8-12
9-11
10-14

LESSON 1-13 CHIP

To the Teacher

Ryan is wondering what his computer looks like on the inside. Chip arrives and tells Ryan about himself — what he is made of and how he looks under a microscope. Chip compares it to using an x-ray machine for humans. The history of vacuum tubes, transistors, and integrated circuits is a part of Chip's family history. Chip tells about his centipede carrier and the different kinds of chips. Ryan looks inside his computer and sees a plastic board with the centipedes and transistors. He learns a lot about Chip and how important he is.

New words in this lesson:	integrated circuit	x-ray
	silicon	centipede
	microscope	

I. Objectives

- Describe the inside of a computer chip.
- Know computer generation history.

II. Instructional Input and Learning Activities

- Make overhead transparencies for each page of the story.
- Place the transparency on the stage of the overhead projector and cover the portion of the page you are not using.
- Read the story to the children.

III. Check for Understanding

Use the review questions at the end of the story to test for story comprehension. Cover the questions as you read the last page of the story. Answers are in parentheses.

IV. Guided Practice

The "Chip-O" game reviews how chips are fabricated.

Materials - Chip-O board, one die, and markers for players

Copy and laminate the game board. Put markers in the "Beginning" box. Roll the die and follow the directions on the board. The first player to reach the "Learn & Fun" box is the winner.

V. Independent Practice and Application Using the Computer

Play a software game that reinforces the lesson.

LESSON 1-13 CHIP

One day Ryan was using his computer, and he wondered what a computer looked like on the inside.

It doesn't have any wheels. It doesn't have any light bulbs. It doesn't have any buzzers or bells.

"What makes it work?" asked Ryan.

"I do. I'm Chip — Silicon Chip."

"What's a CHIP?" asked Ryan in surprise.

"A chip is like a square inside a square. Well I'm really more than that. You need a microscope to see what is inside," said Chip.

"A microscope!" said Ryan.

"A microscope lets you see tiny, tiny things — really tiny. In the microscope I look like a map of a city's streets. That's what you'd see in me with a microscope."

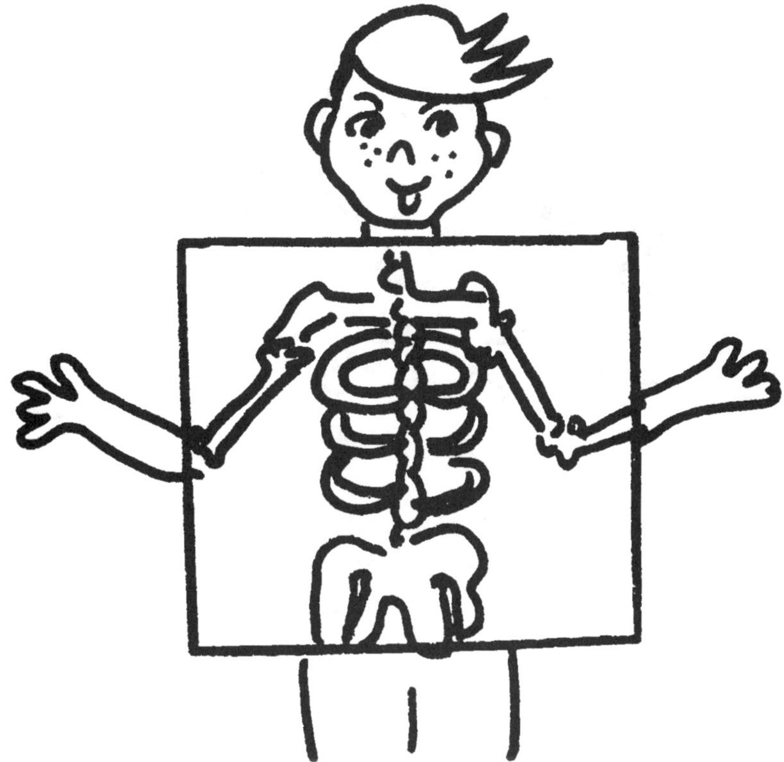

"If you looked at your body with an x-ray, you would see bones, and other things."

"There aren't any cars or buses on my streets — only electricity. Electricity travels on my streets very fast because I am so small," said Chip.

"There are different kinds of chips, too. Some do the arithmetic, some remember, and some follow directions," said CPU.

"We all have to work together to make your computer do anything," said Chip.

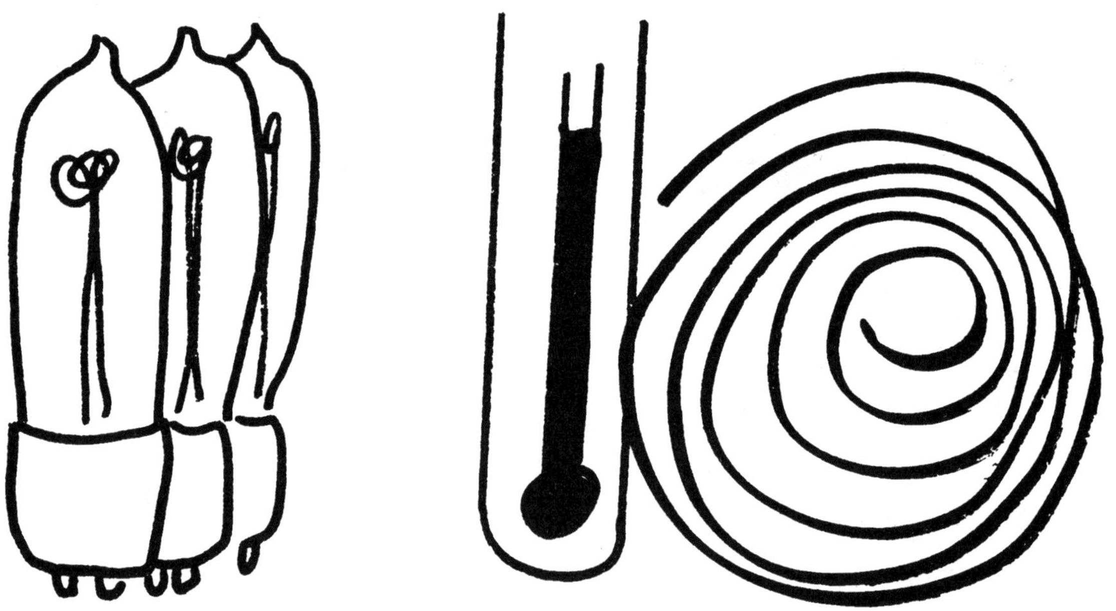

"A long time ago computers didn't have chips. A long time ago computers were as big as rooms. They had hundreds of vacuum tubes, like light bulbs, and miles and miles of wire. They were very hot and had lots of problems."

"Then came integrated circuits — no more vacuum tubes. Then transistors replaced integrated circuits. Transistors carried electricity like vacuum tubes and integrated circuits, but they were smaller and looked like thimbles with wires."

"And then my family and I came along. We are the smallest. I can fit on the tip of your finger, and because of that I need a plastic carrying case."

"The plastic carrying case has a funny name; it is called a centipede, because it looks like a bug with lots of legs. The legs connect me to a board and to the other chips."

"Without Chip and his family computers would be used only by governments, big hospitals, and big businesses. Chip has made computers small and cheap enough for everyone to have and use," said CPU.

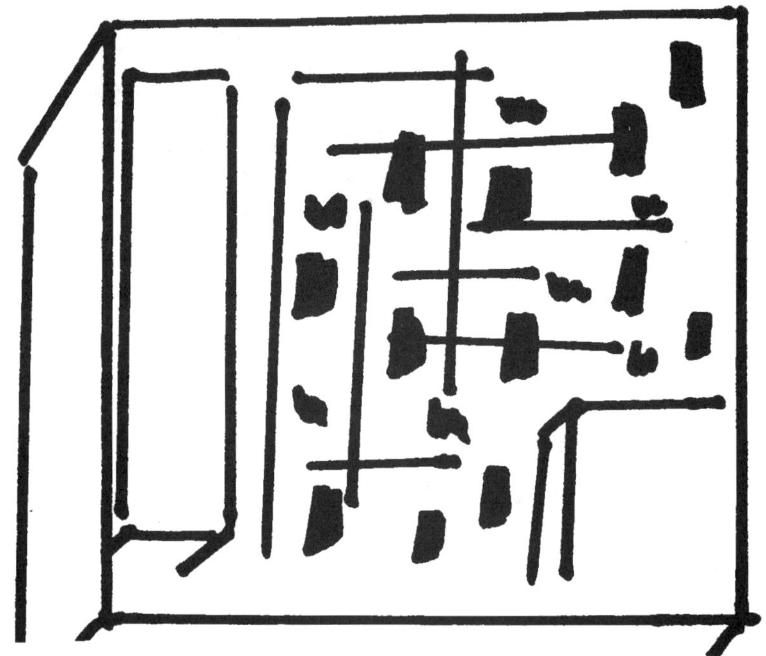

Ryan said, "My computer looks like a board with plastic squares."

"Yes," said CPU, "there are a few special wires, but nothing is moving inside — only electricity."

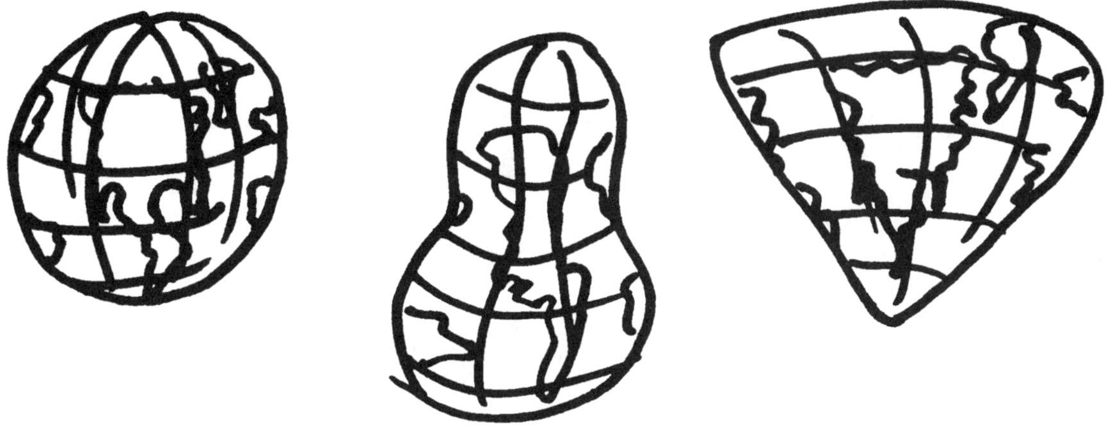

"The computer is a machine that has changed the world because it can do so many things for so many people," said CPU.

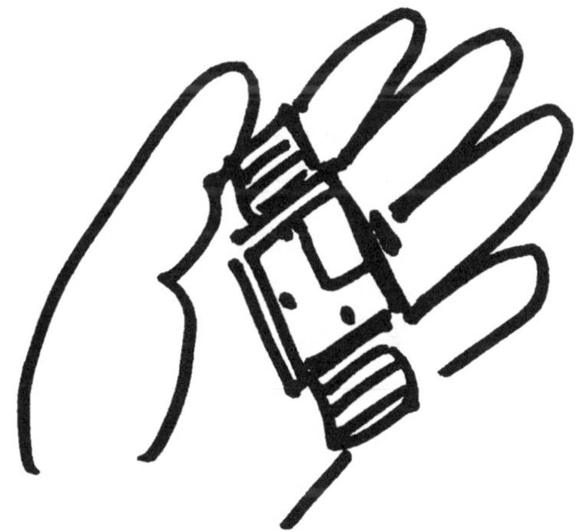

"Computers can fit in your hand. They can play games. They can teach. They can tell time," said Chip.

"I get the idea," said Ryan.

"But," said CPU, "COMPUTERS ARE ONLY AS GOOD AS THE PEOPLE MAKING AND USING THEM."

Lesson 1-13 Questions

1. What does a computer look like on the inside? (big square of plastic with other squares of plastic, and raised lines and bumps)
2. Are there moving parts inside a computer? (no)
3. What are chips made of? (silicon)
4. What does the surface of a chip look like? (map of streets)
5. Do cars travel on these streets? (no — electricity)
6. What was inside CPUs before chips? (vacuum tubes, wires, and transistors)
7. Without chips who would own computers? (governments, hospitals, and big businesses)
8. Chips are so small that they need a carrying case. What is it called? (centipede)
9. What is a computer? (a machine that can do many things to help save time, and make life easier)
10. How good are computers? (only as good as the people making and using them)

Name ______________________________

1-13 Chip-O

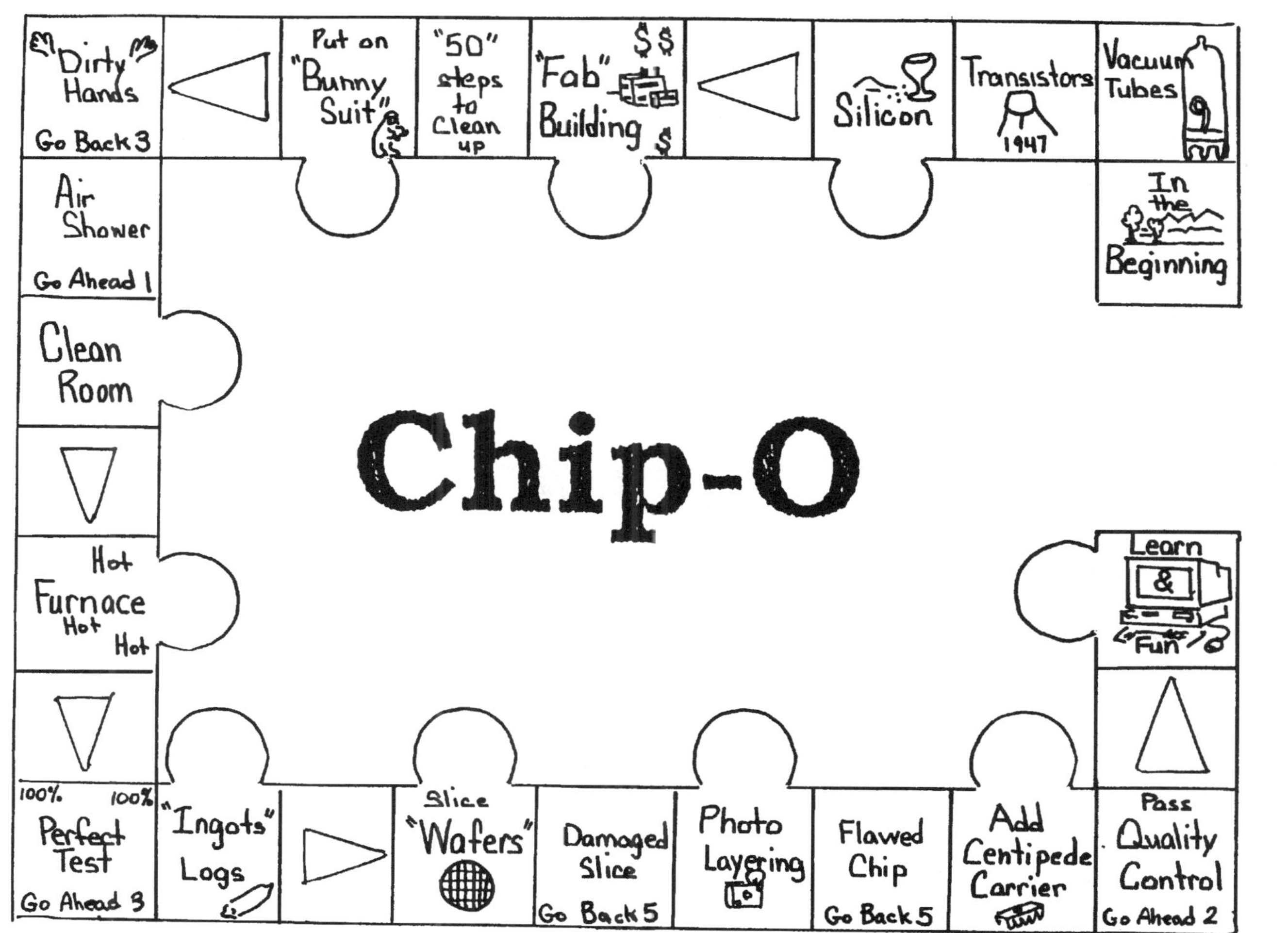

LESSON 1-14 MEMORY CONTEST

To the Teacher

The parts are going to have a contest to see who can remember the best — Kiki Keyboard, Mo Mouse, Monty Monitor, CPU, and Peter Printer (the Hardware Team) versus Susie Software. Susie feels she has an edge because CPU is the only part that can remember and he doesn't have a hard drive. CPU doesn't think a hard drive will make a difference. Data Base has all kinds of things for Susie and CPU to remember. One year passes. CPU has been turned off and on many times during that year. CPU did not remember because when the electricity is turned off, the information is gone. Susie has saved the information on her disk and she remembers everything. Susie wants CPU to have a hard drive. CPU worries that if he has a hard drive Susie will go away. CPU and Susie decide to work together.

New words in this lesson: hardware data base

I. Objective

- Understand the difference between saving information on the hard drive and saving it on floppy disks.

II. Instructional Input and Learning Activities

- Make overhead transparencies for each page of the story.
- Place the transparency on the stage of the overhead projector and cover the portion of the page you are not using.
- Read the story to the children.

III. Check for Understanding

Use the review questions at the end of the story to test for story comprehension. Cover the questions as you read the last page of the story. Answers are in parentheses.

IV. Guided Practice

The "What's in the Box?" game tests human memory.

Materials - game pictures, boxes to put pictures in, timer

Duplicate, laminate, and cut apart the pictures. Students are divided into teams, and each team has a box. Place five different pictures in each box. One member of each team comes to the box and studies the items for five to fifteen seconds. Students say, write, or draw pictures of what they remember. One point is given for each correct guess. Twenty points win the game, or the team with the most points wins. Teams can exchange boxes at the end of the time you have allotted.

V. Independent Practice and Application Using the Computer

Play a software game that reinforces the lesson.

LESSON 1-14 MEMORY CONTEST

One day all the parts of the computer got together. They were going to have a contest. The contest was going to show who could remember best.

The parts decided to call themselves the Hardware Team, because they were all made of hard plastic.

The Hardware Team was very pleased with itself. They wondered who was going to be on the other team. They had the best team and everyone in Computer Land was on their team.

"Who will be on the other team? We are all here. There isn't anyone left to play against," said the Hardware Team.

Then Susie Software spoke up. "I'll be on the other team with my sister softwares," she said.

"That is not going to be fair," said Mo Mouse. "Look how many of us there are."

Susie said, "Just a couple of you have good memories. Kiki Keyboard, Mo Mouse, and Monty Monitor can't remember anything. Peter Printer can't remember anything himself; he has to put it on paper. That leaves CPU. Our friend CPU doesn't have a hard drive and that will make a difference."

"What are the rules?" asked Susie.

The Hardware Team said, "Whoever remembers the most is the winner. We will tell you things to remember today, and we will come back in one year to see who remembers best."

"I do feel I am going to beat CPU," said Susie. "After all CPU doesn't have a hard drive."

"Let the contest begin!" shouted CPU. He was a little upset at Susie's thinking he couldn't win because he didn't have a hard drive. After all what is a hard drive?

Dizzy said, "A hard drive is a cousin of mine that lives in certain computers. It spins a disk like Susie only it is made of metal, and you can't see it because it is inside the CPU. Our friend CPU doesn't have a hard drive because they didn't give him one at the factory."

"So a hard drive is how CPU remembers without you," said Mo.

"That is right," said Dizzy.

It was agreed that Susie could ask Dizzy Disk Drive to help, because after all, Susie is just a piece of round plastic inside a square piece of plastic.

The judge for the contest was Data Base. He had all kinds of things for Susie and CPU to remember. Data Base gave all the information to CPU. The information showed on Monty's face.

Susie said, "I'm ready; I said SAVE," and she spun around and around.

Data Base said, "You all have the information. Peter Printer will make a paper copy but that doesn't count. He just makes the backup copy of the contest information; paper isn't a computer part."

One year passed very quickly and the Hardware Team and Susie Software met to see who won.

CPU had been turned on and off many times during that year. He had done many things like playing games, teaching math, and writing stories, and he didn't think too much about the contest.

Now Data Base said, "Let's see who can remember the most. CPU you go first."

CPU flipped his switch on and tried to remember, but nothing happened.

Susie spun around and there on Monty's face was everything Data Base had told her — one year later.

"It could be ten years, or fifty," said Susie. "I am the winner."

Then she looked at CPU.

"You would have won also if you had a hard drive," said Susie.

"If I have a hard drive, then I won't need you anymore. You are a real friend and I don't want you to go away," said CPU.

Susie said, "You can have a hard drive put inside. Dizzy and I will work together. Sometimes things that need saving shouldn't be on a hard drive. All the new programs you need will still be on me and I will still give you the program first; then you can put it on your hard drive. You can pick and choose what you want to remember on your hard drive and what you want me to remember."

"I'll have the best," said CPU. He had a hard drive put inside. It felt good to know he could remember. It also felt good to know that Susie Software would still remember for him. She was a real friend.

Lesson 1-14 Questions

1. What kind of contest were the parts going to have? (memory contest)
2. How did the parts decide to be on the same team? (All the hard plastic parts were together.)
3. Which parts were on the same team? (CPU, Dizzy Disk Drive, Monty Monitor, Mo Mouse, and Kiki Keyboard)
4. What did they call their team? (Hardware Team)
5. Who was going to be on a team by herself? (Susie Software)
6. How does Peter Printer remember? (puts information on paper)
7. Susie had a reason for being happy to be a team all by herself. What was it? (Only CPU would be able to remember.)
8. What will make a difference in CPU's remembering? (CPU doesn't have a hard drive.)
9. What will happen to CPU's memory when he is turned off? (All the information will be lost.)
10. Who won? (Susie)

Name ______________________________

1-14 What's in the Box?

Section 2

Hardware

LESSON 2-1 COMPUTER BRAIN GETS LONESOME

To the Teacher

CPU isn't his usual self. He isn't bragging the way he usually does. CPU wants to go places, just like Ryan or one of the other computers that he knows. A new computer part moves into the computer room. Ms. Barbara installs the new computer part in CPU. It is Molly Modem. Molly helps CPU talk to his friends all over the world with the help of the telephone. Molly explains how she works to help CPU visit his friends. CPU is happy. The first computer that he wants to talk to is Library Computer.

New words in this lesson:	modem	Internet
	signals	World Wide Web

I. Objective

- Describe how computers communicate with modems.

II. Instructional Input and Learning Activities

- Make overhead transparencies for each page of the story.
- Place the transparency on the stage of the overhead projector and cover the portion of the page you are not using.
- Read the story to the children.

III. Check for Understanding

Use the review questions at the end of the story to test for story comprehension. Cover the questions as you read the last page of the story. Answers are in parentheses.

IV. Guided Practice

The "Do You Need Two?" work sheet develops the idea of pairs. Duplicate the work sheet for students. Instruct students to draw a circle around the pictures of those items that need two to be complete. Example: a pair of shoes. The answer sheet follows the work sheet.

V. Independent Practice and Application Using the Computer

Play a software game that reinforces the lesson.

LESSON 2-1 COMPUTER BRAIN GETS LONESOME

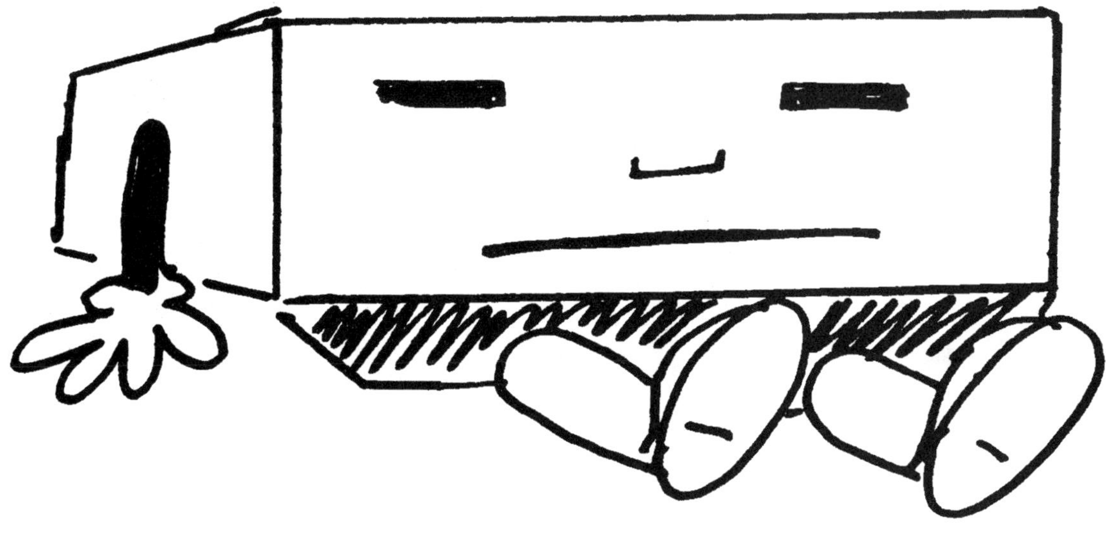

One day Computer Brain, better known as CPU, wasn't his usual self. He wasn't bragging. He wasn't writing letters, or adding really big numbers really fast, and he wasn't playing a game. He was just sitting.

All the other parts looked at Computer Brain. They were usually very busy, but today was different.

"What is wrong?" they all asked.

Computer Brain looked at them and said, "I really wish I could go someplace. Ryan, the boy who comes in and plays games with us, can run around. He can walk in. He can sit in his chair in front of me. He can use his hands and make Kiki Keyboard's letter keys jump up and down. He can point, click, and drag Mo Mouse.

He can go outside, but I just sit here. I'm a school computer. I'm not a computer in an airplane, or a car. I'm not a watch computer. They can go all over the world. I just have to sit here. I wish I could go somewhere — and I don't mean to get repaired."

The parts liked being in the computer room. They liked helping the boys and girls learn adding and reading. They really liked playing games with the children, but they understood how CPU might feel when all of the other computer brains he knew about could move around.

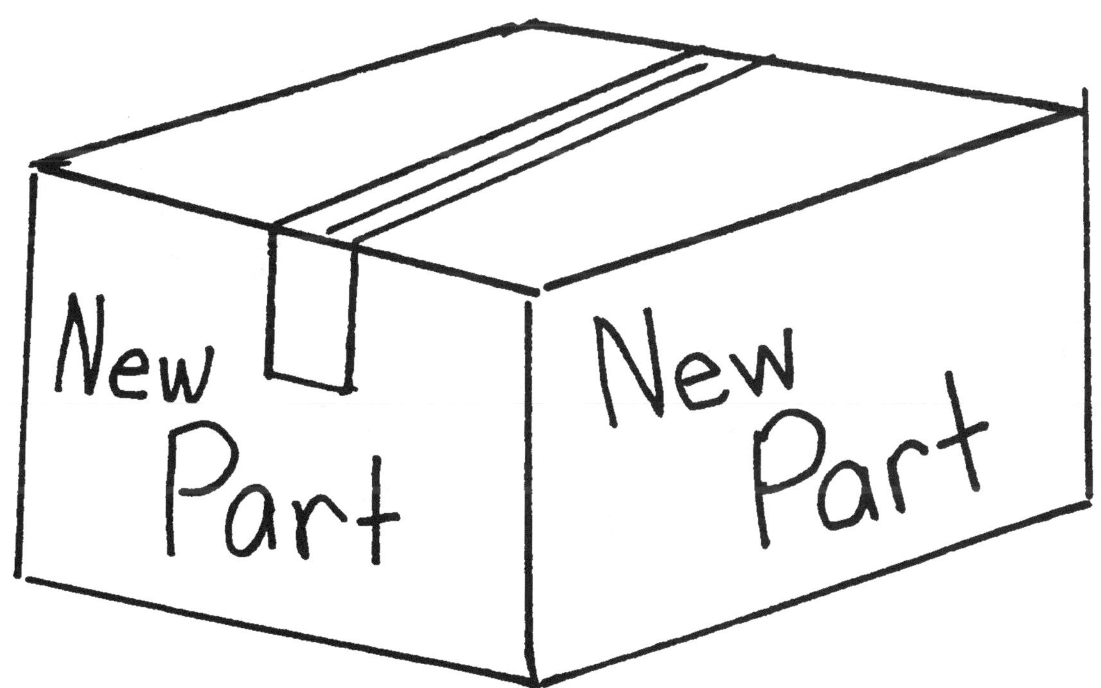

Someone must have heard CPU's wish, because a new part arrived in Computer Land. She didn't look like the rest of the parts. She wasn't big, or square.

Ms. Barbara carefully opened CPU's case and attached the new part to CPU's brain board. The new part looked like a green board with little square pieces of plastic on it. She carefully closed CPU's case and ran a wire to where the telephone wire came into the room.

All the parts wondered what was going on.

"I feel different," said CPU. "I've never felt this way before. What happened?"

The parts told CPU what Ms. Barbara had done.

Then the new part spoke up.

"My name is Modem, Molly Modem, I hope you don't mind that I've come to live with you?"

CPU said, "What if I do mind? Can anything be done?"

"Probably not," said Molly. "Let me tell you about myself. I can let you talk to computers anyplace in the whole world."

CPU was surprised. He said, "The whole world. How can you do that?"
Molly said, "First I need to be hooked up to a telephone line."
The other parts said, "Ms. Barbara did that."

"Then I dial the telephone number of another computer with a modem like me. Once we are connected, someone will type on the keyboard, and I will change the words into tiny sound signals. The sound signals go to the other computer and your message appears on its screen. I use my telephone link — the Internet and the World Wide Web — to get information and talk with computers all over the world."

CPU was happy. "I want to talk to my friend Library Computer. I haven't seen her in ages."

CPU was happy. He wouldn't be able to leave the room, but he would be able to talk to other computers. He said, "This is terrific. When do we get started?

Lesson 2-1 Questions

1. Why was CPU unhappy? (He was a school computer and couldn't go anyplace.)
2. What was the name of the new computer part? (Molly Modem)
3. Where did Ms. Barbara put her? (inside CPU with a wire to the telephone line)
4. What did Molly look like? (like a green board with plastic squares)
5. What does Molly do? (lets CPU talk to other computers that have modems)
6. How do you talk with a modem? (keyboard and telephone line)
7. Was CPU happy with Molly Modem? (yes)
8. Whom did CPU want to talk to first? (library computer)
9. What do we call the telephone link to computers all over the world? (Internet — World Wide Web)
10. What is the purpose of the Internet and the World Wide Web? (You can get information and talk with people all over the world.)

Name ____

Do You Need Two?

Do You Need Two? (Answers)

LESSON 2-2 MONTY MONITOR

To the Teacher

Monty Monitor and CPU are having an argument about who is more important. Peter Printer reminds CPU that before Monty, everyone had to wait until CPU was finished working and Peter made a hard copy. Monty remembers how Great-grandfather Television helped out in the "old days" and then Monty took over. Everyone agreed they all needed to work together to play the game.

New words in this lesson: There are no new words.

I. Objective

- Understand the need of a monitor to see what the computer is doing.

II. Instructional Input and Learning Activities

- Make overhead transparencies for each page of the story.
- Place the transparency on the stage of the overhead projector and cover the portion of the page you are not using.
- Read the story to the children.

III. Check for Understanding

Use the review questions at the end of the story to test for story comprehension. Cover the questions as you read the last page of the story. Answers are in parentheses.

IV. Guided Practice

The "Computer Puzzle" work sheets familiarize students with computer hardware. Work sheet 1 has the puzzle pieces, and work sheet 2 is for student use. Duplicate work sheet 1 for each student; cut each page into pieces, using the code in the top right-hand corner; and place the pieces in envelopes. Distribute one envelope of puzzle pieces to each student and instruct students to glue the puzzle pieces to work sheet 2.

V. Independent Practice and Application Using the Computer

Play a software game that reinforces the lesson.

Lesson 2-2 Monty Monitor

If you ever wondered who gets up first in Computer Land, it is CPU. Computer Brain works very hard doing math, playing games, writing letters, and hundreds of other things. But no one would know what CPU was doing if Monty Monitor didn't come along.

Without Monty, it would be like trying to read a book with a blindfold on.

One day, Monty and CPU had an argument as to who was more important. Monty shouted, "Without me no one would be able to see what CPU was doing."

CPU shouted, "Without me Monty would be a night light."

Peter Printer heard the shouting. In the early days, before Monty came to town, everyone had to wait for CPU to finish his work — and then Peter Printer would take over and put the information on paper.

"I remember," said Mo Mouse. "The paper was long and it was called 'hard copy.'"

"Paper from me is still called 'hard copy,'" said Peter.

"But it took so long to get answers from CPU," said Mo.

"Then Monty's great-grandfather came to the rescue — Great-grandfather Television. He worked with CPU for a while, but then he said he liked the news, and cartoons, and animal shows better. He said he wasn't a computer person." said Peter.

"I remember," said CPU. "I lost my first friend."

"Great-grandfather thought I could take over for him. I was very proud. I look like a television, but I'm different. I just work with CPU," said Monty.

"You can't let your Great-grandfather down," said Mo. "CPU, you know how fast Monty is and how he never does anything except what you say."

"That is right," said Peter. "I still do all the paper work — hard copies — but only after it is checked on Monty's screen."

"Well, that just shows you we can't do without one another. We are all important and we can't break up a team," said Mo.

"Right," said Peter. "If one of us doesn't play, the game is over."

"Let's make up," said CPU, "I want to play a game."

"It is fun to see what you are doing; I don't like playing in the dark," said Mo.

Lesson 2-2 Questions

1. Who lets you see what CPU is doing? (Monty Monitor)
2. In the early days, how did people know what CPU was doing? (Peter Printer printed the information on paper.)
3. What is printing on paper called? (making a hard copy)
4. What does a monitor look like? (television)
5. If CPU and Monty had a fight and didn't work together, what would Monty look like? (night light)
6. Can Monty Monitor be a television? (no)
7. How quickly can Peter Printer work? (He has to wait until CPU is finished working before he can start.)
8. How do Monty and Peter work together? (You can check work on Monty before Peter makes a copy.)
9. Why is paper from Peter called hard copy? (You can touch it and take it with you.)
10. Can Monty or CPU work without the other part? (no)

Name ______________________________

Computer Puzzle (Worksheet 1)

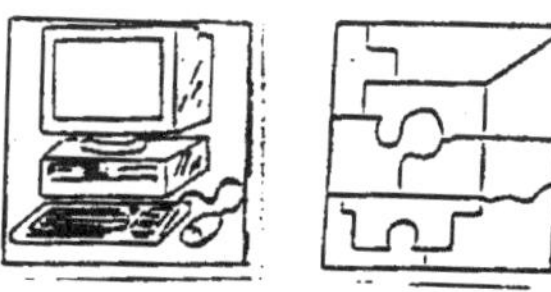

Cut into marked pieces
Keep in envelopes

Name ______________________________

Computer Puzzle (Worksheet 2)

LESSON 2-3 PETER PRINTER

To the Teacher

Monty Monitor has work to do; he can't just sit around and be a sign for wet paint or anything else. Peter Printer steps up and says, "My job is making permanent copies of what CPU and Monty want to save." Susie Software and Dizzy Disk Drive step up and say their job is to make permanent copies, but that you need CPU and Monty Monitor to see them. Peter explains how he and CPU work together. He also talks about track paper and single-sheet paper. The letters are happy that Peter and CPU make the sign to go on the wet paint.

New words in this lesson: track paper soft copy

I. Objectives

- Describe how printers make permanent copies of computer work.
- Distinguish between soft and hard copies.
- Understand that disk information cannot be seen without a computer.

II. Instructional Input and Learning Activities

- Make overhead transparencies for each page of the story.
- Place the transparency on the stage of the overhead projector and cover the portion of the page you are not using.
- Read the story to the children.

III. Check for Understanding

Use the review questions at the end of the story to test for story comprehension. Cover the questions as you read the last page of the story. Answers are in parentheses.

IV. Guided Practice

The "Partners" work sheet emphasizes that computer hardware must work together to complete a task. Duplicate the work sheet for students and instruct them to draw a line between pictures of objects that need a partner to complete a task. The answer sheet follows the work sheet.

V. Independent Practice and Application Using the Computer

Play a software game that reinforces the lesson.

LESSON 2-3 PETER PRINTER

The letters were all playing. It was fun to see their names on Monty Monitor's face, but sometimes they wanted to make signs to help, like WET PAINT, NO LEFT TURN, STOP.

Monty Monitor couldn't go where the wet paint was, or anyplace else. He couldn't just sit around being a sign. He had work to do.

Monty said, "I can go only as far as my cord that connects me to CPU, and CPU doesn't want to make just one sign. He has many things for me to do."

"Well, the paint is still wet. What should we do?" asked the letters.

Peter Printer was sitting beside CPU, Computer Brain, and Dizzy Disk Drive was sitting on the other side. Dizzy didn't say anything, but Peter did.

Peter Printer said, "Pardon me. I've been listening and I think I can help."

"How?" asked the letters.

"My job is to make permanent paper copies of what CPU and Monty make," said Peter.

Dizzy Disk Drive interrupted, "I make copies on disks but that won't help. You can't see anything that I save on my disk without Monty, but it can last forever."

"No, that won't help," said the letters.

"I make the hard copies. Dizzy Disk Drive makes soft copies on disks, and Monty makes soft copies on his face, which disappear. Hard copies last forever," said Peter.

"How does that happen?" asked the letters.

"CPU, Computer Brain, gives me the command PRINT and I do. Anything that is on Monty's face will be on the paper," said Peter.

"Great, the paint is still wet and we need the sign now," said the letters. "Please print one for us."

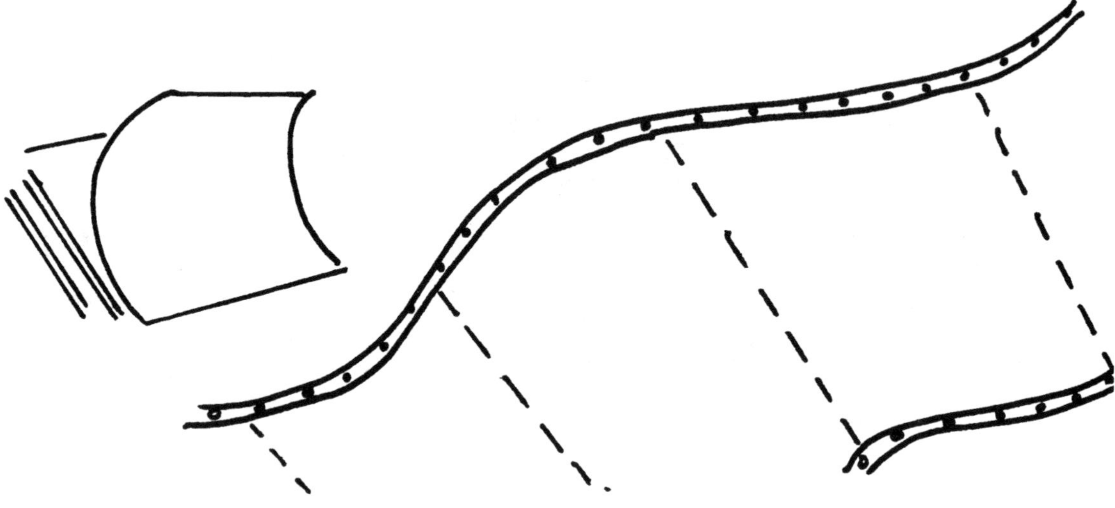

"One more thing," said Peter. "I have two kinds of paper. Which kind do you want?" One kind is like the pages in a book — single sheets. One kind is connected together. It is called track paper, and I can make a sign a mile long."

"Wow!" said the letters. "We don't need one that long. We will be happy to have the words on a single sheet."

"Do you want pictures?" asked Peter. "I can have pictures, too. They can be in color or black and white. I am good at copying anything."

"Just the letters, please," said the letters.

The letters were happy to see themselves on the hard copy. They were happy to help, so people wouldn't get paint on themselves. They were also happy to learn that whenever they wanted to save what they said forever, they could use software or paper.

The letters really like seeing themselves. You're looking at them right now and they think it is GREAT.

Lesson 2-3 Questions

1. Could Monty Monitor be a sign? (no)
2. Could he go where wet paint was and just stand there till the paint dried? (no)
3. What is Peter Printer's job? (make permanent copies of CPU's work)
4. What kind of copies do Dizzy Disk Drive and Susie Software make? (soft copies on disks)
5. What is used to save CPU's work? (paper and disks)
6. What kind of copies does Monty Monitor make? (soft copies on his face)
7. What are Peter Printer's copies called? (hard copy)
8. What kind of paper is connected together in long folded sheets? (track paper)
9. What kind of copies may be carried around for everyone to see? (hard copies)
10. What is the command for Peter Printer to make a hard copy? (print)

Name ______________________________

Partners

Ex. They go together.

Partners (Answers)

Ex:  They go together.

1-20
2-15
3-16
4-17
5-18
6-14
7-12
8-19
9-11
10-13

LESSON 2-4 TO PRINT OR NOT TO PRINT

To the Teacher

Peter Printer looks at a photo album and tells Molly Modem about his relatives Dot-matrix, Inkjet, and Laser. Peter talks about track paper and about hard copies, which enable people without computers to benefit from computer information.

New words in this lesson: dot-matrix inkjet laser

I. Objectives

- Identify the different kinds of printers.
- Understand the differences in their print formation.
- Realize that all printers make hard copies.

II. Instructional Input and Learning Activities

- Make overhead transparencies for each page of the story.
- Place the transparency on the stage of the overhead projector and cover the portion of the page you are not using.
- Read the story to the children.

III. Check for Understanding

Use the review questions at the end of the story to test for story comprehension. Cover the questions as you read the last page of the story. Answers are in parentheses.

IV. Guided Practice

The "Criss-Cross Capture" game is used to review concepts taught in previous lessons. Choose subjects that you feel need reinforcing. Cut apart the letters; you can make them with paper or transparency plastic. There are enough letters to cover all the grid letters. Make an overhead transparency of the grid and put the letters into a container. Make a list of your review questions. Students are divided into teams. Teams take turns in answering review questions. If the student answers a question correctly, he or she picks a letter from the "take" pile and places it anywhere on the grid. For example, an "o" can be placed in the "o" of "computer," "monitor," "mouse," or "keyboard." The object of the game is to complete a word — to capture it. If the letter completes two words, then two words are captured. Strategy is involved in playing to make a short word or a double word. The team with the most captured words is the winner.

V. Independent Practice and Application Using the Computer

Play a software game that reinforces the lesson.

LESSON 2-4 TO PRINT OR NOT TO PRINT

One day Peter Printer was looking at his family photo album with Molly Modem.

Peter said, "We don't look exactly alike but we all do the same thing. We make hard copies."

Peter was very proud of his family. He was proud that he was the only computer part that copied information on paper for Computer Brain.

Peter said, "Here is a picture of Great-grandfather. He waited until Computer Brain was completely finished working and copied rolls and rolls of information on rolls and rolls of paper. He was so big that only governments, hospitals, and big businesses had room for him and Computer Brain."

"Here are pictures of my cousins Dot-Matrix, Inkjet, Color Inkjet, and me — Peter "Laser" Printer," said Peter.

"How are you different, and how are you alike?" Molly asked.

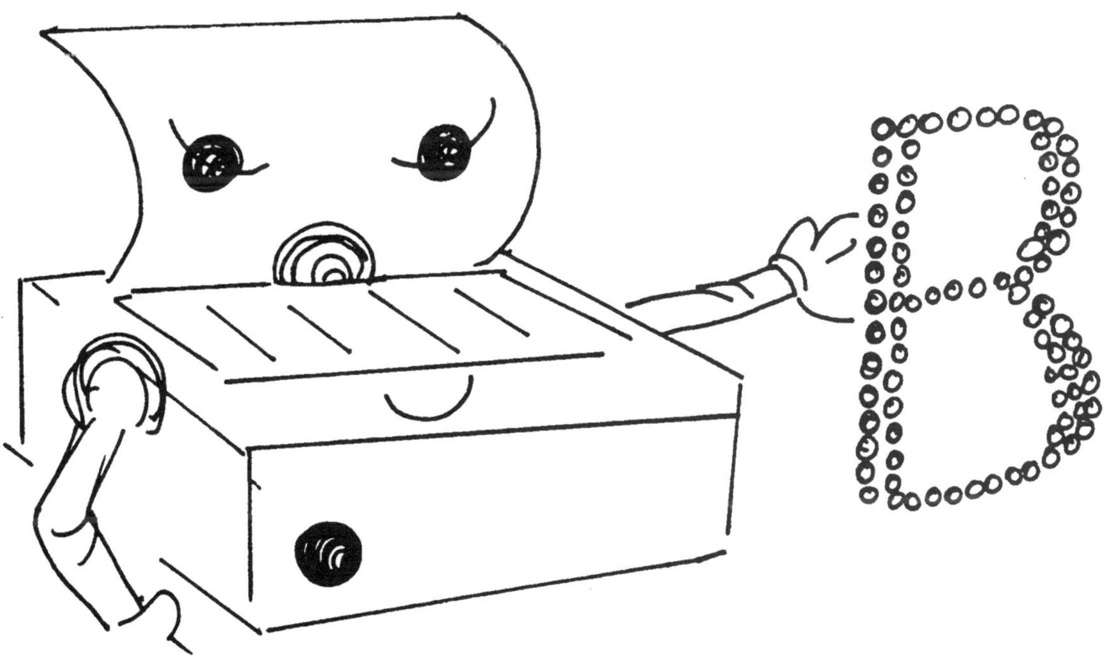

"Dot-Matrix costs the least amount of money. Dot uses a pattern of tiny dots to form images on paper. Dot uses the same kind of paper as Great-grandfather," said Peter.

"What do you call the paper?" asked Molly. Peter said, "It is called track paper, because it is all connected together, with holes to pull it through the printer the way a train is pulled along tracks."

"Inkjet is faster, and sprays ink on the paper through small holes. The ink takes time to dry, but it is high-quality work," said Peter. "His twin, Color Inkjet, mixes colored inks together to make rainbow words and pictures."

"And then of course, there is Me. I'm a laser high-speed printer. I use a beam of light to form images on paper," said Peter, bragging again.

"We can all do the job. We put Computer Brain's work on paper so it can be seen by anyone — not just people who have a computer. You can take the paper with you. You can fold it, color it, or save it in a book," said Peter.

Molly said, "Computer Brain needs paper copies — hard copies. I think Computer Brain is happy to have any of your relatives work with him. You have a very important job to do. I think Computer Brain is calling for you to print a letter right now."

Lesson 2-4 Questions

1. How does a dot-matrix printer print information? (patterns of tiny dots to form images)
2. What kind of paper does a dot-matrix printer use? (track paper)
3. What is track paper? (paper connected together, with holes on the sides designed to pull the paper through a printer)
4. How does an inkjet printer print information? (sprays ink through tiny holes)
5. What is a disadvantage of the inkjet printer? (time to dry)
6. How does the color inkjet printer print? (mixes colors to make rainbow words and pictures)
7. How does the laser printer print information? (uses a beam of light to form images)
8. What is the printed work called? (hard copy)
9. What is the advantage of hard copy? (It may be used by people who do not have computers.)
10. When does the printer print? (anytime the computer commands)

Name ______________________________

Criss-Cross Capture

a b c
d d d
e e e e
i i i i
k k
m m
n n
o o o o o
p p
r r r r
s
t t t
u u
v y

							D						
							I						
				M	O	U	S	E					
							K						
	C												
	O						D						
	M	O	N	I	T	O	R						
	P						I						
	U						V						
	T					K	E	Y	B	O	A	R	D
	E												
P	R	I	N	T	E	R							

LESSON 2-5 DIZZY DISK DRIVE

To the Teacher

Dizzy Disk Drive doesn't feel appreciated. He feels that no one tells him anything, and decides to run away. He spits out Susie Software and says he wants to split. Susie tells him about herself. Susie doesn't want Dizzy to run away because they always work together. Peter Printer tells Dizzy they are alike, and Dizzy is really lucky. They both sit on the side of CPU and they are both needed. Dizzy is happy and feels that he is part of the big picture. He is also happy when all the other parts watch as he spins Susie with his red light glowing.

New words in this lesson: versatile

I. Objective

- Identify the purpose of disk drives and software.

II. Instructional Input and Learning Activities

- Make overhead transparencies for each page of the story.
- Place the transparency on the stage of the overhead projector and cover the portion of the page you are not using.
- Read the story to the children.

III. Check for Understanding

Use the review questions at the end of the story to test for story comprehension. Cover the questions as you read the last page of the story. Answers are in parentheses.

IV. Guided Practice

The "Dizzy Disk" game reviews anything you think will help the students to understand the computer.

Materials—Duplicate the three sheets; the background and cover disks should be laminated. Make as many copies as needed of the question wheel. Cut out the question wheel sheet. Cut the cover disk and windows to reveal the questions and answers. Write your questions and answers on the wheels. (Be sure question 1 is opposite answer 1, etc.) The top is shown so they will be revealed in an upright position for reading. This game may be played by an individual or a team. Students spin the wheel. First they open the question door and read the question. The student who can answer the question receives one point. The first team to reach ten points wins the game.

V. Independent Practice and Application Using the Computer

Play a software game that reinforces the lesson.

LESSON 2-5 DIZZY DISK DRIVE

Sitting next to Computer Brain was a small box-shaped part called Disk Drive — Dizzy Disk Drive. In some computers Dizzy is connected to the computer, or inside its main case.

Dizzy had a big mouth. It went from one side of his face to the other. He had one red eye, which lit up whenever CPU wanted Dizzy to spin a disk for him.

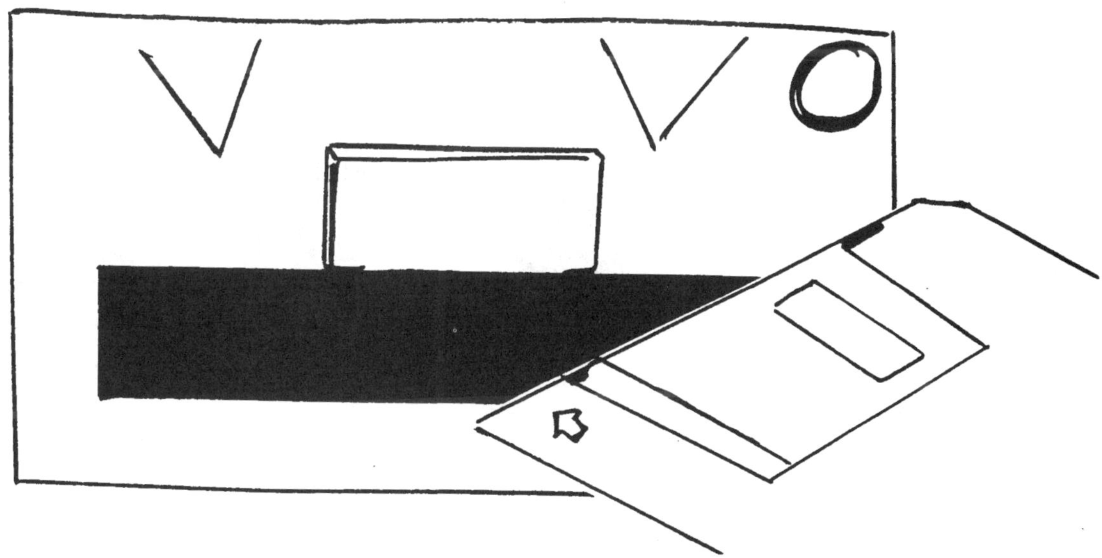

Dizzy loved to help CPU by spinning disks. Disks can be made of floppy plastic, or stiff, shiny CD-ROMs.

Dizzy always waited patiently. "No one tells me anything," he said. "I don't think anyone likes me or appreciates me. I think I'll run away."

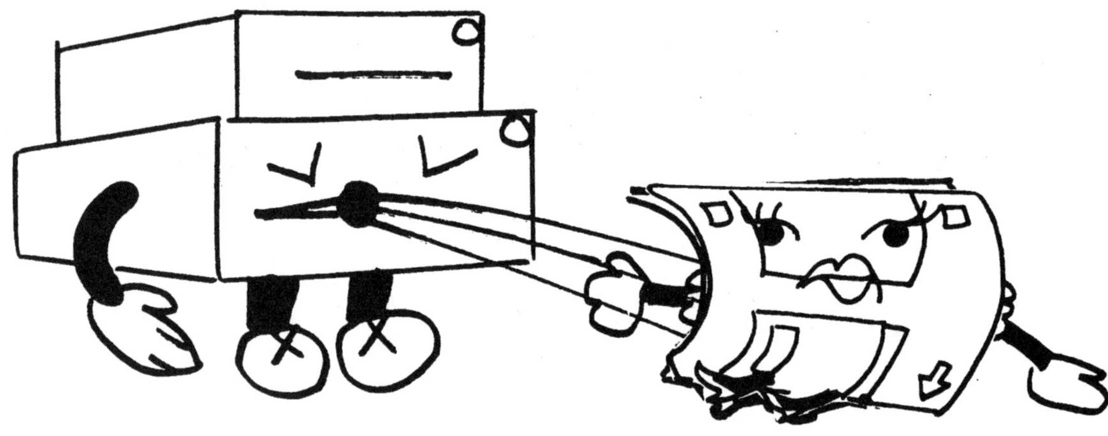

He spit out the disk he was spinning.
"Hey, what are you doing?" asked Susie Software.
"I'm running away. Who are you?" asked Dizzy.
"My name is Susie Software," said the disk.

"Susie, you and I have been spinning together and I don't know anything about you," said Dizzy.

Susie said, "I am versatile; I can do many different things. I can be an adding and subtracting game. I can draw pictures, and so on, and so on."

"I get the idea. So when you and I are together, we make good things happen," said Dizzy.

"If you run away, how will I be able to give my information to CPU?" asked Susie.

"I guess you can't," said Dizzy.

"Then you can't run away," said Susie. "I'll tell CPU and he won't let you."

"CPU won't care," said Dizzy.

Just then CPU got the message from Susie Software.

CPU said, "Dizzy I need you. I can get information from Kiki Keyboard and Mo Mouse, but without you and Susie I can't do anything. Susie has all the instructions I need and she can't give them to me alone. You're a pair that can't be separated. Together we make it work."

Dizzy looked around. He saw Monty Monitor, Kiki Keyboard, and Mo Mouse all wanting him to stay.

Then he saw Peter Printer, who also sat beside CPU. "CPU needs me when he wants to make paper copies of work, but he needs you all the time. You are really LUCKY," said Peter.

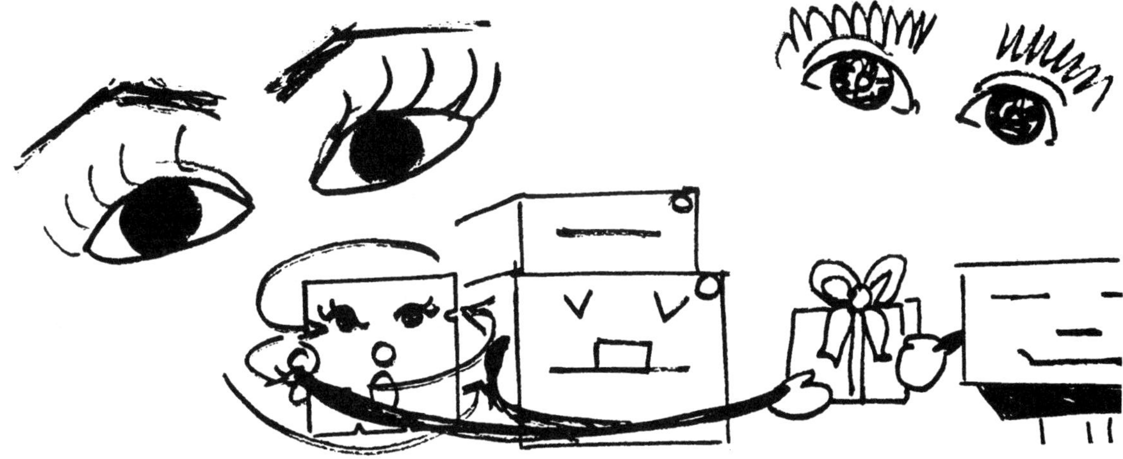

"And wanted, and needed," said all the other parts.

Dizzy smiled and jumped into his place. He no longer felt alone. He was part of a Big Picture, and his red light would shine brightly every time he spun Susie around. All the parts would stop everything and watch and wait as Dizzy and Susie gave the information to CPU.

It was fun to have everyone stop and notice how well Susie and Dizzy worked together.

Lesson 2-5 Questions

1. Who gives disk information to CPU? (Dizzy Disk Drive spins Susie Software.)
2. How do you know to stop and wait while Dizzy is working? (light glows)
3. Describe a disk. (floppy plastic or stiff, shiny CD-ROM)
4. What is Peter Printer's job? (make hard copies — permanent copies of CPU's work)
5. Why did Peter Printer think Dizzy Disk Drive was lucky? (Dizzy and Susie are working all the time, and Peter works only when a hard copy is needed.)
6. Where does all the information CPU uses come from? (Susie Software, hard drives, CD-ROM, and you)
7. How do we talk to CPU? (Kiki Keyboard and Mo Mouse)
8. What does versatile mean? (A disk can do many different things.)
9. Are the disk drives always separate from the CPU case? (No, they can be inside the main case.)
10. Why can't Dizzy Disk Drive and Susie Software be separated? (They are a pair; you can't use software without a disk drive.)

Name ____

Dizzy Disk (Background Disk)

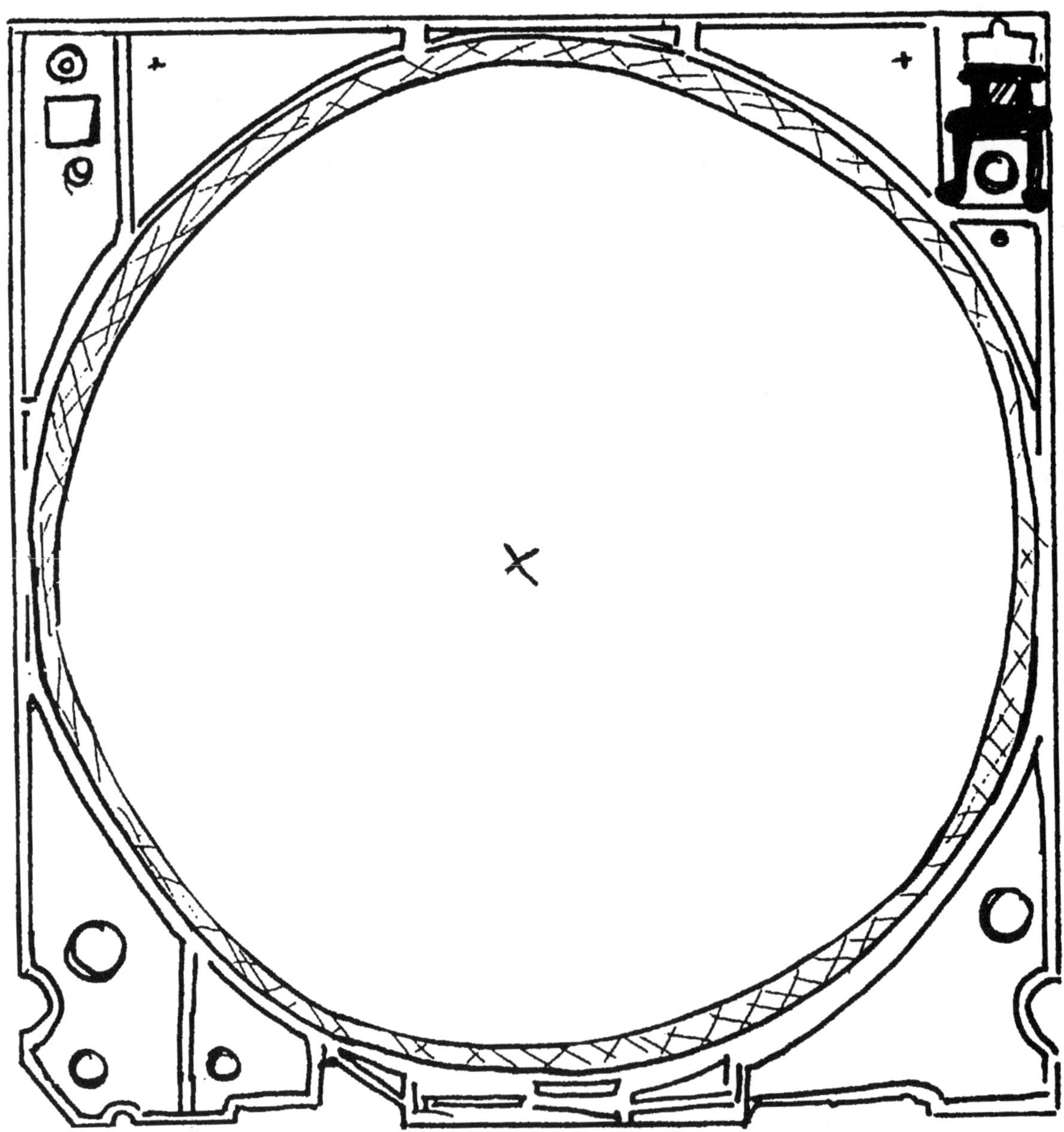

Name ____

Dizzy Disk (Cover Disk)

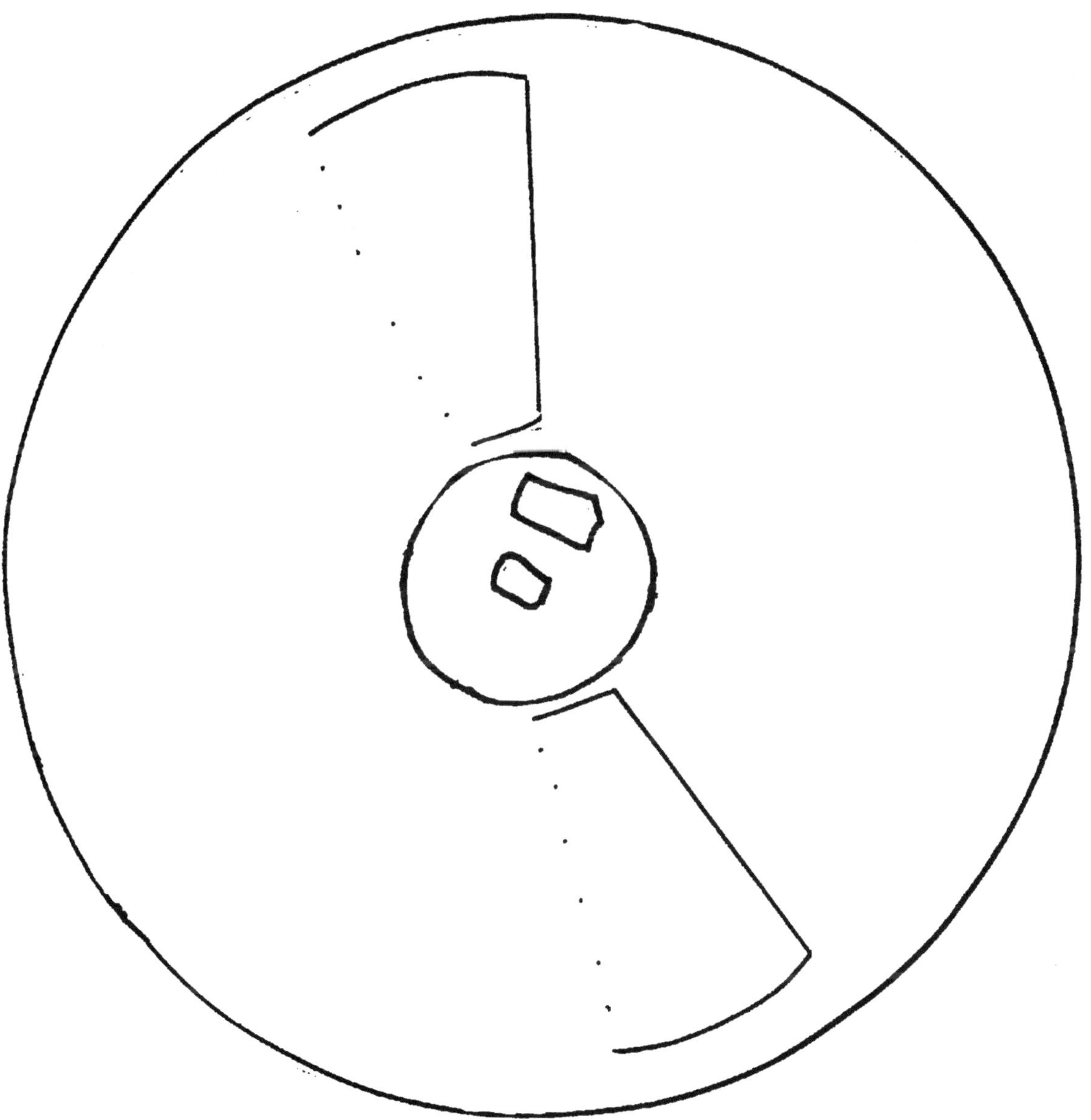

Name ______________________________

Dizzy Disk (Question Disk)

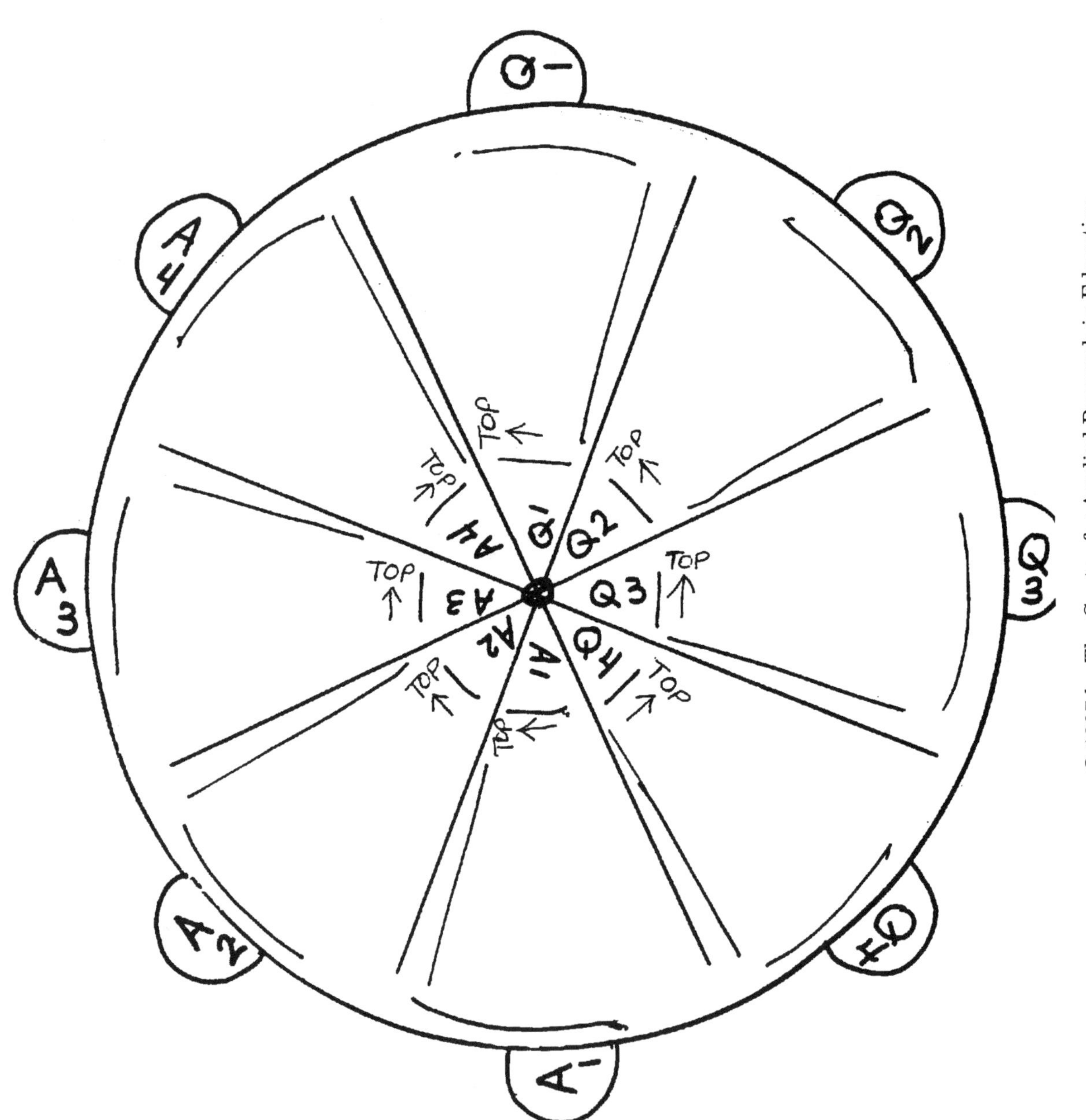

LESSON 2-6 GENTLE TOUCH - I HAVE A HEADACHE

To the Teacher

Kiki Keyboard has a headache, and it is caused by fingerprints on her keys, someone pressing too hard on her keys, and pencil and ink smudges on her keys. Mo Mouse sometimes has a headache, too, from being pressed too hard or being dropped. The computer parts help Kiki get cleaned up and make a sign with the GOLDEN RULE on it to be hung in the computer room. They decide it is a good rule for the computer room, the school, and the whole world.

New words in this lesson: golden rule

I. Objective

- Be clean and use a gentle touch on the keyboard.

II. Instructional Input and Learning Activities

- Make overhead transparencies for each page of the story.
- Place the transparency on the stage of the overhead projector and cover the portion of the page you are not using.
- Read the story to the children.

III. Check for Understanding

Use the review questions at the end of the story to test for story comprehension. Cover the questions as you read the last page of the story. Answers are in parentheses.

IV. Guided Practice

The "Pick Up Sticks" game builds a gentle touch when using computers. It is also a review of computer parts. Students will know the hardware they use.

Materials—sticks with names of computer parts, containers to hold sticks. Duplicate, color, laminate, and cut apart stick sets, allowing three pages of stick sets for each group of three to four students. Place in containers. An alternative is to use commercial game or colored wooden meat skewers (you will need six colors to create your code). Students try to assemble their own computer by picking a stick, following Pick Up Sticks rules. Shake the stick container and let the sticks fall between the players. They may take only one stick at a time, and must not disturb the other sticks. If other sticks move, the student loses a turn. The set is made up of six sticks labeled "monitor," "keyboard," "mouse," "cpu," "disk drives," and "printer." The first child to complete his or her computer set wins the game. If you are using commercial sticks, you can use the following code: green (1 point) = CPU, yellow (2 pts) = monitor, blue (3 pts) = keyboard, red (4 pts) = mouse, white (5 pts) = printer, orange (6 pts) = disk drives. Twenty-one points equal one computer.

V. Independent Practice and Application Using the Computer

Play a software game that reinforces the lesson.

LESSON 2-6 GENTLE TOUCH - I HAVE A HEADACHE

It was a bright and sunny day in Computer Land, but Kiki Keyboard was not feeling bright and sunny.

"What is wrong?" asked Peter Printer.

Kiki said, "I have a headache."

"Someone has been pressing my keys very HARD. Someone has made the letter keys make a lot of noise, and the number keys jump up and down too fast. Someone has slapped the special keys without caring how the keys felt. I feel bad, very bad," said Kiki.

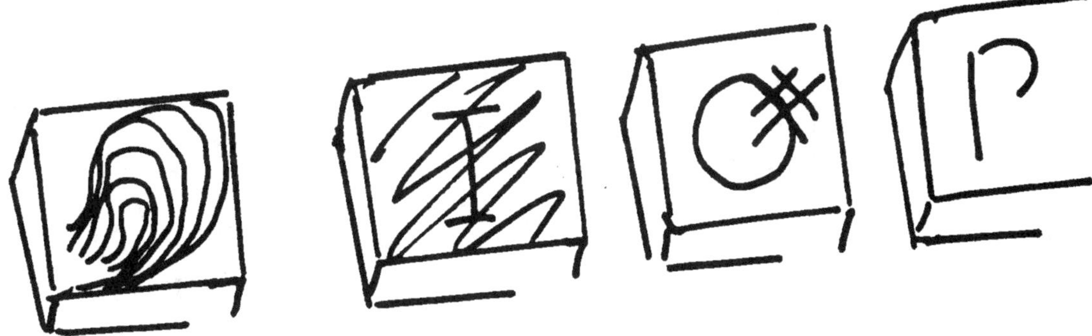

Peter looked at Kiki. He saw big, ugly fingerprints on some of the keys. He saw pencil and ink smudges on some of the special keys. He said, "Someone has really been hard on you. What are you going to do?"

Kiki said, "If someone hits my keys too hard, or smudges up the keys too badly I will have to go to get repaired. It isn't quite that bad YET."

Peter said, "Maybe some of the other computer parts have seen who did this to you. Let's ask the other parts." So Kiki and Peter called the other parts and asked, "Have any of you had problems with someone touching you too hard? Kiki Keyboard has a headache from someone touching her keys too hard, and she wants to know if anyone else has had a problem."

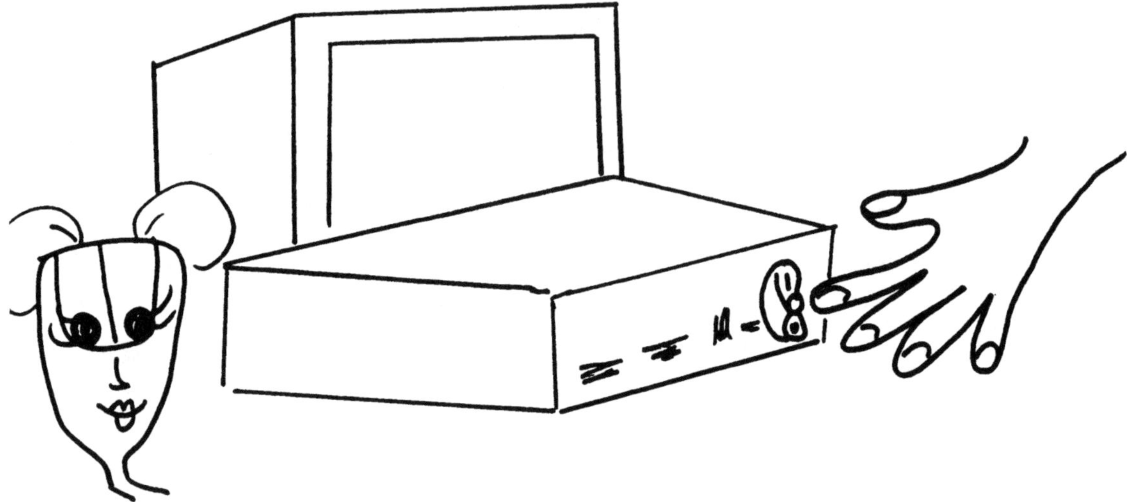

The parts all looked at each other.

Computer Brain, better known as CPU, said, "No one touches me except to flip my switch on and off. Sometimes there is a dirty hand but that is all."

"A dirty hand can be bad," said Peter.

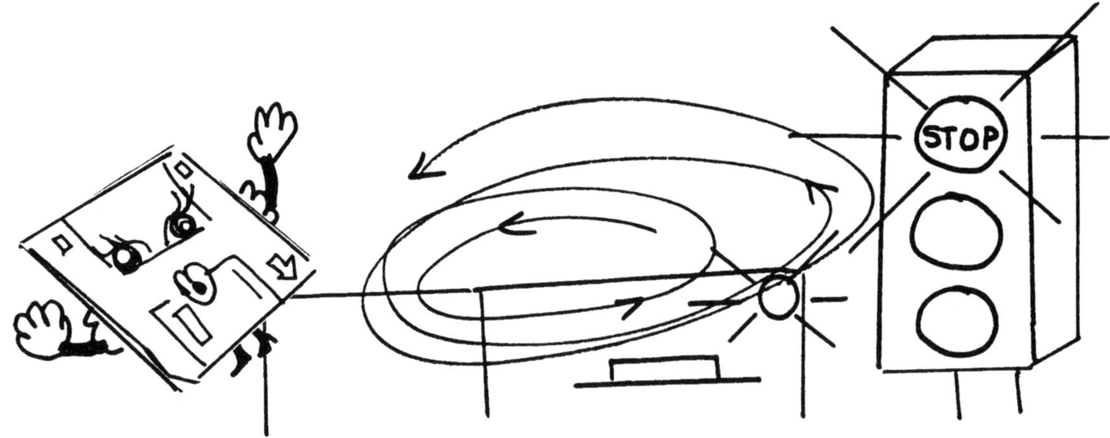

Dizzy Disk Drive said, "Sometimes people don't wait for my red light to stop before they touch Kiki's keyboard. That is bad. I am still spinning Susie Software and we both can get hurt."

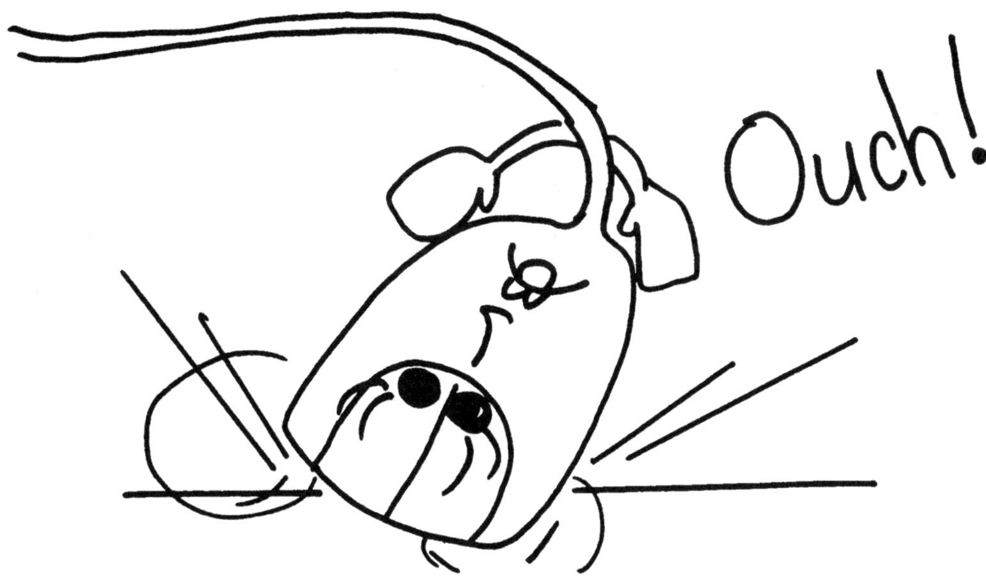

Mo said, "I work like Kiki, and sometimes someone presses my button too hard. Sometimes I have been dropped and that really hurts."

"What can we do to help Kiki and Mo? It sounds as if someone isn't treating them well, and we don't want them to get hurt and have to get repaired," said Dizzy.

"Don't forget Dizzy. If they don't wait for your red light you will have to be repaired also. And Susie might have to go away without her program," said CPU.

All the parts tried to make Kiki feel better. They got a clean cloth and wiped each key's face so it was very shiny. They jumped up and down very carefully to see which key was hurt, and then they said, "How can we help you stay clean and not get hurt?"

Susie Software said, "Make a sign to say, 'Wait for the red light to stop.'" CPU said, "That will help you and Dizzy. But what about Kiki and Mo?"

Mo Mouse thought a long time. She went over and talked quietly with Kiki. They both had button problems. They both got dirty, and they both got headaches if someone touched them too hard.

They put their heads together for a long time.

"I have a headache from thinking too much," said Mo. "I don't want you to get my headache. I like you too much."

"That's it," said CPU. "You don't want Kiki to get a headache because you like her too much. Kiki doesn't want you to get a headache. The rest of us don't want you to get sick. We all want to be treated the same so . . . the best rule is the GOLDEN RULE."

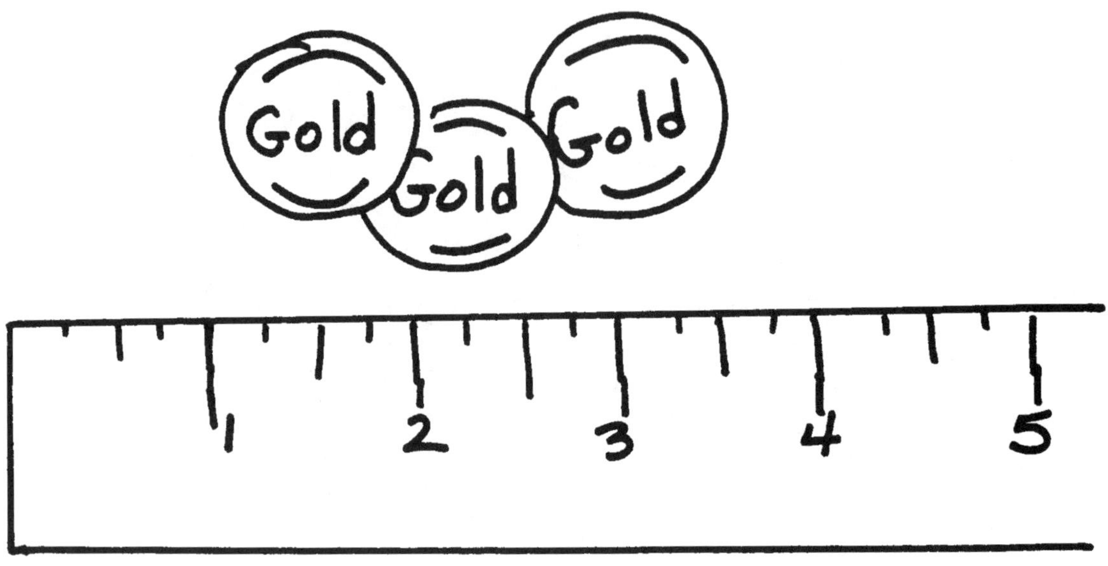

"The GOLDEN RULE means: I don't want to be pressed or hit hard. You don't want to be pressed or hit hard. I don't want to get your dirt on me. You don't want my dirt on you. I want to be treated with kindness. You want to be treated with kindness," said Kiki.

Mo said, "That is a great idea. The GOLDEN RULE will work for everyone. Be nice and you will be treated nicely."

"It is so easy, too," said CPU.

"And I won't get a headache and stop working," said Kiki.

Lesson 2-6 Questions

1. How did Kiki Keyboard get a headache? (Someone pressed her keys very hard.)
2. What are some other ways to hurt the keyboard? (food, drinks, fingerprints)
3. What happens if Kiki gets hurt? (She has to get repaired.)
4. Did any of the other parts have the problem of being touched too hard? (yes)
5. Which part did? (Mo Mouse)
6. What kind of sign did Susie Software want? (wait for warning light to stop)
7. Whom does that help most? (Susie Software and Dizzy Disk Drive)
8. What was the rule that the parts agreed on? (golden rule)
9. What does it mean? (be nice to one another)
10. Who should follow the rule? (everyone)

Name ______________________________

Pick Up Sticks (Labels)

CPU
Monitor
Keyboard
Mouse
Printer
Disk Drives
CPU
Monitor
Keyboard
Mouse
Printer
Disk Drives
CPU
Monitor
Keyboard
Mouse
Printer
Disk Drives
CPU
Monitor
Keyboard
Mouse
Printer
Disk Drives

LESSON 2-7 A TO Z MEET KIKI KEYBOARD

To the Teacher

Kiki Keyboard tries to help the letters say their names when Pencil says he has a hard time keeping up. She paints the letters on her keys and runs to show the letters, but she falls down and the letters are all mixed up. When she gets up, the letters are arranged in QWERTY keyboard order. The letters don't care that they are mixed up. They are happy because Kiki can say their names very fast. She says she will not get too tired and wants to help all the time.

New words in this lesson: QWERTY

I. Objectives

- Describe the keyboard as an input to CPU.
- Know the mixed-up letters on the keyboard.

II. Instructional Input and Learning Activities

- Make overhead transparencies for each page of the story.
- Place the transparency on the stage of the overhead projector and cover the portion of the page you are not using.
- Read the story to the children.

III. Check for Understanding

Use the review questions at the end of the story to test for story comprehension. Cover the questions as you read the last page of the story. Answers are in parentheses.

IV. Guided Practice

The "A to Z" keyboard work sheets are used to fill in letter key names. This activity acquaints the students with the placement of the letters on the keyboard. Duplicate the first work sheet for students. Instruct them to look at their computer keyboard and then copy the letters of the alphabet into the same position on the work sheet. As an alternative, students may be instructed to copy one row at a time, as on the work sheet following the full keyboard work sheet. Answer sheets follow the work sheets. (*Note:* While your keyboard may not look exactly like the Apple keyboard work sheet, the letter and number keys will be the same for the students' use.)

V. Independent Practice and Application Using the Computer

Play a software game that reinforces the lesson.

LESSON 2-7 A TO Z MEET KIKI KEYBOARD

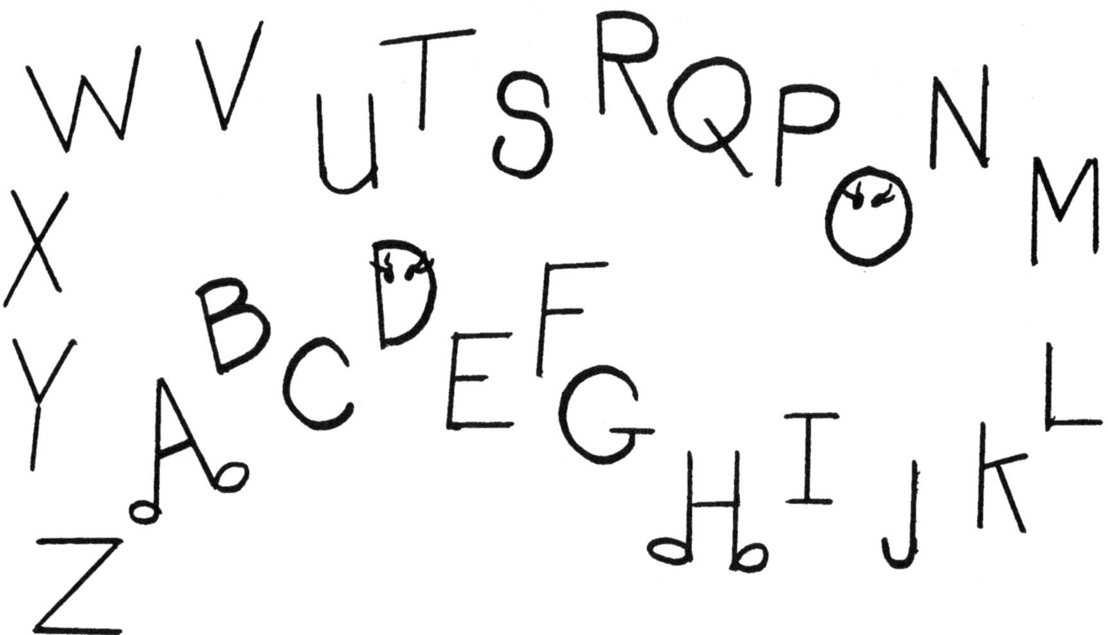

A, B, C, D, E, F, G . . . the alphabet letters were all saying their names.

"This is fun," said A.
"I like it too," said Z.

"When we get together we can make every word in the world in every language. We are SUPER, TERRIFIC, GREAT," said all the letters, but it takes so long for Pencil or Pen to write our names on paper."

"It sure does," said A.

"I get tired," said Pencil. "You talk very fast. There must be an easier and faster way."

Kiki Keyboard heard what Pencil and the letters were saying. She wanted to help. She painted the name of each alphabet letter on her keys and ran to show everyone.

Kiki called, "I have a surprise for you."

The letters saw Kiki running to them, and then they saw Kiki fall. When Kiki got up, she had a surprise, too. All the letters were mixed up.

Kiki knew the letters liked to say their names one after the other, but the letters on her keys didn't look like that now.

The letters looked at Kiki. Kiki looked at the letters.

Kiki said, "I can type your names really fast but . . ."

The letters knew Kiki was trying to help.

"I like the way we got mixed up," said Q, W, E, R, T, and Y. "Look, we make a funny word — QWERTY."

Kiki said, "Kiki — QWERTY. I like it. How about the rest of you?"

"We don't mind. It is fun to be next to different letters," said A.
"It is like hide and seek," said Z.

"Kiki can say our names fast, even if we are not in ABC order, so it doesn't matter that Kiki got us all mixed up," said A.

"And I won't get tired," said Kiki.

"Let's see how fast we can say our names and how long it will take Kiki to get tired," said Z.

As long as no one stopped her, Kiki could go on, and on, and on, and on.

Lesson 2-7 Questions

1. What tools write letters on paper? (pencil, pen, crayon)
2. Are the letters on Kiki Keyboard in ABC order? (no)
3. Why did the letters want to give Kiki Keyboard a chance to say their names? (It took Pencil a long time to write their names on paper.)
4. What reason did Pencil give for taking a long time? (He got tired because the letters talked very fast.)
5. What did Kiki do to help the letters say their names faster? (painted the letters on her keys in alphabetical order)
6. What happened to Kiki when she ran to show the letters? (She fell, and the letters got mixed up.)
7. What did the letters say to make Kiki feel better? (they liked it)
8. The letters' new order made a funny word. What was it? (QWERTY)
9. What are the names of the letters of the first six top-row letter keys? (QWERTY)
10. Are the letters slowed down because they are mixed up and not in alphabetical order? (no)

Name ______________________________

A to Z (Worksheet 1)

A to Z (Worksheet 1—Answers)

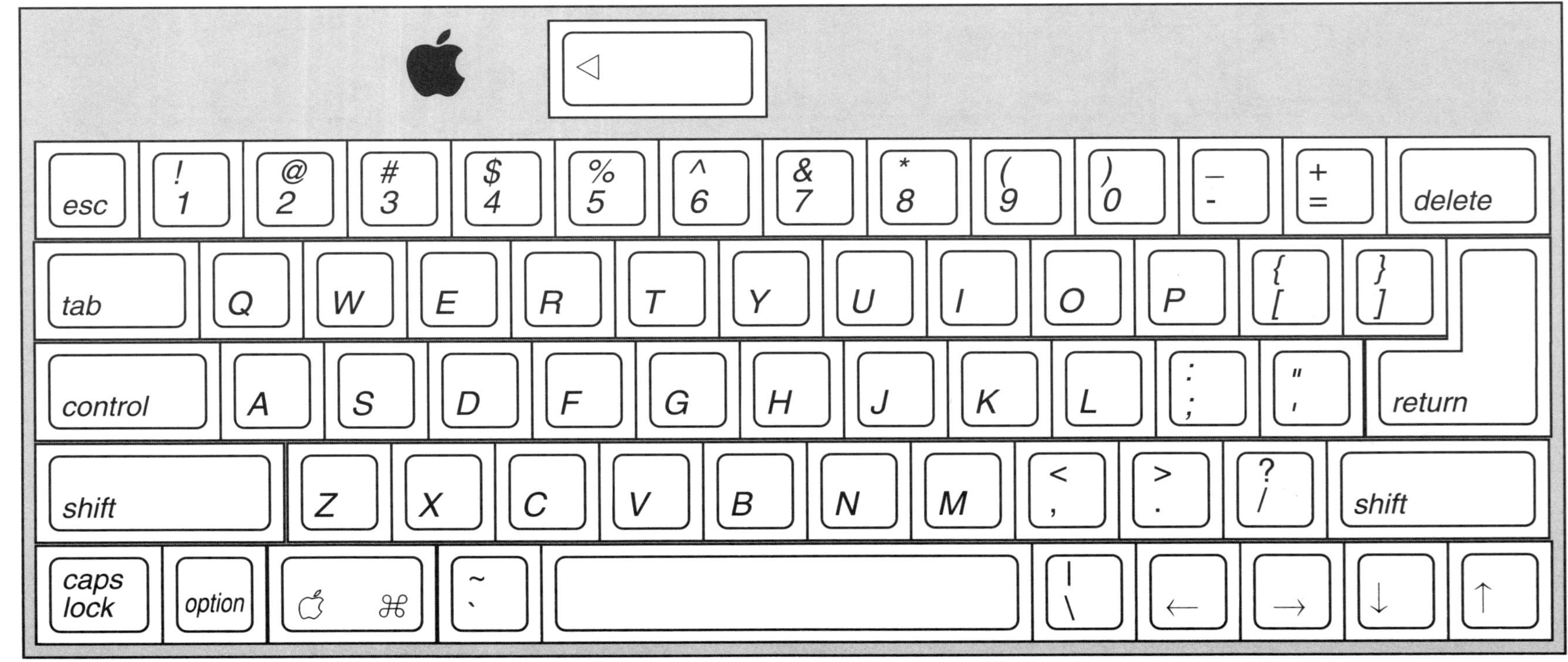

Name ______________________________

A to Z (Worksheet 2)

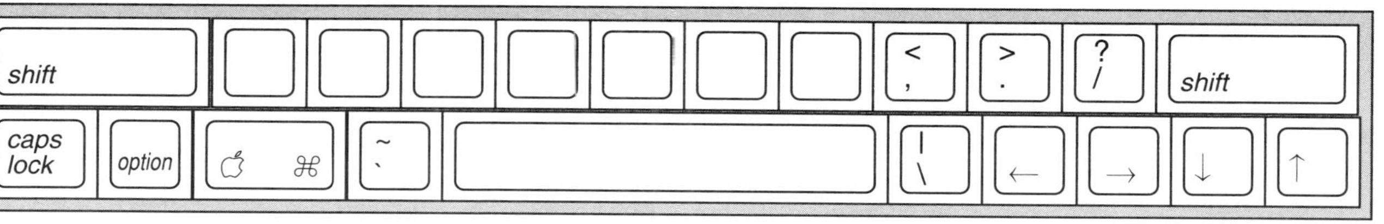

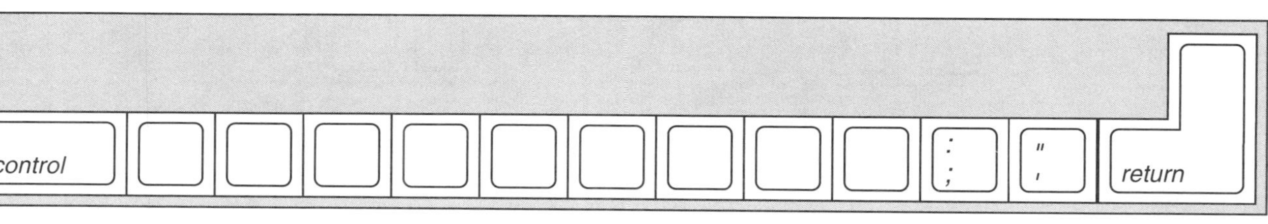

A to Z (Worksheet 2—Answers)

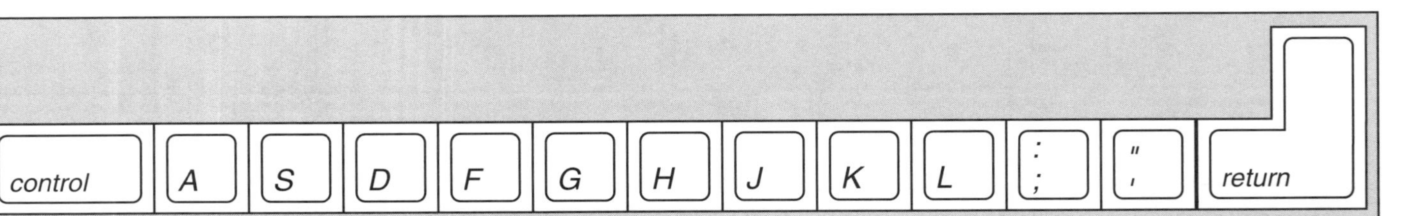

LESSON 2-8 THE HANDS MEET KIKI KEYBOARD

To the Teacher

The hands find their home in the home-row keys. All the fingers are assigned jobs by Timmy Thumb. Timmy doesn't want to play, but he has good ideas for everyone else. The pointers want to do the most work and each pointer is assigned six letters. All the fingers practice to get fast at typing the letters, so they'll know their keys and where their homes are, even in the dark.

New words in this lesson: home-row

I. Objective

- Describe the placement of hands in the home-row position.

II. Instructional Input and Learning Activities

- Make overhead transparencies for each page of the story.
- Place the transparency on the stage of the overhead projector and cover the portion of the page you are not using.
- Read the story to the children.

III. Check for Understanding

Use the review questions at the end of the story to test for story comprehension. Cover the questions as you read the last page of the story. Answers are in parentheses.

IV. Guided Practice

The "Home-Row Letters" work sheet is designed to help students learn the home-row keys. It also teaches the QWERTY keyboard positions. Duplicate the work sheet for students and instruct them to write the letters of the home row in the correct position on the work sheet. After you check for accuracy, instruct the students to add the QWERTY row, and then the bottom row. Check for accuracy after each row is added. You may also have students circle the letter keys that would be used to type their names, or devise a code they can use to indicate the correct finger for each key on the work sheet. The answer sheet follows the work sheet. (*Note:* While your keyboard may not look exactly like the Apple keyboard work sheet, the letter and number keys will be the same for the students' use.)

V. Independent Practice and Application Using the Computer

Play a software game that reinforces the lesson.

LESSON 2-8 THE HANDS MEET KIKI KEYBOARD

The hands heard how Kiki Keyboard tried to help the ABC's by painting their letter names on her keys, and how she got the letters all mixed up.

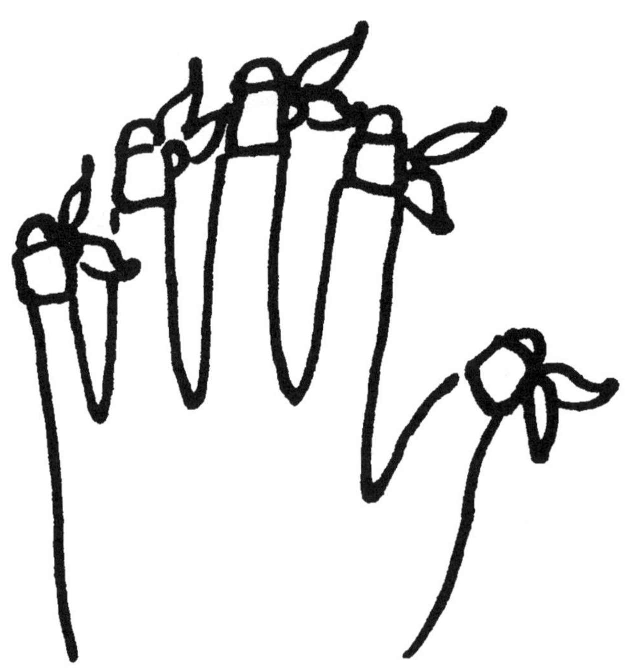

The hands thought it would be fun to find each letter without even looking. They thought they could do it with their eyes blindfolded. They wanted to be able to write anything anytime after they learned where the letters were located.

Tommy Thumb, better known as Right Thumb, said, "I like to press BIG keys, so I want to press Space Bar."

Timmy Thumb, better known as Left Thumb, said "I just like to watch. I don't want to press any keys."

"That is all right, too," said the other fingers. "We can choose what we want to do; after we decide, we will always be counted on to do it."

Tommy lined up on Space Bar. The other fingers touched keys close to Space Bar.

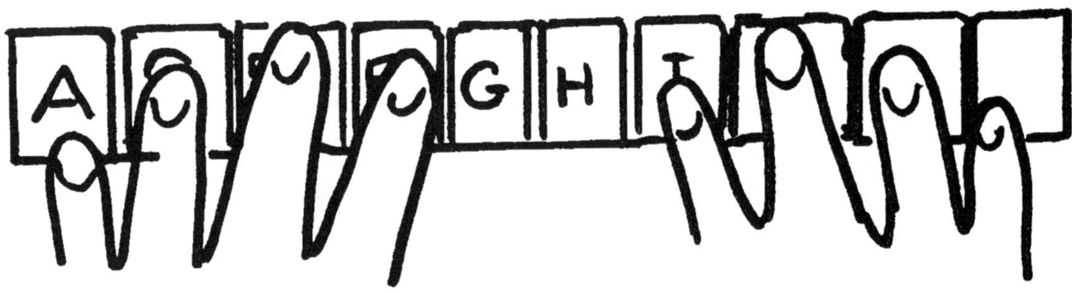

Timmy said, "Why don't you line up on the middle row of keys? And left fingers why don't you do the same?"

Timmy didn't want to play, but he did have good ideas for Right Pointer; Tall/Middle Man; Ring Finger, and Little Finger (sometimes known as Pinky). They all gently touched the middle row of keys. Left Hand fingers did the same.

"I feel right at home," said Little Finger Left Hand.

"That is what we will call where we start. We are at HOME," said Pinky.

"Home, Home Row; we can always come back home. We can jump up to more letters or down to more letters and come back here — home," said Pointer.

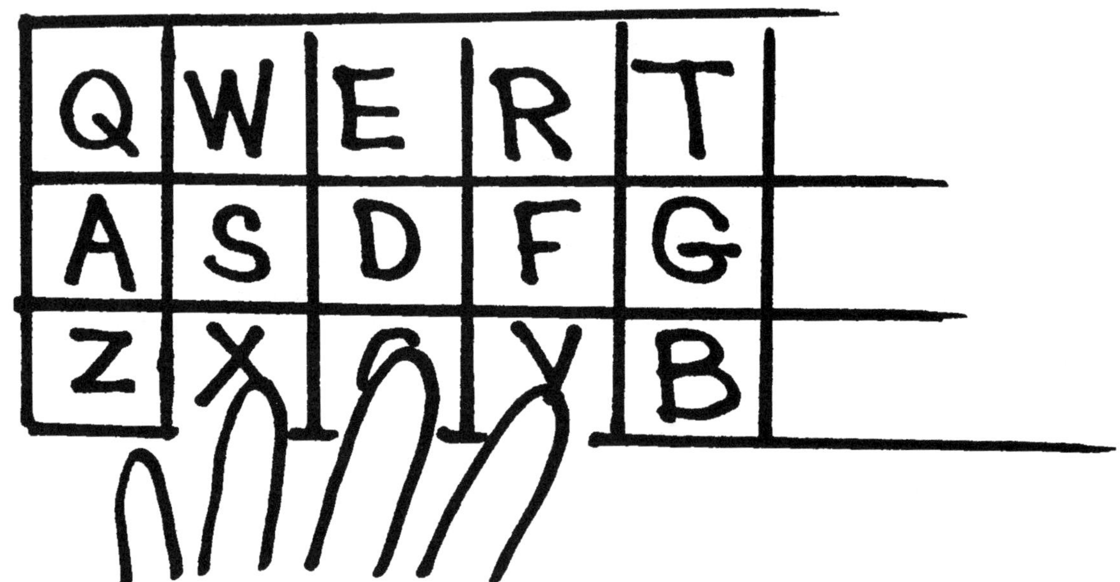

"I bet we can learn the keys nearby and press them even with our eyes closed — and fast," said Pointer.

"It will be fun to learn to spell and work together, and Tommy can make spaces between the words," said Timmy.

"That is terrific," said Tommy.

"I'll paint lines on Kiki to show you fingers which letters will be your job," said Timmy.

Timmy was good at organizing.

"Good idea," said the fingers.

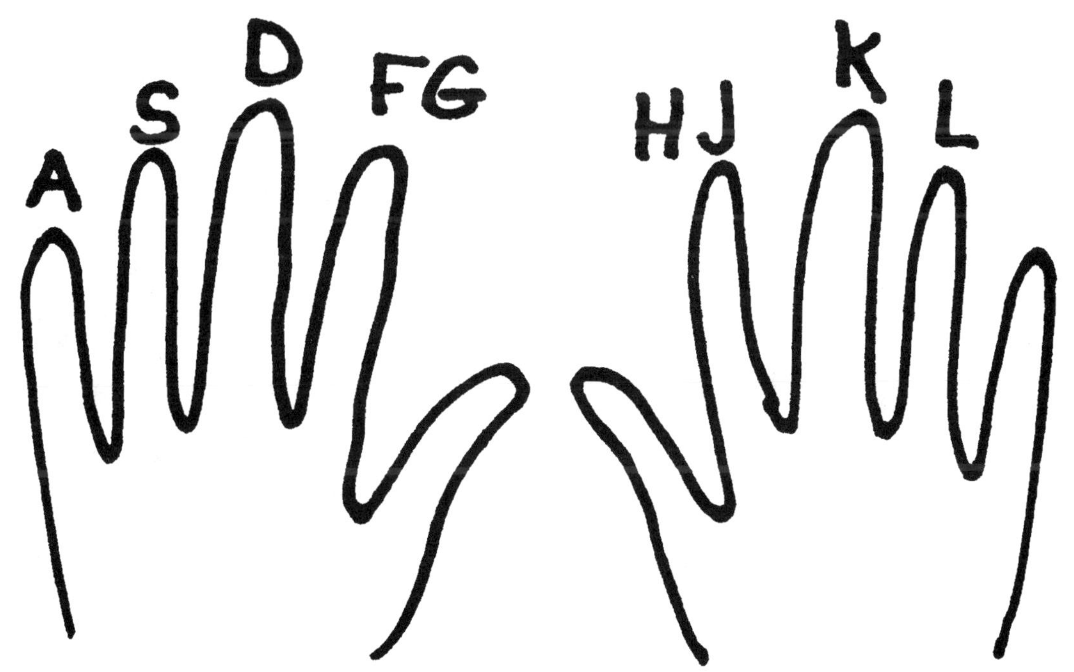

The fingers practiced until they could find the ABC's very quickly. They loved their home, Home-Row, and said the letters over and over: ASDFGHJKL — ASDFGHJKL — ASDFGHJKL.

The fingers were very happy with the letters Timmy assigned them.

The pointers said they wanted to do the most because they were the strongest. Timmy assigned them six letters each. They were happy. Everyone was happy — even Timmy.

The letters said, "Now we all know where our home is, and we can type every letter and go back to our home, Home-Row — ASDFGHJKL — ASD-FGHJKL — even in the dark!"

Lesson 2-8 Questions

1. What key does Tommy Thumb, better known as Right Thumb, press? (space bar)
2. Why did Tommy Thumb want to press the space bar? (He liked really big keys.)
3. What key does Timmy Thumb, better known as Left Thumb, press? (none)
4. Where did the fingers line up? (middle row of keys)
5. What do you call the middle row of keys where the fingers line up? (home row)
6. What are the letters in the home row? (ASDFGHJKL)
7. Why is lining up on the middle row of keys a good idea? (easy to reach all the other letters)
8. Which fingers do the most work? (pointers)
9. How many keys does each pointer press? (six)
10. Why do the pointers do the most letters? (They are the strongest.)

Name ______________________________

Home-Row Letters

Home-Row Letters (Answers)

LESSON 2-9 THE ARROW BROTHERS

To the Teacher

The Arrow Brothers are arguing about who is the biggest and who can point the best. All they can really do is make Cursor jump up and down and laugh. CPU says no one wins and they are silly for thinking they are different. The brothers agree that they are all alike and are needed to help Cursor.

New words in this lesson: arrow keys

I. Objective

- Recognize that the arrow keys move the cursor around the screen.

II. Instructional Input and Learning Activities

- Make overhead transparencies for each page of the story.
- Place the transparency on the stage of the overhead projector and cover the portion of the page you are not using.
- Read the story to the children.

III. Check for Understanding

Use the review questions at the end of the story to test for story comprehension. Cover the questions as you read the last page of the story. Answers are in parentheses.

IV. Guided Practice

The "Little Arrow" story, with the matching activity, teaches listening skills and directions.

Materials - Little Arrow story and arrow models. Duplicate and laminate enough arrows to give to all your students. Tell the "Little Arrow" story and model arrow directions.

V. Independent Practice and Application Using the Computer

Play a software game that reinforces the lesson.

LESSON 2-9 THE ARROW BROTHERS

Four little brothers live all together at the bottom of the keyboard. Their names are Up Arrow, Down Arrow, Left Arrow, and Right Arrow. They stand together every day and every night. They wait very patiently for someone to need them.

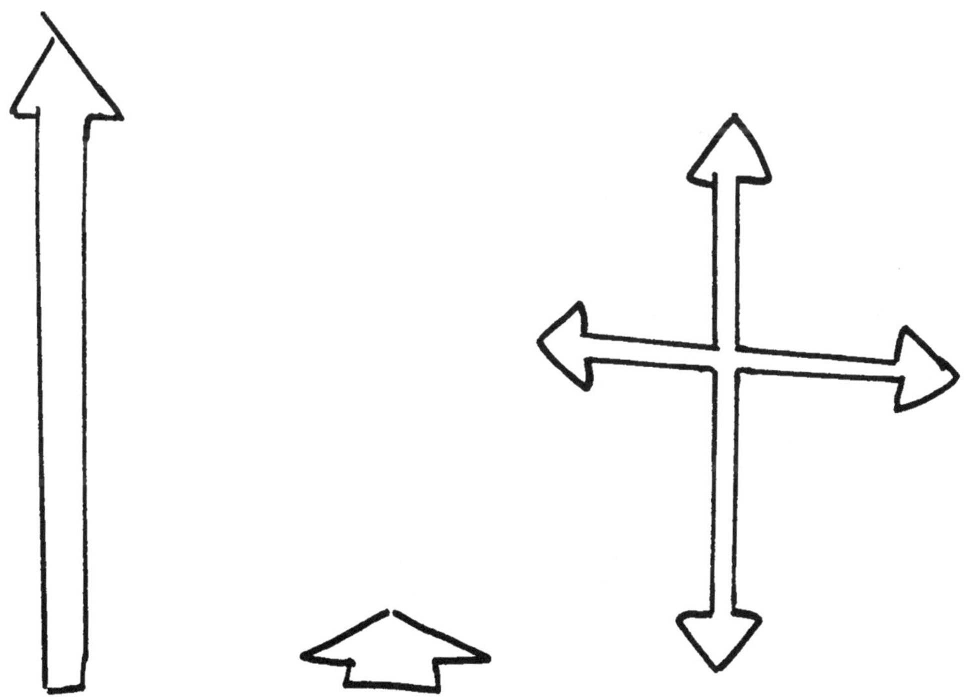

While they wait, they compare. They argue about who is the tallest, and who is the smallest, and who can point the best.

Computer Brain, CPU, heard all the arguing. He said, "All you do is talk, talk, talk. When you jump up and down no one sees any marks."

"What do you mean?" said Up Arrow.

CPU called Monty Monitor. He said "The Arrow Brothers are arguing. Can you help settle their argument?"

"Of course," said Monty, "Glad to help people see what they are doing."
Monty's smiling face lit up, bright and ready.
Cursor also lit up on Monty, ready to help.

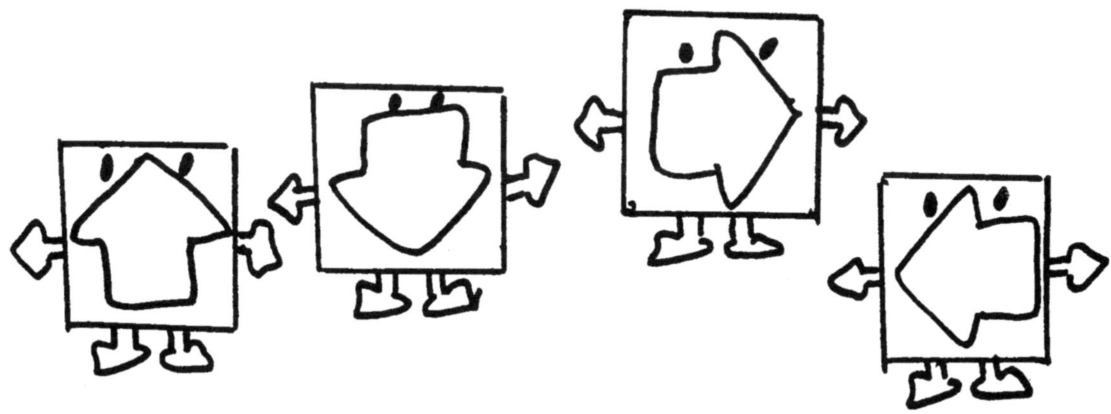

"OK," said CPU. "We are going to have a contest to see who is the best once and for all. Then I don't want to hear anymore arguing. Who wants to be first?"

"Me, Me, Me," they all said.

"I will pick," said CPU. "Up Arrow, you go first."

"Fine," he said, and jumped up and down many times.

Cursor jumped up and down on Monty's face, but no marks followed.

Right Arrow went next. He jumped and jumped, but he didn't leave marks. Down and Left Arrow tried and tried, but no one was able to leave a trail to mark who was the longest, or widest, or anything on Monty's face.

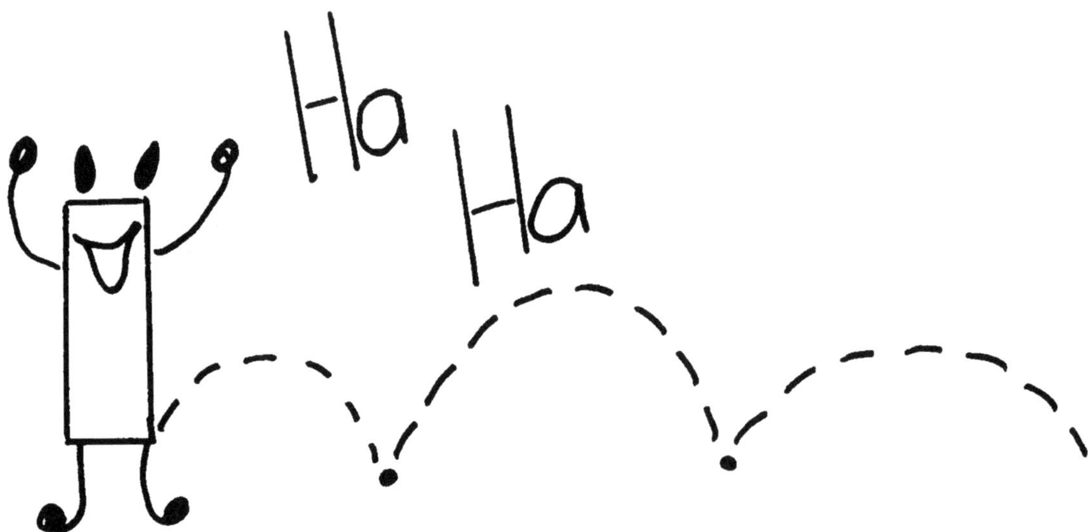

Cursor jumped and jumped as each brother took a turn. He laughed and laughed as he moved from one place to another.

"That was fun," said Cursor.

"Who won ?" asked the Arrow Brothers
"No one," said CPU.

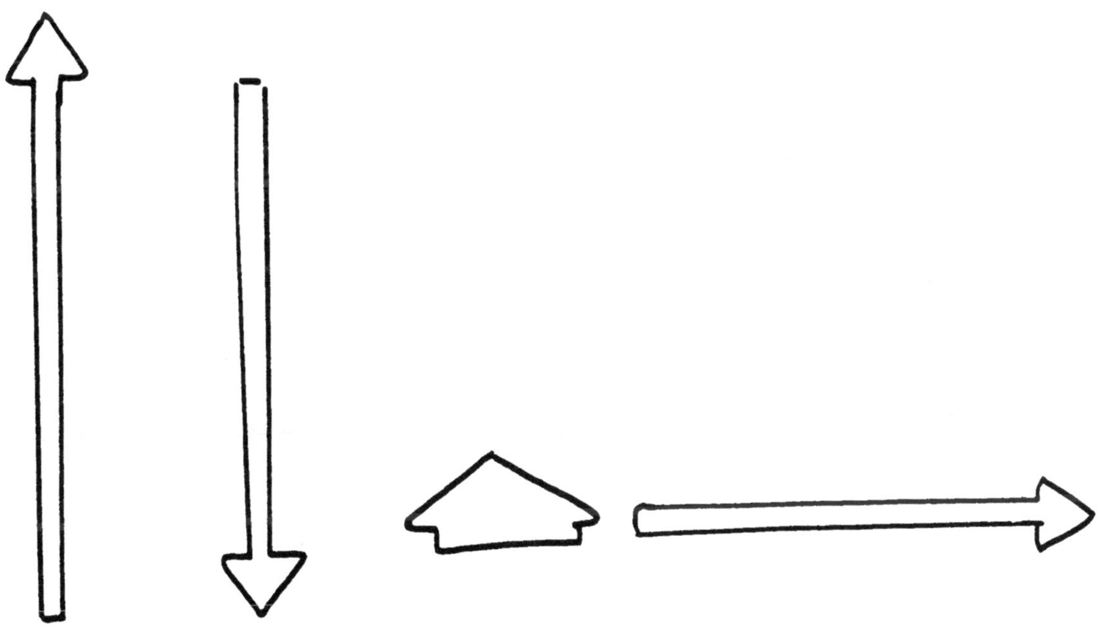

"What do you mean?" asked Right Arrow.

"No one made any marks, but you did make Cursor jump around. No one is bigger, faster, thinner, or anything. You are all exactly alike," said Monty.

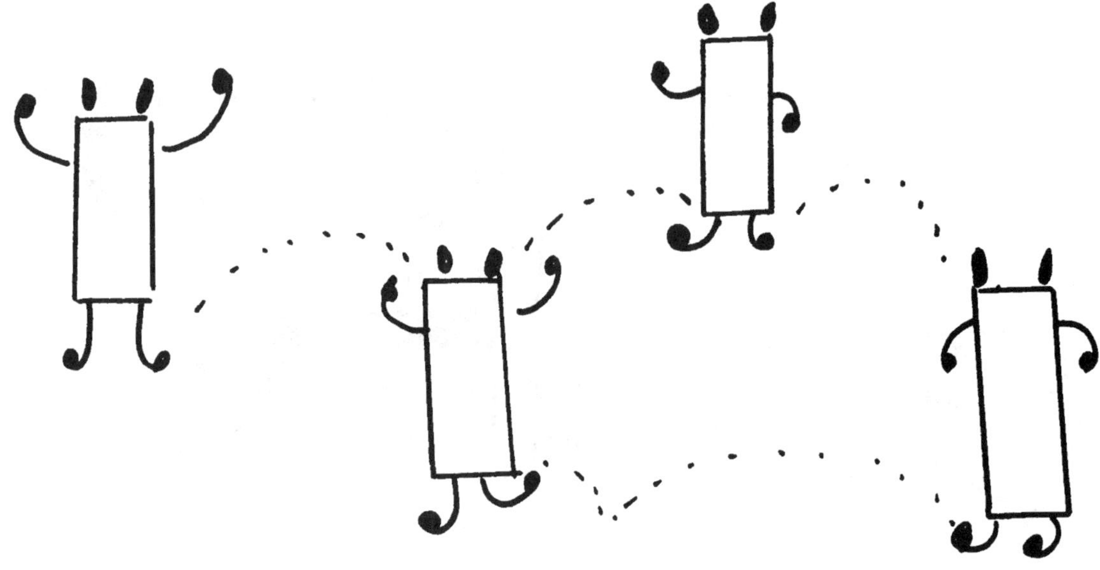

"No one wins, and no one loses. You are all winners, because each of you can make Cursor laugh and move to a new place without leaving a mark. That can be very important," said CPU.

"From now on, each of you can just jump to help Cursor when he needs you, and I won't tell the other keys how silly you were to be arguing," said Monty.

Up Arrow, Down Arrow, Left Arrow, and Right Arrow agreed, because after all they were brothers — and they were all exactly alike. They were proud of it, because they had an important job — to help Cursor.

Lesson 2-9 Questions

1. What is Monty Monitor's job? (show what Computer Brain is doing)
2. What does Cursor look like? (a blinking square on Monty Monitor's face)
3. What kind of jobs do the Arrow Brothers do? (move Cursor up and down Monty Monitor's face)
4. Who is the best Arrow? (none — they are all alike)
5. Why is it difficult to see who is the tallest, longest, and so on? (no marks on the screen)
6. Who wanted to have a contest to see who was the best arrow? (Computer Brain)
7. Which arrow went first? (Up Arrow)
8. Is it important to move the Cursor without having marks? (yes)
9. Where are the Arrow Keys located? (bottom of the keyboard, usually)
10. What is the order of the keys? (Left Arrow, Down Arrow, Up Arrow, and Right Arrow; Up and Down may be stacked)

Little Arrow

This is a story of a little American Indian boy named Little Arrow. Today, you are going to help me tell the story in sign language. You all have an arrow and you will point in the same directions that the story gives. When an old story teller told a story, he used sign language to be sure the boys and girls were paying attention. In those days, the children always wanted to look interested, because if they were not, they were sent to bed. I will help you at first, but you must listen very carefully so you can do a good job. Let's pretend we are sitting around a fire. It is a dark evening, and the wind is gently blowing and making the fire do a beautiful dance. Here is the story. Don't forget to help.

Little Arrow was a brave Indian. He wanted to grow UP. Here, you point up, because UP is a direction. I will also say DOWN, and LEFT, and RIGHT, and you will point those ways also. Let's begin again.

Little Arrow was a brave Indian. He wanted to grow UP (model for students) big and strong to take care of the gifts of the forest. He watched everyone and everything. He went for a walk. He looked RIGHT and saw three bears eating golden honey on a fallen log. He looked LEFT and saw two ducks swimming in the blue lake. He looked DOWN and saw many tiny red flowers under his brown moccasins. He looked UP and saw the bright, orange sun. He was very happy. As he enjoyed the beautiful sights, the sky became dark. It wasn't night. Little Arrow had seen the sun go DOWN at the end of the day. He had seen the sun come UP in the morning, until his head got so hot at midday that he sat DOWN under the shade of a big pine tree. Little Arrow wondered why the sky was dark, so he thought he would climb UP to the top of the tree to see more. He climbed UP until he could see his eagle friend's nest. The eagle flew RIGHT to the giant mountain to find food for her babies. He looked DOWN at the babies and wondered how hungry baby eagles could be. He did not want to bother the nest, so he climbed DOWN before the eagle would worry about her family. Little Arrow looked LEFT. The ducks flew UP in front of him. The bears stood UP high to smell the air. The honey dripped DOWN to the ground from their mouths and paws. What could be causing the excitement? Then a bright light flashed high UP in the sky, and a bright line of light flashed from LEFT to RIGHT across the sky. Then DOWN came many drops of cool rain. The bears ran RIGHT to their cave. The ducks flew DOWN to the lake to swim in the large circles of dropping rain. The mother eagle flew DOWN to her babies and covered them UP with her large wings. Little Arrow looked DOWN at his feet and saw the tiny red flowers reaching toward the sky to catch the cool, wet gift of life. It was good. Little Arrow was happy as he ran home. The story is ended, and all the little boys and girls must go RIGHT to bed. The End. Did you keep up with all the arrow directions? Let's see if you can make UP an arrow story.

Name ______________________________

Little Arrow (Molds)

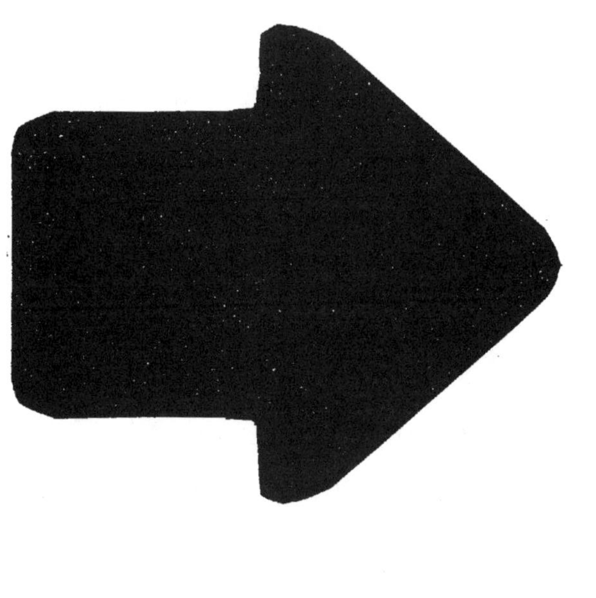

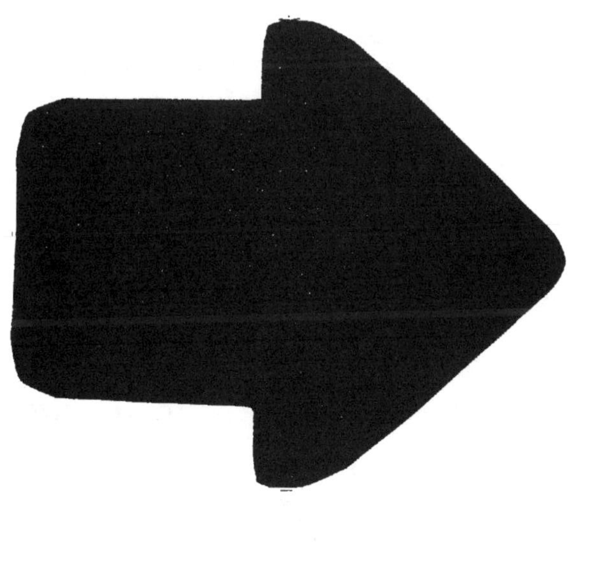

LESSON 2-10 DOTTIE DELETE

To the Teacher

Dottie Delete learns that she is important in erasing mistakes of both letters and numbers, because after all, NO ONE IS PERFECT.

New words in this lesson: delete backspace

I. Objective

- Understand that the delete key is used to erase mistakes.

II. Instructional Input and Learning Activities

- Make overhead transparencies for each page of the story.
- Place the transparency on the stage of the overhead projector and cover the portion of the page you are not using.
- Read the story to the children.

III. Check for Understanding

Use the review questions at the end of the story to test for story comprehension. Cover the questions as you read the last page of the story. Answers are in parentheses.

IV. Guided Practice

The "Reboot" game teaches descriptions of the computer parts.

Materials—Reboot deck—make four copies of each card. Students try to make sets. A set consists of at least three of the same card. Deal five cards to each player and place the remaining cards in the center of the playing surface. Players acquire cards by asking the player to their left a question. *Example:* "Do you have a card with a part that shows what a computer is doing?" (*not* "Do you have any monitor cards?") If the answer is "yes," the player on the left has to give the asking player any of that card he or she has. A player may not ask for a card unless she or he already has two. If the answer is "no" when the player on the left is asked, he or she will answer, "Reboot." The asking player then picks a card from the deck, and play passes to the next player. The first player to be out of cards is the winner.

V. Independent Practice and Application Using the Computer

Play a software game that reinforces the lesson.

LESSON 2-10 DOTTIE DELETE

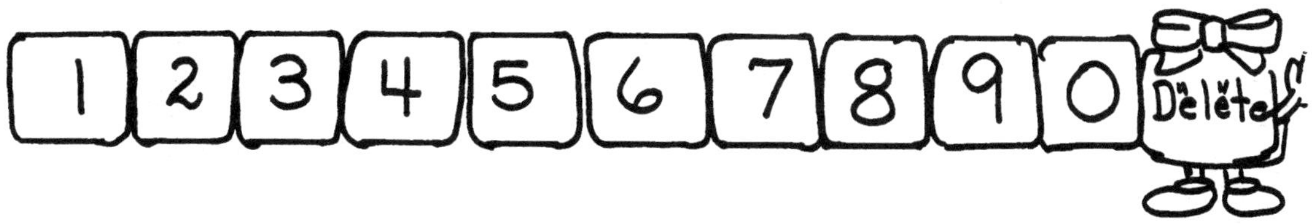

Dottie Delete lived at the very top of the keyboard. She lived with the number keys 1, 2, 3, 4, 5, 6, 7, 8, 9, and 0.

Dottie Delete might be called Backspace on your keyboard, but Backspace and Dottie Delete do the same job. It doesn't matter what the name of the key is. What matters is getting the job done. This is Dottie's story.

All the numbers had fun counting and making really big numbers like millions, and trillions, and zillions.

Dottie was not sure how she fitted in with all the numbers — or even the letter keys. She began to cry.

Return Key heard her and asked, "What is the matter?"

Dottie said, "Where do I fit in? The number keys don't need me; they can make every number in the whole world without me. The letter keys don't need me; they can make every word in the whole world without me. Boo hoo, boo hoo."

"Now cut that out," said Return Key. "You are needed."

"Where?" cried Dottie.

"Right here," said Return Key.

"How?" asked Dottie.

"Let me see," said Return Key. "We can make all the numbers and all the words but what happens if we make a mistake?"

"I don't know," said Dottie.

"Let's ask around," said Return Key. "One, what happens if you add 1 + 2 and you really want to say 1 + 1?"

"One said, "I call . . . uh."

"Who?" asked Return Key.

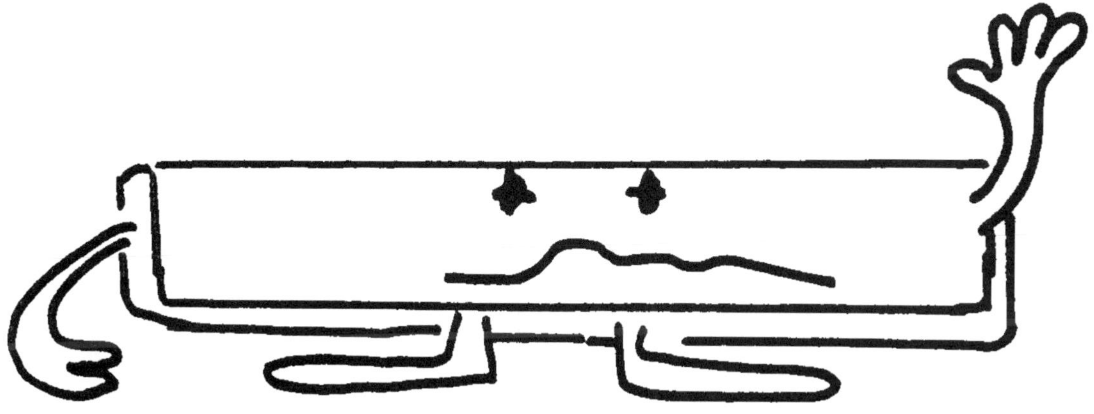

"Maybe Space Bar," said One.

"Oh, no," said Dottie. "Space Bar would just run away and leave big spaces."

"Then who?" said Return Key. "Any volunteers? It is an important job."

Dottie looked around. No one raised a hand, so Dottie did.
"What do I have to do?" asked Dottie.
"Just erase everyone's mistakes," said Return Key.

Pencil had been listening. "It is the same job my eraser does. When I write the wrong letters, eraser rubs them off the paper," said Pencil.

"How will I do it?" asked Dottie.

"You don't have an eraser but if you back up on the wrong letter or number maybe it will disappear. Try it," said Pencil.

Dottie said, "OK, let's try it."

Dottie had numbers 1, 2 and 3 write their names, and then 5.

"Five is not the next number," said Dottie. "Now I will make the mistake go away."

Dottie took a deep breath and jumped up and down. The 5 disappeared.

"Terrific," said Return Key.
Then the letters got together and typed SURPRIZ.
"That is not how you spell 'surprise,'" said Dottie.

"OK," said the letters, "fix it."
Dottie jumped up and down, and like magic, the "z" disappeared.
The letters said "Great job."

"We will need you to be right by our side all the time," said the numbers.

"Wait a minute. We need Dottie, too," said the letters.

"I LOVE IT," said Dottie. "Everyone needs me. Don't worry. Anytime anyone needs me, I'll be ready and, just like magic, your mistakes will disappear."

Dottie still lives at the very top of the keyboard with the numbers. She is very happy knowing she can help when anyone makes a mistake.

After all NO ONE IS PERFECT. We all make mistakes.

Lesson 2-10 Questions

1. Where does Dottie Delete live? (top right corner of the keyboard)
2. With whom does she live? (the number keys)
3. How does a pencil get rid of mistakes? (eraser)
4. Does Space Bar make mistakes go away? (no)
5. What does Space Bar do? (leaves spaces and runs away)
6. Which key erases mistakes? (Dottie Delete)
7. Do the number keys need Dottie? (yes)
8. Do the letter keys need Dottie? (yes)
9. Do we need Dottie? (yes)
10. Why? (No one is perfect.)

Name ____

Reboot

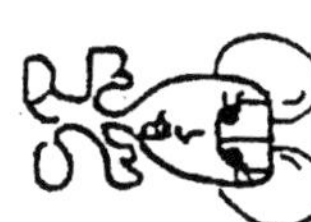

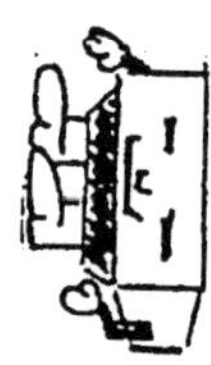

Name ______________________________

Reboot (Continued)

Name ______________________________

Reboot (Continued)

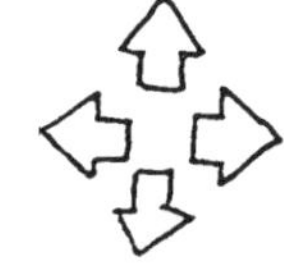

Name ______________________________

Reboot (Continued)

Name ______________________________

Reboot (Continued)

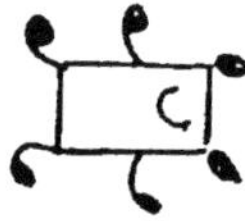

LESSON 2-11 RETURN KEY

To the Teacher

Return Key is different. He is trying to fit in. Cursor helps Return Key fit in. When the letters are saying their names and need a way to tell CPU they are ready, Return Key wants the job. Space Bar comes to help Return Key in games, and all the keys learn that they need each other. CPU says he likes Return Key because he is different.

New words in this lesson: return key

I. Objectives

- Identify the return key as the messenger to CPU.
- Understand that arrow keys move the cursor around the screen.

II. Instructional Input and Learning Activities

- Make overhead transparencies for each page of the story.
- Place the transparency on the stage of the overhead projector and cover the portion of the page you are not using.
- Read the story to the children.

III. Check for Understanding

Use the review questions at the end of the story to test for story comprehension. Cover the questions as you read the last page of the story. Answers are in parentheses.

IV. Guided Practice

The "Return May I?" game teaches the importance of the return key.

Materials - game boards, spinners, markers, coin. Duplicate and laminate game board 1, separate game board 2 from the spinner before laminating it, and laminate and assemble the spinner. The game has two boards. The first game board keeps track of the players' progress to the finish line. The first player to the finish line is the winner. Place players' markers in the START boxes on game board 1. Game board 2 has the spinner and the flip coin circle and boxes. Players in turn start by placing a coin in the black circle and using the pointer finger to flip the coin. The object is to land the coin in the "Esc" box to move two spaces on game board 1. The space bar box allows the player to move one space. If the coin lands on the board but not in a space bar or escape box, the player may try again. If the coin is flipped off the board, the player loses a turn. When the coin lands in either the space bar or escape box, the player spins the spinner and asks "Return May I?" If the pointer points to "yes," the player may move the marker; if "no," the player must wait till her or his next turn and try the process again.

V. Independent Practice and Application Using the Computer

Play a software game that reinforces the lesson.

LESSON 2-11 RETURN KEY

Return Key was sitting on the side of the keyboard. He saw square-shaped keys all around him. Some square keys had letters on them; some had numbers; some had arrows; and some had words.

Return Key was not far from Space Bar. Space Bar sat at the bottom of the keyboard. He was very long and straight. He liked sunning himself under the bright light.

Return Key looked at himself. He looked more like Space Bar than the other keys.

All the square keys looked at Return Key. They said to one another, "Why do we need him around here? We make letters and numbers. Space Bar makes spaces. But what does Return Key make?"

They began to point and laugh.

Return Key didn't know what to say. He wanted to be with all the other keys.

Space Bar was a little bit friendly, but he was always busy getting in between the letters to make words, so he didn't have a lot of time for Return Key.

Return Key was almost ready to cry. He said, "Please, please, please," but no one listened.

The letter keys all got together and began to say their names. Each letter said its name and jumped up and down, and then its name showed on the big screen of Monty Monitor. When the last letter was finished, they all looked at one another.

"Now what do we do?" A said to Z.

"I don't know," Z said. "There has to be a way for all of us letters to talk to Computer Brain when we want to tell him to work with us."

They all looked at Monty Monitor. The letters saw their names and the blinking light square called Cursor.

Just then Return Key spoke up. “You need a key to tell Computer Brain that you want him to work,” he said.

“What key?” asked A. “We tried all the letters.”

“Did you try any other keys?” asked Return Key.

“No. How about using the arrow keys?” said Z.

We know the directions,” said Up Arrow.

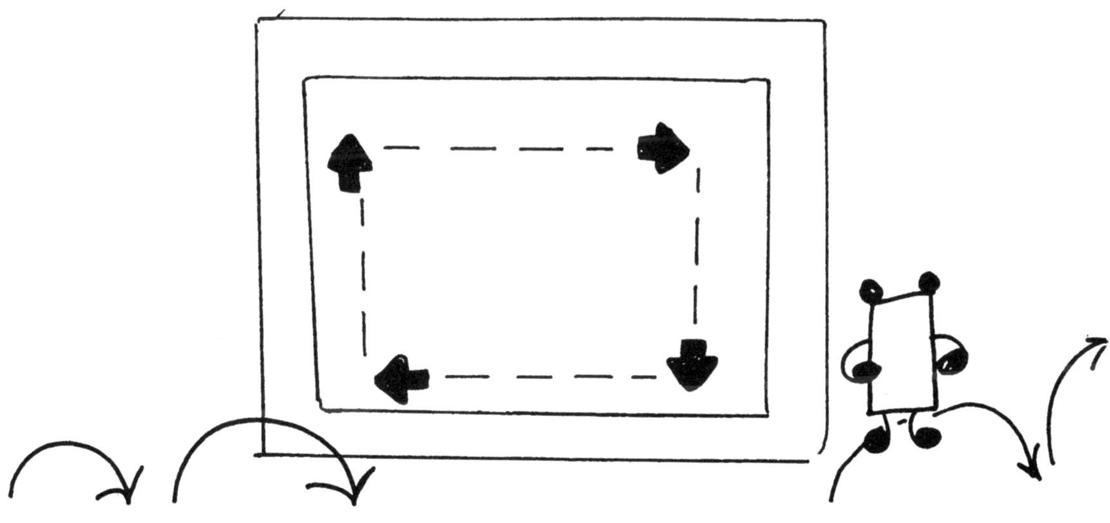

Each arrow key jumped up and down, but all that happened was that Cursor jumped in the same direction.

"That didn't work," said Dottie Delete. "Let me try." She jumped up and down and some of the letters started disappearing.

"Wait a minute," cried Q. "Where did X, Y, and Z go?"
The keys said "Here we are," and jumped up and down again.
The letters said "How about you, Escape Key — can you help?"

Escape Key said, "Dottie Delete makes one letter at a time disappear. I can make everyone disappear. Do you want me to do it?"

All the letters shouted, "NO!"

"We tried all the keys," said A.

"How about me? How about me?" pleaded Return Key. "I'm big. I'm as big as three of you together. Don't you think it's worth a try?"

"Go ahead," said Space Bar, stretching out a little longer.

Return Key looked so unhappy and X, Y, and Z didn't want to disappear again, so they all said, "Go ahead — try."

X, Y, and Z held hands.

Return Key took a deep breath and jumped up and down. Then Computer Brain said in a loud voice, "What do you want?"

All the letters didn't say anything. They were afraid.

Return Key said in a small voice, "Please Sir, the letters want you to say their names."

Computer Brain said, "I will certainly work and say your names because Return Key asked in such a polite way. From now on, whenever you keyboard letters want me to work, you will have to ask Return Key to ask me. You letters will all have to be polite to him also."

Return Key will have the most important job of all. He will talk to me and tell me to work. I LIKE HIM. HE IS POLITE.

Lesson 2-11 Questions

1. Are all of the keys on the keyboard the same size and shape? (no)
2. Who is as different looking as Return Key? (Space Bar)
3. Where does Space Bar sit? (at the bottom of the keyboard)
4. What does Space Bar do? (gets between letters to make words)
5. What is the blinking square on the screen called? (Cursor)
6. What happened when the Arrow Keys tried to help? (Cursor jumped all over the screen of Monty Monitor.)
7. What happened when Dottie Delete tried to help? (letters disappeared)
8. What did Escape Key do? (made everything disappear)
9. Why did the letters give Return Key a chance? (He looked so unhappy, and X, Y, and Z didn't want to disappear again.)
10. What is Return Key's job? (tell CPU to work)

Name ______________________________

Return May I? (Game Board 1)

S									F
T									I
A									N
R									I
T									S
									H

Name ______________________________

Return May I? (Game Board 2)

MISS TURN IF COIN IS FLIPPED OFF PAPER.
TRY AGAIN IF COIN DOES NOT LAND IN A BOX.

1. Put Marker in Start Box.
First Person in Finish Box = Winner

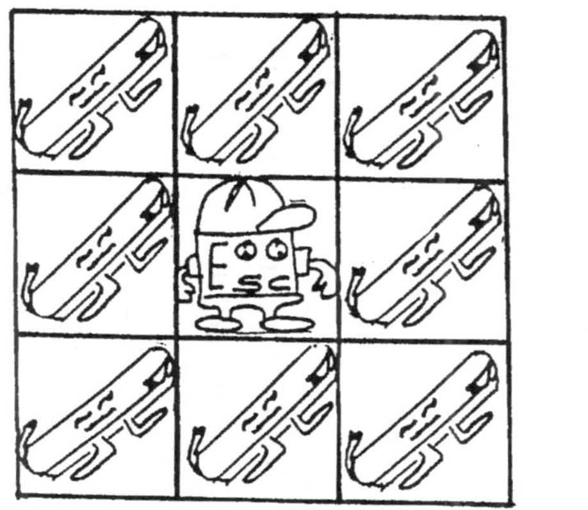

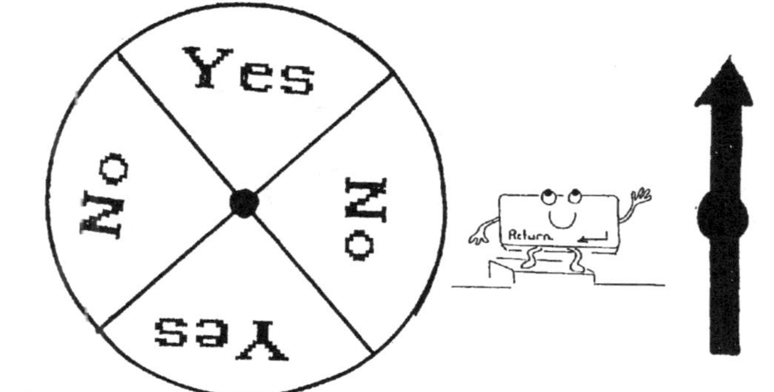

2. Flip coin to a square
* Space Bar = 1 Move
* Escape = 2 Moves

** 3. Spin Spinner –
Yes = Move Marker
No = Do not move Marker

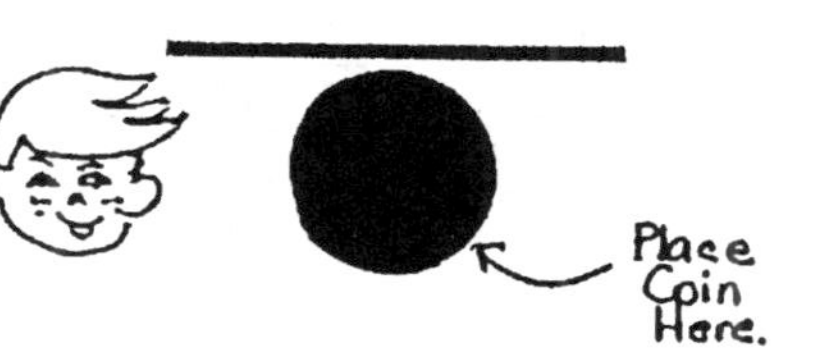

LESSON 2-12 TWINS

To the Teacher

Return Key is still trying to fit in. The numbers of the numerical key pad are going to do a lot of really fast work. Return Key doesn't know how he can help because the numerical key pad is not close to him. Enter Key speaks up and says that he is Return Key's twin brother, and even though they don't look exactly alike, they can do the same thing. Return Key and Enter Key are happy to be twin brothers.

New words in this lesson: enter key, numerical key pad, rectangle

I. Objective

- Understand that the return and enter keys serve the same function.

II. Instructional Input and Learning Activities

- Make overhead transparencies for each page of the story.
- Place the transparency on the stage of the overhead projector and cover the portion of the page you are not using.
- Read the story to the children.

III. Check for Understanding

Use the review questions at the end of the story to test for story comprehension. Cover the questions as you read the last page of the story. Answers are in parentheses.

IV. Guided Practice

The "Find the Twins" work sheet is designed to use the students' powers of observation to find clowns that look exactly alike — that are twins. Instruct students to draw lines to connect pictures of clowns that are exactly alike. One clown does not have a match.

V. Independent Practice and Application Using the Computer

Play a software game that reinforces the lesson.

LESSON 2-12 TWINS

Return Key is shaped like a rectangle. A rectangle is a square that is longer then it is tall.

He wants to look like the rest of the keys.

He knows he has a big, important job; he has to tell CPU, Computer Brain, to work with the information Kiki Keyboard has been typing.

He likes his job.

Space Bar is a good friend. He is a rectangle, too.

Sometimes, when Return Key helped Kiki Keyboard write letters or stories, he would jump up and down, and his little friend Cursor would jump down the page. That was fun.

Big spaces would appear in the places where Return Key jumped, and then Kiki would ask Return Key to keep an eye on Cursor. Cursor is the one who says, "Ready — type."

Return Key liked writing stories.

One day, the numbers said they were going to do a lot of work in a special program that would let them add, subtract, multiply, and even divide. They were really excited. They were not going to use the number keys at the top of the keyboard. They were going to use special keys.

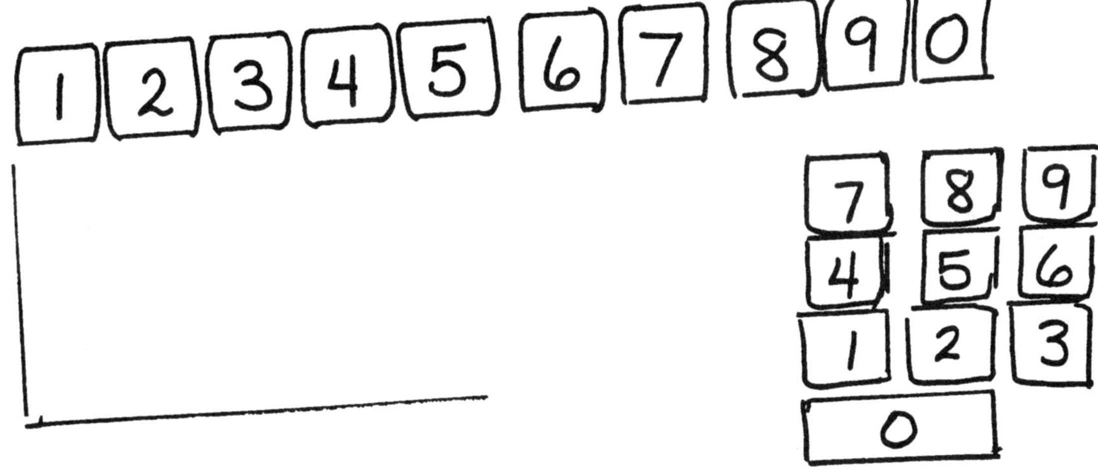

Some keyboards are different; they have number keys both at the top of the keyboard and in a group on the side of the keyboard. The number keys on the side have a special name — Numerical Keypad. Numerical means numbers, and you know what keys are.

"This will be fun. We will jump really fast," said the numbers.

Return Key said, "If you are using numbers all the way over there, how will it be fast if you have to come back to me to tell CPU to work?"

"We never thought of that," said Zero.

Just then a voice spoke. It sounded like Return Key, but it wasn't Return Key. It came from the side of the Numerical Keypad.

"Who are you?" asked Return Key.

"I'm your twin brother, Enter Key," said Enter Key.

"Twin?" asked Return Key. "You don't look like me."

"I am your twin," said Enter Key. "We can do the same thing. — Return Key — Enter Key. Enter Key — Return Key."

"Wow, my twin — SUPER!" said Return Key. "I can do the stories and you can do the number work. Wow!"

"Or I can do the stories and you can do the number work," said Enter Key.

"Return Key — Enter Key. We are the same. We are twins. We are special," said Return Key.

Return Key is very happy to have his twin brother with him. They are alike. They do the same thing.

Lesson 2-12 Questions

1. How are some keyboards different? (two sets of number keys)
2. Who is Return Key's twin? (Enter Key)
3. Do they do the same thing? (yes)
4. Do they have the same shape? (depends on your computer)
5. What do they look like? (Enter Key looks like an up-and-down rectangle. Return Key looks like a side-to-side rectangle — or sometimes a backward 'L'.)
6. How did Return Key meet his twin, Enter Key? (The numbers were going to do a lot of adding, etc.)
7. What other key helps Return Key? (Space Bar)
8. What other jobs does Return Key do? (moves Cursor down the page)
9. How can you tell Cursor is moving down the page? (the blinking square jumps)
10. What does Cursor say? (Ready — type.)

Name ______________________________

Find the Twins

Find the Twins (Answers)

LESSON 2-13 THE NUMBER STORY

To the Teacher

The number keys are bragging about themselves. The letters try to write the same numbers as the number keys. They compare the space and readability that each has. Comma trys to settle the argument. He decides it is easier to read numbers in word form, but it is easier to add, subtract, multiply, and divide using the number keys. The numbers in the numerical keypad and the other number keys think they are really important because there are two different sets of them.

New words in this lesson: comma symbols

I. Objectives

- Recognize that there are two sets of number keys on the keyboard.
- Identify the numerical keypad.

II. Instructional Input and Learning Activities

- Make overhead transparencies for each page of the story.
- Place the transparency on the stage of the overhead projector and cover the portion of the page you are not using.
- Read the story to the children.

III. Check for Understanding

Use the review questions at the end of the story to test for story comprehension. Cover the questions as you read the last page of the story. Answers are in parentheses.

IV. Guided Practice

The "Are the Pictures Changed?" work sheet is designed to help students improve their visual acuity. Duplicate the work sheet for students or make a transparency. Students view the left-column picture of the transparency for 20 seconds; then cover this half and show the right-column picture for 20 seconds. Ask students if both pictures are the same. If the work sheet is used, cut the work sheet into the left and right columns and have the students view only one part at a time. The answer sheet follows the work sheet.

V. Independent Practice and Application Using the Computer

Play a software game that reinforces the lesson.

LESSON 2-13 THE NUMBER STORY

The number keys thought they were very SPECIAL. They could tell how many, do arithmetic — even help you choose a program from the Main Menu.

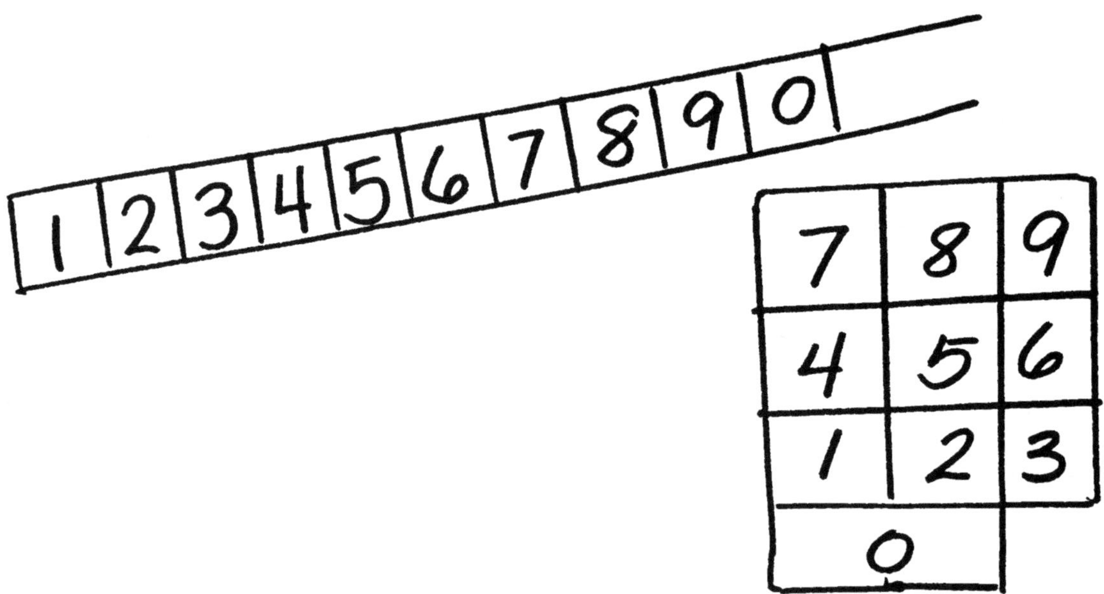

Some computer keyboards have two sets of number keys. One set of the number keys is over the letter keys. They have symbols, too. The other set of number keys is on the right side, in a group.

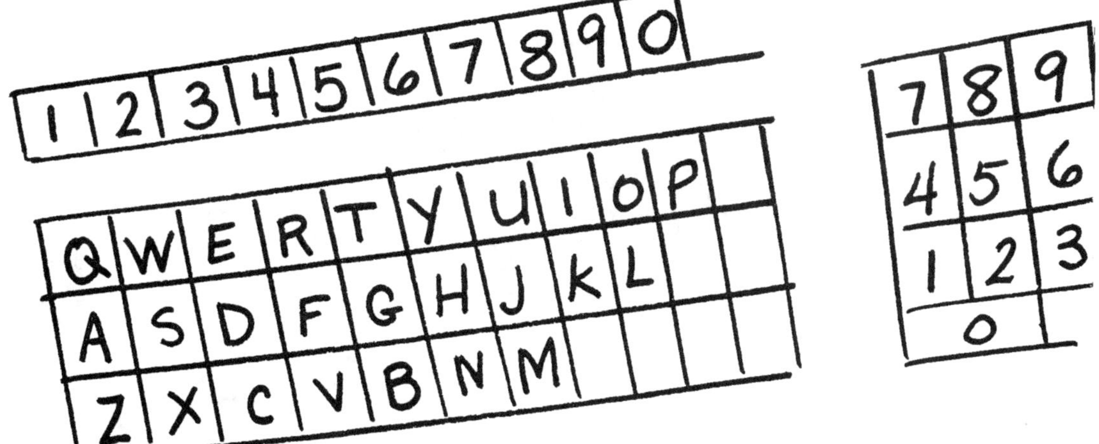

The number keys thought they were very SPECIAL because there were two ones, two twos, and so on, but only one A, one B, one C — only one of each letter.

The number keys began to brag.

"We really are important. We are at the very top of the keyboard, no matter which computer you have. We make BIG numbers."

The other keys got tired of hearing the number keys brag. They sat around trying to think of ideas to put the numbers in their place.

The letter keys began to think very hard. Then Z said, "We can make very big numbers too."

"That's right; we can," all the other letter keys agreed.

The number keys got together and made a really big number.

Nine billion, eight hundred seventy-six million, five hundred forty-three thousand, two hundred ten

"Let's see you make that number," said the number keys.

The letter keys knew they could do it, but it was a really big number. Each letter looked carefully and took its place.

"There we did it," said the letters.

"Look how much space you used," said the numbers. "We can do really big numbers in a little, tiny space."

"I'm important, too," said Comma. "You both say the same thing in different ways, and both ways are important. But without ME all the numbers and letters run together and are hard to say," said Comma. "Number keys can make really BIG numbers in small spaces, but letter keys can write it so it is easy to read."

"You can't add words easily," said Plus Sign Key.

"That is true," said the number keys. "We are more important, and we forgot all about how we can add and subtract, so add that to our list."

The number keys began to brag again.

"We really are important. We are at the top of the keyboard, and our numerical keypad is even better at doing math."

"We make BIG numbers. WE ADD AND DO ARITHMETIC."

"We are really, really important."

Lesson 2-13 Questions

1. When do you use numbers? (tell how many, do arithmetic)
2. Why did the number keys think they were really special? (Some keyboards have two sets of numbers.)
3. Where are the number keys on the keyboard? (above the letter keys, top row, with a numerical keypad to the right of the letters on some keyboards)
4. How do the number keys help to choose programs? (by numbers on the main menu)
5. Are there only numbers on the number keys? (No, there are also symbols: ! @ # $ % ^ & * ( ))
6. Can you write numbers only with these keys? (No, you can write the numbers as words with the letter keys.)
7. What takes less space to write a number — letter keys or number keys? (number keys)
8. What key helps when you want to write really big numbers? (comma)
9. What is very hard to do with letter numbers? (adding, arithmetic)
10. Which set of numbers — top row or numerical keypad — is better for doing math? (numerical keypad)

Name ______________________________

Are the Pictures Changed?

Is the B picture changed from A?

Are the Pictures Changed? (Answers)

Is the B picture changed from A?

LESSON 2-14 SHIFTY SHIFT

To the Teacher

The number and letter keys have a contest to guess whether Shifty Shift or Caps Lock is helping to make the numbers or letters on Monty Monitor's face. Caps Lock does not change numbers to characters. Shifty Shift does. Caps Lock and Shifty Shift both make lower-case letters upper-case letters. That is the secret to the contest. Can you guess which key will win the contest?

New words in this lesson: shift key character symbol caps lock

I. Objective

- Describe the difference between using the shift key and using the caps lock key with numbers and letters.

II. Instructional Input and Learning Activities

- Make overhead transparencies for each page of the story.
- Place the transparency on the stage of the overhead projector and cover the portion of the page you are not using.
- Read the story to the children.

III. Check for Understanding

Use the review questions at the end of the story to test for story comprehension. Cover the questions as you read the last page of the story. Answers are in parentheses.

IV. Guided Practice

The object of the "Shift-O" game is to know whether the shift key or the caps lock key is used to produce an image.

Materials—cards with the upper-case and lower-case letters, numbers, and symbols. Duplicate and laminate the cards. Divide the class into teams. Shuffle the deck and place it face down. A student from each team takes a turn, picks a card, and states, "shift key," "caps lock key," or "none." The team with the most correct answers wins. Students must know that the shift key changes letters from lower-case to upper-case, and numbers to symbols. The caps lock key changes letters but not numbers.

V. Independent Practice and Application Using the Computer

Play a software game that reinforces the lesson.

LESSON 2-14 SHIFTY SHIFT

a b c d e f g h i j k l m n o p q r s t u v w x y z

1 2 3 4 5 6 7 8 9 0

The numbers and letters were all having fun printing their names on Monty Monitor's face.

They did it over and over. Then one of the letters said, "Look at Kiki Keyboard, and then look at the letters on Monty's face. They look different."

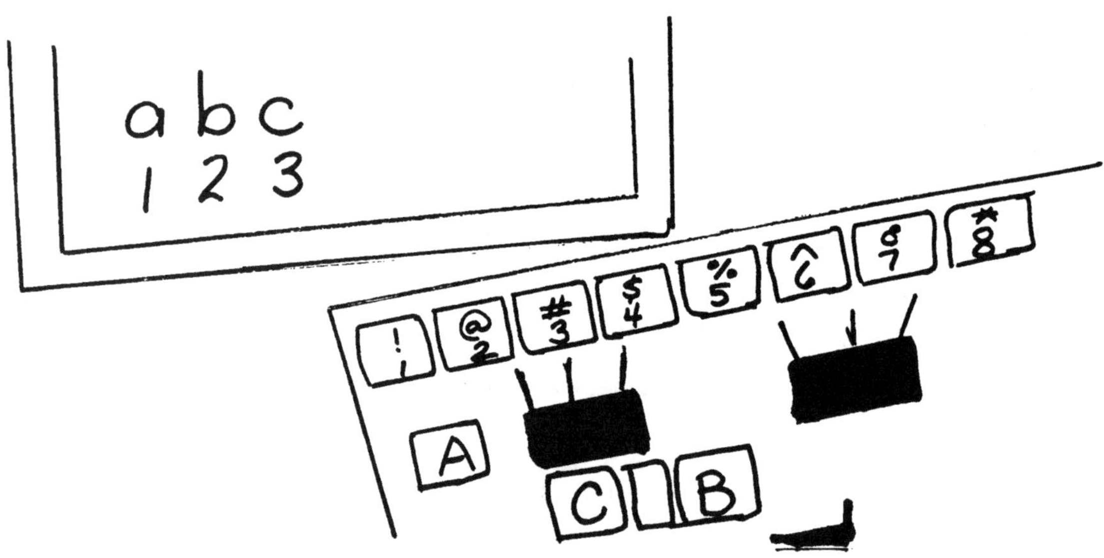

"You are right," said the numbers. "You are little on Monty's face and big capital letters on Kiki Keyboard. Why don't you look the same in both places?"

Kiki Keyboard stepped up. "I have been waiting for you to notice the difference," she said. "Look at the number keys, too. They have a number and another character on them."

"Character! What is a character?" asked letter A.

"A character is a symbol for something else, for example, '$' is dollars, and '&' is the word 'and,'" said Kiki.

$ or Dollar

% or Percent

"When are they used?" asked letter A.

"They are used when someone is in a hurry — and also because sometimes it is the right way to write things. Money is written like this: $576.98. That's the way it is always done," said Kiki.

"How am I going to print my BIG name?" asked letter A.

Kiki said, "There are two different ways. One way is to ask Caps Lock key to press on, so all of you will be capital letters. 'Caps' stands for 'capitals' and 'Lock' means you can do only capitals."

A B C D E F G H I J K L M N O P Q R S T U V W X Y Z

1 2 3 4 5 6 7 8 9 0

"Let's try it," said the numbers and letters. Caps Lock key pressed on, and they jumped up and down and saw themselves on Monty's face again.

A B C D E F G H I J K L M N O P Q R S T U V W X Y Z

1 2 3 4 5 6 7 8 9 0

"Hey! Something is very strange," said the letters. "We letters all did our BIG name, but you numbers didn't change at all. Try it again."

ABCDEFGHIJKLMNOPQRSTUVWXYZ
1234567890

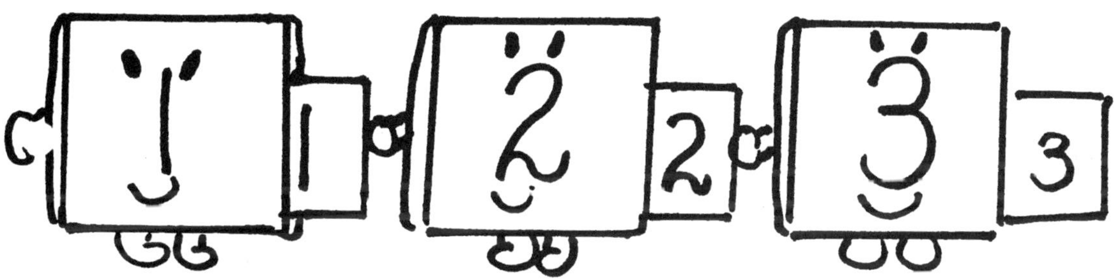

"Same thing. Why?" asked the letters.

The numbers said, "We don't have BIG names. We are 1234567890 when we are little and 1234567890 when we are big."

"Well, your keys say 1 is !; 2 is @; 3 is #; 4 is. . ." said the letter A.

"Stop! We already know what our keys say," said the numbers.

Kiki said, "I want you to meet a new key. He is a cousin to Caps Lock. Caps Lock likes to press and stay on while the new key likes to jump up and down like the rest of you."

"Who is it?" asked the letter A.

Caps Lock said, "I would like you to meet my cousin Shift, Shifty Shift. He is going to sit on Kiki Keyboard right by me."

Shifty waved hello to everyone.

Letter A said, "Let's try again and see what we look like with Shifty's help. How will we do it? Caps Lock just pressed down and stayed down. How do you work Shifty?"

Shifty said, "I like to hold hands and jump up and down with each letter, or I can go first and wait for each of you. I can hold down while each of you says your name."

"Let's try it," said the numbers and letters. Each one jumped at exactly the same time as Shifty, or Shifty got a little head start.

A B C D E F G H I J K L M N O P Q R S T U V W X Y Z

! @ # $ % ^ & * ( )

The letters said, "We all said our BIG name, but you numbers changed to your characters. It is like magic. Caps Lock doesn't change you, but Shifty does. You both are SPECIAL KEYS to do SPECIAL JOBS."

"I bet we could play a game," said the numbers. "You can guess if it is Caps Lock or Shifty who is with us. Want to try?"

"Sure," said the letters. "This should be really easy. We just have to remember that Caps Lock doesn't change the numbers, but Shifty Shifty does. Easy!"

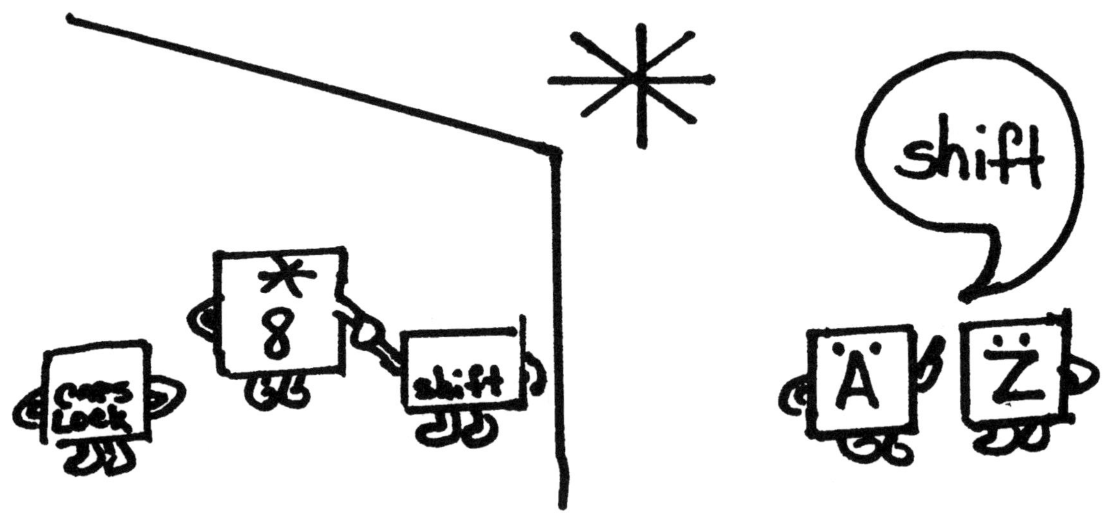

It was easy for the letter keys after they learned the secret. But the numbers couldn't guess at all when it was the letters' turn to be BIG, because with Caps Lock and Shifty Shift they looked exactly alike in their BIG names.

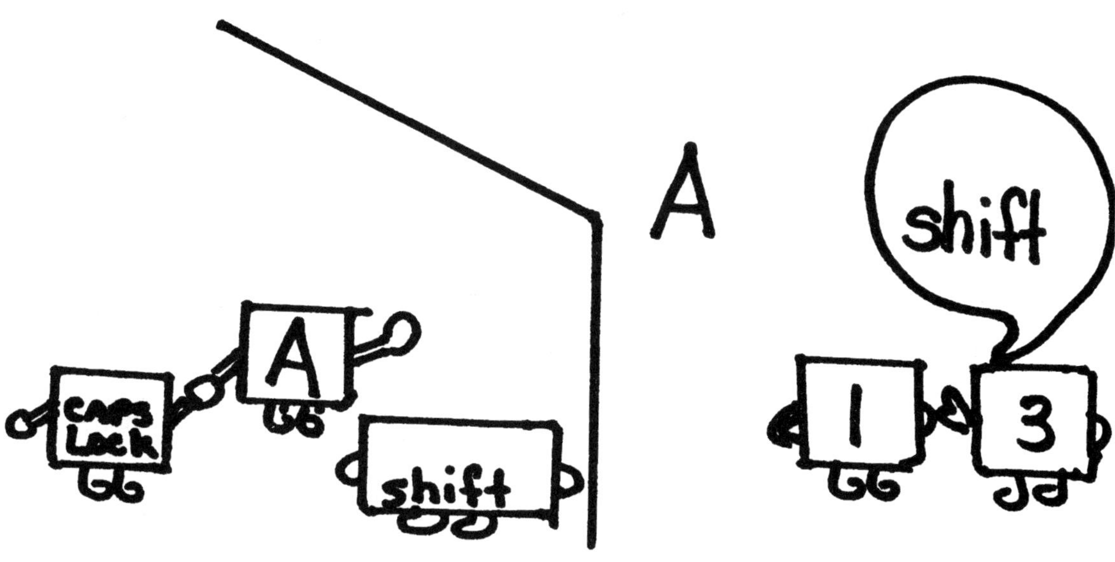

The numbers would have to peek to see which key was helping the letters. The letters always knew who was helping the numbers.

Who do you think won the game?

Lesson 2-14 Questions

1. What is a character? (a symbol for something else)
2. When do you use characters? (in a hurry, looking for a short cut, just because it's the way we do it)
3. What is one way of making a capital letter? (caps lock key and letter key)
4. What is another way? (shift key, together with letter key)
5. Do the numbers change when Caps Lock is used? (no)
6. Do the letters change when Caps Lock is used? (yes)
7. Do the numbers change when Shifty Shift is used? (yes)
8. Do the letters change when Shifty Shift is used? (yes)
9. What was the secret? (Caps Lock doesn't change the numbers, but Shifty Shift does.)
10. Who do you think won the game? (Letter Keys)

Name ______________________________

Shift-O

A	K	U
B	L	V
C	M	W
D	N	X
E	O	Y
F	P	Z
G	Q	
H	R	
I	S	
J	T	

Name ______________________________

Shift-O (Continued)

a	k	u
b	l	v
c	m	w
d	n	x
e	o	y
f	p	z
g	q	
h	r	
i	s	
j	t	

Name ______________________________

Shift-O (Continued)

1	!	
2	@	
3	#	
4	$	
5	%	
6	^	
7	&	
8	*	
9	(	
0	)	

LESSON 2-15 RYAN AND THE SECRET CODE MYSTERY

To the Teacher

Ryan is playing a mystery game on his computer. He realizes he has a "real world mystery" right in front of him. He asks about the function keys and wants to know why they are part of the keyboard. Ms. Barbara encourages Ryan to solve the mystery by trying the keys to find the "secret codes" and short cuts — each key by itself, or in combination with the shift key, the control key, or the alt key.

New words in this lesson: function keys control key alt key

I. Objectives

- Identify the purpose of function keys as keyboard short cuts for certain tasks.
- Understand that the function keys do different tasks with different software.
- Realize that function keys do not print anything on the screen.

II. Instructional Input and Learning Activities

- Make overhead transparencies for each page of the story.
- Place the transparency on the stage of the overhead projector and cover the portion of the page you are not using.
- Read the story to the children.

III. Check for Understanding

Use the review questions at the end of the story to test for story comprehension. Cover the questions as you read the last page of the story. Answers are in parentheses.

IV. Guided Practice

The "Scavenger Hunt" game lets the students be detectives and find items right under their noses. Students use the software to find listed items and learn a different approach to looking at things. Divide students into teams and give them a list of things to find in a computer program that the class has used. Students use the program to find an item and you check it off. Examples you might use are shapes, sounds, words, or pictures. The winner is the team or student with the most checks.

V. Independent Practice and Application Using the Computer

Play a software game that reinforces the lesson.

LESSON 2-15 RYAN AND THE SECRET CODE MYSTERY

Ryan was having fun playing a mystery game on his computer. He was busy looking for clues.

Then he looked at his keyboard and said, "I see a mystery right here."

Ms. Barbara was happy to see Ryan being a "real detective" in the "real world." "What is the mystery?" she asked.

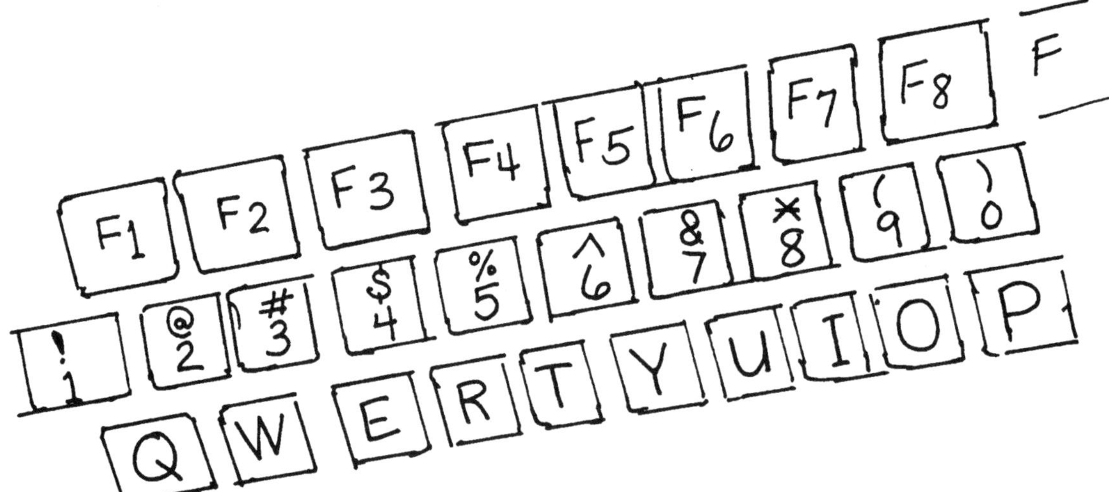

Ryan said, "Look at my keyboard. I know the letter keys make letters, and the number keys make numbers. But, what do the keys do that have F and a number together — the keys above the number key row — and what are they called?"

Ms. Barbara said, "These keys are called Function Keys because they do certain jobs depending upon the software and other keys that work with them; that is their function. They tell the printer to print, the hard disk to save, the helper to help, the spell checker to spell check. They do not print their names, but I could go on and on with all the jobs they can do."

"How many function keys do you see?" Ms. Barbara asked.

Ryan looked at his keyboard and said, "There are twelve function keys—F1, F2, F3, F4, F5, F6, F7, F8, F9, F10, F11, and F12.

I'll bet they do more than twelve jobs. What happens if I press these keys?" asked Ryan.

"You have a mystery," said Ms. Barbara. "Try typing each key to find out what they do. First type each one by itself, and then type it with a combination of the shift key and the function key, and then the control key, and then the alt key. You will be surprised. Different things will happen."

Ryan had a "real mystery" to try to solve. He was going to press each function key and write down what happened. He was going to be a "real detective" and learn some of the SECRET CODES of these function keys.

But he had one more question before he got started. "Why don't we use these keys every day, and learn the codes?" asked Ryan.

Ms. Barbara said, "New programs and mouse buttons can do almost all the same tasks, so everyone doesn't need to learn the function key codes."

Ryan said "It is fun to solve mysteries and know secrets. I am going to find out what each function key can do. I am going to know the secrets and short cuts."

Lesson 2-15 Questions

1. What was Ryan's "real mystery"? (purpose of function keys)
2. How many function keys are on the keyboard? (twelve)
3. What do the function keys do? (short-cut keyboard commands to the computer)
4. Do the function keys print their names on the screen? (no)
5. Are the commands the same for every program? (no)
6. Where are the function keys located on the keyboard? (above the number key row)
7. Do the keys only work alone? (They work alone, and in combination with shift key, control key, and alt key.)
8. Why doesn't everyone know the "secret codes?" (New programs and mouse buttons can do almost the same tasks.)
9. How was Ryan going to learn the "codes?" (try each key and write its purpose)
10. Why was Ryan going to solve the mystery? (He said it was fun to solve mysteries and know secrets.)

LESSON 2-16 POINT, CLICK, AND DRAG

To the Teacher

The story of Mo Mouse tells about the three things she can do - point, click, and drag. Mo tells about her magic arrow that moves on Monty Monitor's face when she moves on her mouse pad. She explains how pictures stick to her arrow until she wants to let go. Mo and Kiki Keyboard need to work together. Mo does not totally replace Kiki, and Kiki can't totally replace Mo.

New words in this lesson: point click drag

I. Objectives

- Understand that a mouse and a keyboard can't replace each other totally.
- Compare the use of different tools for different jobs.

II. Instructional Input and Learning Activities

- Make overhead transparencies for each page of the story.
- Place the transparency on the stage of the overhead projector and cover the portion of the page you are not using.
- Read the story to the children.

III. Check for Understanding

Use the review questions at the end of the story to test for story comprehension. Cover the questions as you read the last page of the story. Answers are in parentheses.

IV. Guided Practice

The "Point, Click, and Drag" game teaches the three movements of the mouse — point, click, and drag.

Materials—Point, Click, and Drag board, spinner, markers. Laminate the board and spinner. Only three players can play this game on a board. One player starts on Point; one on Click; and one on Drag. Players in turn spin the spinner. If the pointer ends on Point, the point person moves one square; if it ends on Drag - drag moves; if it ends on Click - click moves. The first player to go all around the board and back to her or his starting point is the winner.

V. Independent Practice and Application Using the Computer

Play a software game that reinforces the lesson.

LESSON 2-16 POINT, CLICK, AND DRAG

Mo Mouse lives in Computer Land. She is very important for talking to Computer Brain, better known as CPU. She is not the only part that talks to Computer Brain. Kiki Keyboard also talks to CPU. We could not talk to Computer Brain if we did not have Kiki or Mo. The computers we use in school, or at the library, or at home have a keyboard, and sometimes a mouse.

When Mo Mouse first arrived in Computer Land, everyone thought she could just take over and do Kiki Keyboard's job, and that we wouldn't need Kiki anymore. That isn't true. Mo can't always be used with the games we play and, of course, you can't spell your name with Mo. Mo doesn't have any letters on her. She usually has one button — like Return Key.

Mo Mouse is happy to share the work with Kiki Keyboard. Kiki's keys write words on Monty Monitor's face. Space Bar and Return Key get CPU to work.

But how does Mo work?

Mo is called a mouse because she is little and has a long wire connecting her to Kiki or CPU that looks like a tail.

Mo is very smart, although she can only do three things. Those three things are POINT, CLICK, and DRAG. POINT, CLICK, and DRAG. POINT, CLICK, and DRAG.

When Monty Monitor met Mo, he asked her, "How will we work together?"

Mo said, " I do only three things — POINT, CLICK, and DRAG."

"POINT, CLICK, and DRAG — how will that work?" asked Monty.

"Well," Mo said, "I do have a magic arrow with me. It was given to me by the Computer Wizard a long time ago when I was born. The Wizard said to use it only for good. I guess talking to CPU would be a good reason."

Monty said, "It is a very good reason. How do you use your magic arrow?"
"Put a word or picture on your face," said Mo.
Monty thought for a minute and put a picture of a dog on his face.

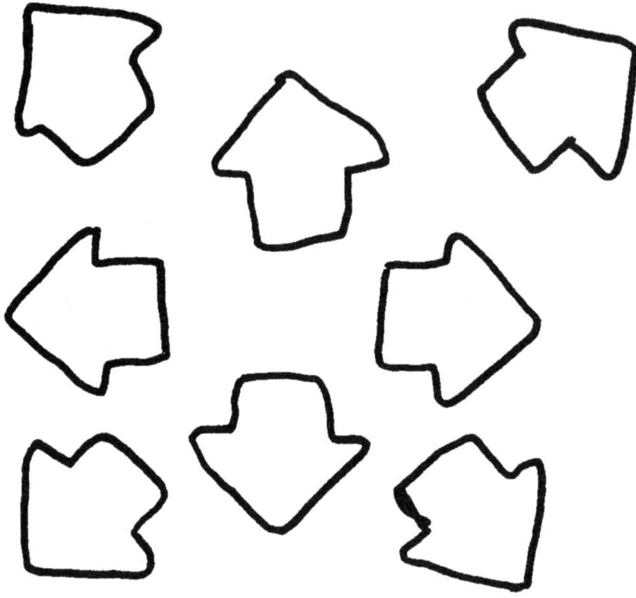

"Let us say you want to put the dog in his house. I can do it with my magic arrow," said Mo. Mo started moving around on the table, and soon on Monty's face a little magic arrow made the same movements. If Mo went right, the arrow went right. If Mo went down, the magic arrow went down.

"That is terrific," said Monty. "How will you get the dog in the house?"

Mo said, "I can do only three things with my magic arrow — POINT, CLICK, and DRAG — so first I will POINT on the dog; then I will hold my magic arrow button down hard and slide — DRAG — the dog to the house."

When Mo held her magic arrow button down hard and slid to the right, the dog picture stuck to her arrow and slid along, too.

Monty said, "It looks as if your magic arrow is sticky, and the dog can't get away."

"No, he can't until my button is let go. Everything sticks to my magic arrow until I want to drop it. When I let go, that's where it will stay," said Mo.

"That is great, but that is only POINT and DRAG, what does CLICK do?" asked Monty.

"CLICK works like Return Key. It is the same as saying, 'Do this now.'"

"So with POINT, CLICK, and DRAG you can do everything Kiki Keyboard can do," said Monty.

"Not exactly. I can't write letters with my magic arrow. I can only POINT, CLICK, and DRAG. You still need Kiki to do letter work. I can only POINT, CLICK, and DRAG — POINT, CLICK, and DRAG," said Mo.

"I get the picture," said Monty.

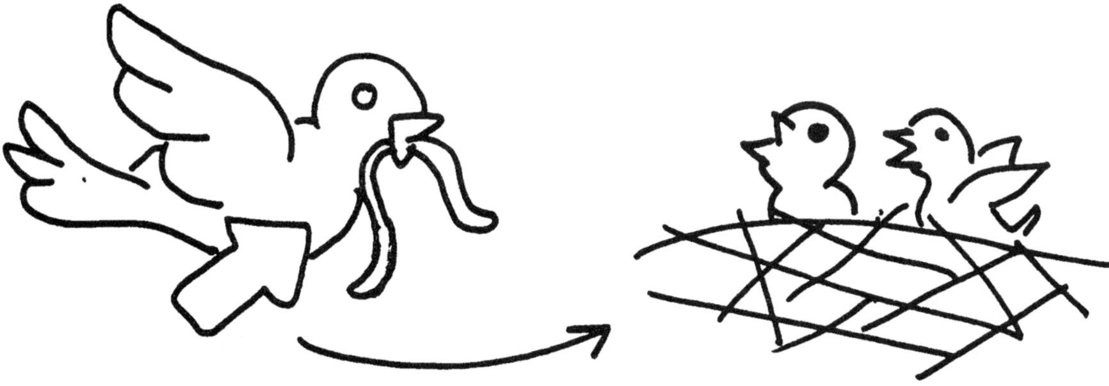

"No, I'll get the picture and move it wherever you want it, or I'll pick the picture by clicking. . ." said Mo.

Monty interrupted, "Now I know that all you can do is POINT, CLICK, and DRAG — POINT, CLICK, and DRAG. So when I want you to work, you will POINT at the picture or word; CLICK, or hold your mouse button down; and DRAG anything with your magic arrow. I like that."

Lesson 2-16 Questions

1. Who helps us talk to CPU? (Mo Mouse and Kiki Keyboard)
2. Can Mo take over completely for Kiki Keyboard? (no)
3. How many things can Mo Mouse do? (three)
4. What are the three things? (point, click, and drag)
5. What do you do to point? (move the mouse around the screen of the monitor to a picture or word)
6. What do you do to drag? (hold the mouse button down and pull across the screen)
7. What do you do to click? (press the mouse button like a key on the keyboard)
8. What does Mo Mouse look like on Monty's face? (an arrow)
9. Can all software games and programs use the mouse? (no)
10. Does Mo Mouse look like a real mouse? (no)

Name ______________________________

Point, Click, and Drag

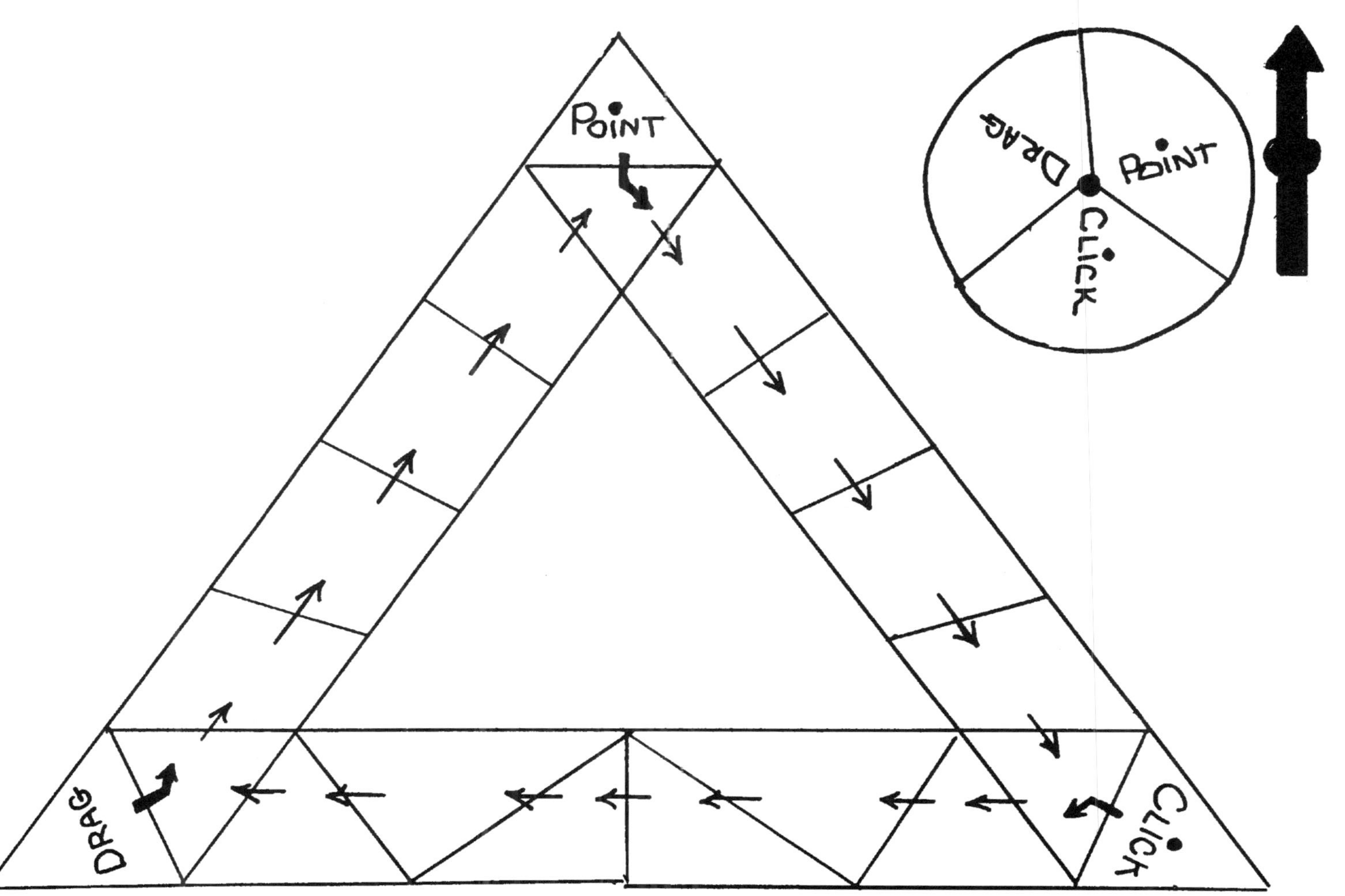

LESSON 2-17 MO MOUSE TO THE RESCUE

To the Teacher

One day Kiki Keyboard feels sick and goes home to bed. CPU says he needs her, but she is too sick. While she is in bed, she hears a click, click sound. It is Mo Mouse. Kiki finds out that even though Mo doesn't have as many keys as Kiki, she can take her place to do certain things. Kiki is very happy and when she is well, she asks Mo to stay and be her friend and helper.

New words in this lesson: There are no new words.

I. Objective

- Recognize that a mouse may be used in place of the keyboard for inputting information with some software programs.

II. Instructional Input and Learning Activities

- Make overhead transparencies for each page of the story.
- Place the transparency on the stage of the overhead projector and cover the portion of the page you are not using.
- Read the story to the children.

III. Check for Understanding

Use the review questions at the end of the story to test for story comprehension. Cover the questions as you read the last page of the story. Answers are in parentheses.

IV. Guided Practice

The "Mouse-O" game reviews the names of the parts and functions of the computer. You may want to use the glossary for definitions.

Materials—fifteen different game boards for students, covers or overhead pens, calling pieces. All the parts are on all the boards. Duplicate the calling pieces and cut them apart. Duplicate the game boards and laminate them. Students cover or X out pictures as the piece is called. The winner is the first student to cover five squares across, up and down, diagonally, or four corners plus the free space. *Example:* Caller pulls a monitor picture piece and says, "Monitor — the part of your computer that lets you see what your computer is doing."

V. Independent Practice and Application Using the Computer

Play a software game that reinforces the lesson.

LESSON 2-17 MO MOUSE TO THE RESCUE

One morning Kiki Keyboard wasn't feeling well. She looked around. She saw CPU, better known as Computer Brain.

She said, "Oh, CPU, I think I need to rest in bed today."

CPU said, "What do you mean? You can't stay in bed. Monty Monitor, Dizzy Disk Drive, and I need you. What will we do without you?"

"I don't know," said Kiki, "but I have to stay in bed to get well."

Kiki went home and climbed into bed. She pulled the covers over her head.

"I wish there were someone who could help when I don't feel well," said Kiki.

After a little while Kiki heard a click, click, click. She peeked over the covers but didn't see anything. She tried to go back to sleep.

Again she heard a click, click, click. This time Kiki decided she wasn't going back to sleep until she found out who or what was making that click, click, click sound.

Kiki waited for a long time, and then she heard the click, click, click. She looked and listened very carefully. Then she saw — she saw IT.

IT was different. IT was smaller than Kiki. IT didn't have letter keys or number keys like Kiki. IT had a long, long tail — well, it looked like a tail — but IT didn't look like a kitten or a turtle. IT didn't look like any animal Kiki had ever seen.

Kiki grabbed the tail. "Who are you?" cried Kiki. She tried to be big and brave. A small squeaky voice said, "My name is Mo, Mo Mouse. Put me down. Put me down. I'm a magic mouse."

“Mo Mouse,” said Kiki. “Magic. You don’t look magic, and you certainly don’t look like a mouse — except maybe for the tail.”

“I’m a special mouse. I can take your place while you don’t feel well,” said Mo.

“How can you help? You don’t have alphabet letters, or a big space bar, or a return key,” said Kiki.

"I have one key. It is like a return key. I can point at things with a magic arrow that will show on Monty Monitor's face. When my button goes up and down, CPU will fall under my spell and think I am you," said Mo.

"It is worth a try, because . . . Aaaachooooo! . . . I think I need to go back to bed," said Kiki, grabbing a handkerchief.

Mo Mouse said, "I will go work with CPU and Monty and Dizzy until you are well. Everyone will think I am you. Drink plenty of liquids and stay in bed."

Mo Mouse worked and played so well that Kiki asked her to stay with her and share keyboard duties for playing games, making pictures, and opening and closing files.

Mo was very happy to say yes.

Lesson 2-17 Questions

1. Who was making the click, click, click sound? (Mo Mouse)
2. What does a mouse look like? (a small plastic box with a long tail)
3. Is Mo Mouse really magic? (no)
4. What is Mo Mouse? (part of a computer)
5. What can Mo do? (take Kiki's place in games and other things)
6. Can she do everything? (no)
7. What are some things she can't do? (type letters and numbers)
8. Did Mo take Kiki's place on everything? (No, they shared duties.)
9. Can Mo open and close files? (yes)
10. What does the one button key on Mo Mouse do? (points the arrow on your choices and gives the information to CPU)

Mouse-O

Calling pieces for Mouse-O game. Cut apart.

	Computer	Arrows - Direction	CPU Computer Brain	Centipede
Chip	Cursor	Dottie Delete	Dizzy Disk Drive	Enter Key
Eddie Escape	History	Home Row	Kiki Keyboard	Letter Key
Molly Modem	Monty Monitor	Mo Mouse	Track Paper	Peter Printer
Return	Rules	Susie Software	Space Bar	Red Light

Name ______________________________ **Mouse-O**

Name ______________________________ **Mouse-O**

Name ______________________________ **Mouse-O**

Name ________________________________ **Mouse-O**

Name ______________________________ **Mouse-O**

Name ____________________ **Mouse-O**

Name ______________________________ **Mouse-O**

Name ______________________________ **Mouse-O**

Name ______________________________ **Mouse-O**

Name ______________________________ **Mouse-O**

MOUSE-O

			Enter	Return
		ASDFGHJKL		STOP
Esc		FREE	RULES	
			Delete	
			Q	

Name ______________________________ **Mouse-O**

Name ______________________________ **Mouse-O**

Name ______________________________ **Mouse-O**

Name ______________________________ **Mouse-O**

Name ______________________________ **Mouse-O**

LESSON 2-18 THE MAGIC WORD – ESCAPE

To the Teacher

Ryan and his friend Rocky learn how to change games and how to stop a game when they want to go outside to play. They know the computer will wait forever for them to return, but it isn't fair for others not to be able to use the computer. They learn how to escape out of their game by using Eddie Escape and returning to the main menu. The words "stop," "quit," and "escape" must be learned so that students can properly exit software; some programs have the word "quit" or "stop" on each screen; other programs use the escape key. The escape key is on all keyboards. Dedicated keys such as "enter," "shift," and "escape" have the same application on all computers. "Escape," "quit," and "stop" may in some cases be interchangeable in teaching correct closing of software.

New words in this lesson: main menu

I. Objective

- Comprehend how to stop games and return to the main menu.

II. Instructional Input and Learning Activities

- Make overhead transparencies for each page of the story.
- Place the transparency on the stage of the overhead projector and cover the portion of the page you are not using.
- Read the story to the children.

III. Check for Understanding

Use the review questions at the end of the story to test for story comprehension. Cover the questions as you read the last page of the story. Answers are in parentheses.

IV. Guided Practice

The "Stop Sign Dominoes" game acquaints the students with the different special keys and ways to stop games.

Materials—set of dominoes cards. Duplicate at least one set of dominoes for each group of four to five students. Shuffle and deal four cards to each student. Place one domino face up in the middle. Students build on the ends with a matching picture. If they do not have a matching picture, they pick another domino from the deck. If they have a double, they place it sideways. If there is a stop sign, they cannot build. Stop signs end the trail. Play ends when one player is out of dominoes, or when no further moves can be made because of stop signs. The player with the fewest dominoes in his or her hand is the winner.

V. Independent Practice and Application Using the Computer

Play a software game that reinforces the lesson.

LESSON 2-18 THE MAGIC WORD – ESCAPE

It was a very long day in Computer Land. The game One, Two, Three, Hop was playing and playing.

"This game is fun to play," said Ryan.

"I really like it too, but you promised we could play Circles and Squares," said Rocky.

Ryan and Rocky were having a good time but it was time to change games. Neither boy knew what to do.

"How can we change games?" said Ryan.

Ryan and Rocky looked around. They both wanted to stop, and they knew you shouldn't just turn off your computer in the middle of a game, because it would damage the software.

"What should we do?" asked Ryan.

"I'd like to run away, or hide, or give up, or stop, or quit," said Rocky.
"I want to escape from here," said Ryan.

"You just said the Magic Word."

Ryan looked around. "Magic Word — I did? What do you mean? Where are you? Who are you?" Ryan asked.

"I am Eddie Escape," said a key with ESC on his chest. "Yes, I heard the magic words quit, stop, and ESCAPE," said Eddie. "I guess you want to stop your game."

"We sure do. You're right. What do we do?" asked both boys together.

"Well, you need me," said Eddie. "Like magic, if you press me twice — two times — the game you are playing will go back to its beginning. I tell CPU to go back to the Menu," said Eddie.

"The Beginning, the Menu?" said Rocky.

"Yes," said Eddie. "The beginning of any game or program has a Main Menu. A menu is a list of what you can do on a computer. It's just like a food menu that lists the food you can eat. It is safe to change games at the Main Menu. You usually see a choice of QUIT or STOP, and then you can start your new game or stop and go outside and play."

"Great, thank you," said Ryan.

"Now we know how to change games, or stop and go outside to play," said Rocky.

"Let's go outside. We can come back and play another computer game later," said Ryan.

And that is just what they did. The boys were very happy to meet Eddie Escape and learn the best way to stop and change games. They knew it was important to know all the magic words like please, thank you, and ESCAPE.

Lesson 2-18 Questions

1. Should you turn off your computer in the middle of a game if time is called? (no)
2. Why not? (It will damage software.)
3. What is another word for stop? (quit)
4. What is the stop-quit key? (escape key)
5. How many times do you press the escape key to quit? (two times)
6. What happens when you press the escape key two times? (return to main menu)
7. What is the main menu? (beginning of every software program)
8. What is the computer menu like? (a food menu)
9. What is a food menu or a computer menu? (a list of things you want to eat or to do)
10. What are the magic words? (please, thank you, and escape)

Name ______________________________

Stop Sign Dominoes

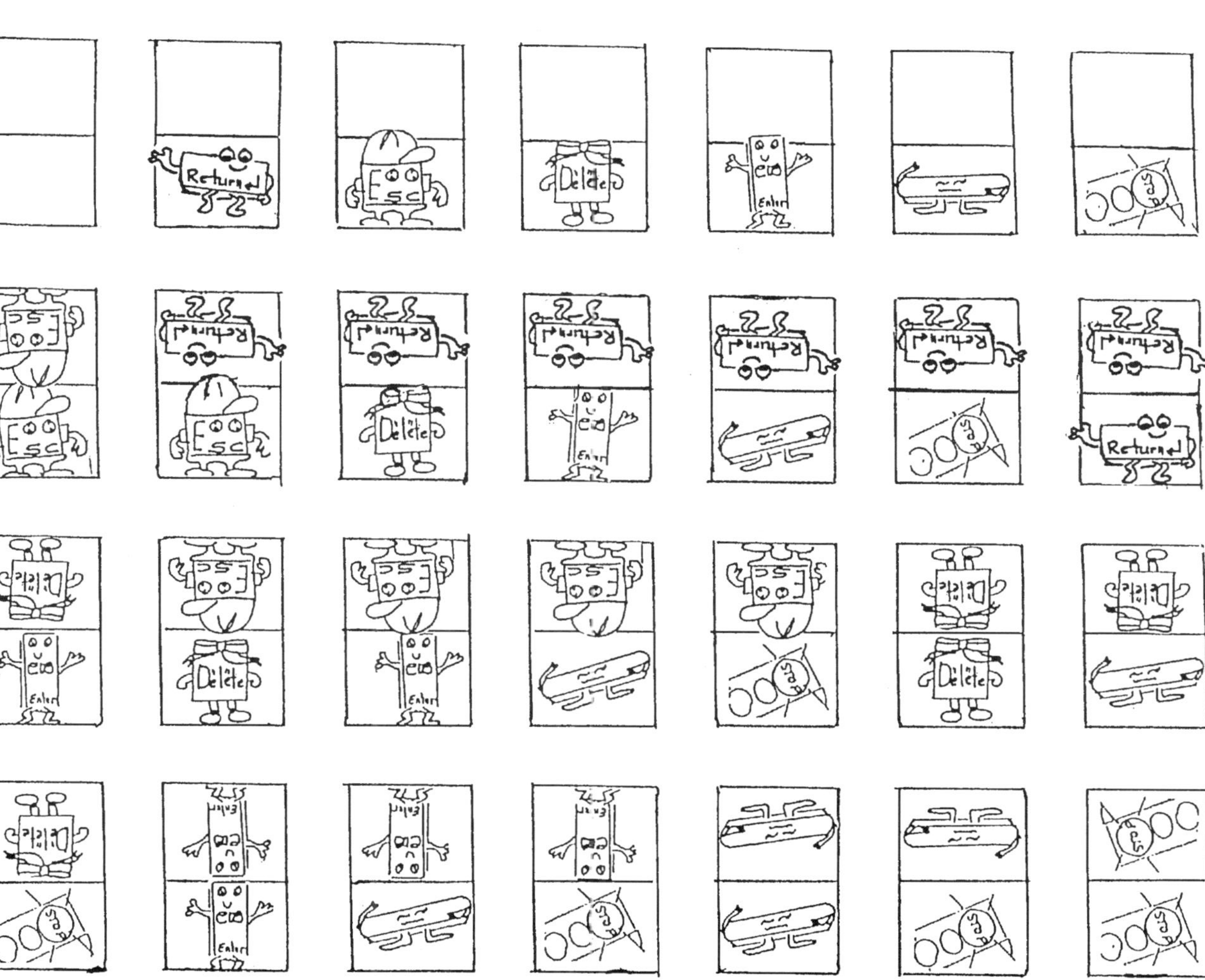

Section 3

Software

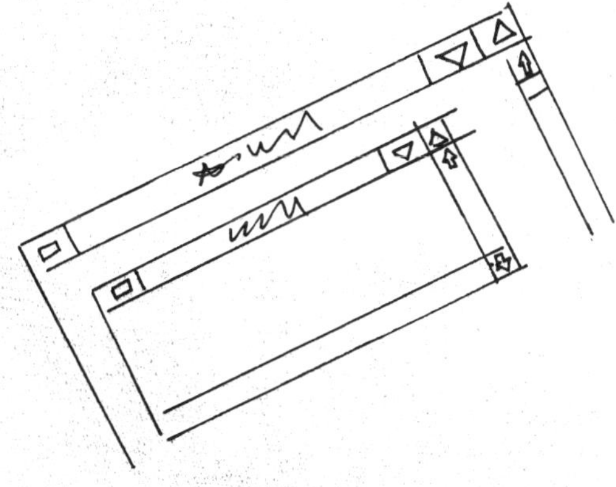

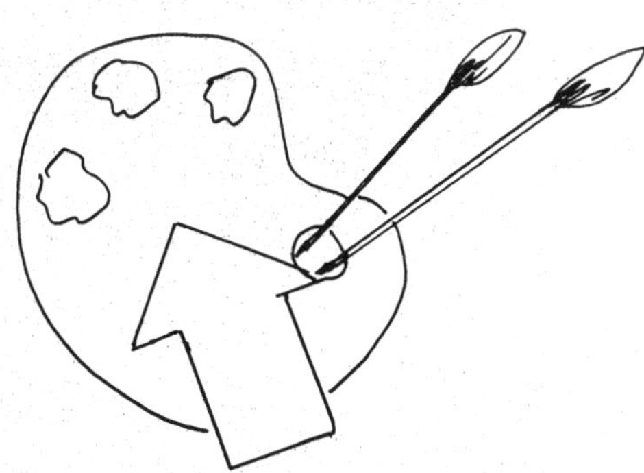

LESSON 3-1 SUSIE SAVES THE DAY

To the Teacher

Tommy Thumb and the other fingers are writing a story about their summer vacation when they see the clock and know they have to go to their piano lesson. Tommy says that it isn't fair for CPU to just wait until they get back. Susie Software and Dizzy Disk Drive say that they can help. Susie says that she saves games, but some disks are meant to keep personal work until you want to use it again. The hands are happy that they can go to their lesson and then come back and finish their story.

New words in this lesson: save

I. Objective

- Describe software storage for saving information.

II. Instructional Input and Learning Activities

- Make overhead transparencies for each page of the story.
- Place the transparency on the stage of the overhead projector and cover the portion of the page you are not using.
- Read the story to the children.

III. Check for Understanding

Use the review questions at the end of the story to test for story comprehension. Cover the questions as you read the last page of the story. Answers are in parentheses.

IV. Guided Practice

The "Inside Story" game teaches the parts of a computer disk, and that "crashing" erases everything.

Materials—Inside Story game board, spinner, and seven markers for each player. Laminate and assemble the spinner. Players spin the spinner and put a marker in each part they earn. If they spin a "crash" all of their markers go back to the beginning square. The first person to have a marker in each of the seven word squares wins the game.

V. Independent Practice and Application Using the Computer

Play a software game that reinforces the lesson.

LESSON 3-1 SUSIE SAVES THE DAY

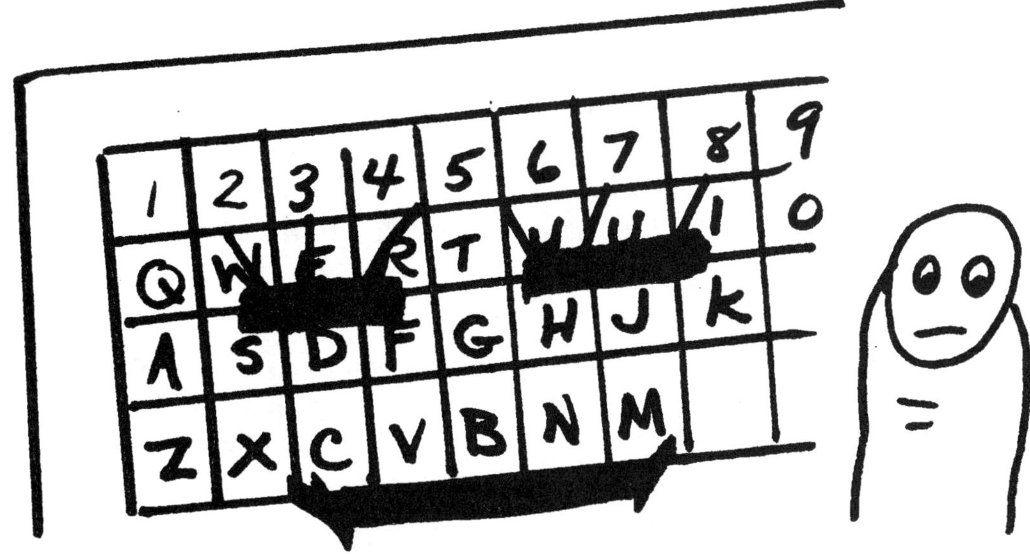

Kiki Keyboard had been very busy with the hands, writing a story about summer vacation, when Tommy Thumb looked up at the clock and said, "Oh my, we have to stop; we must go to our piano lesson."

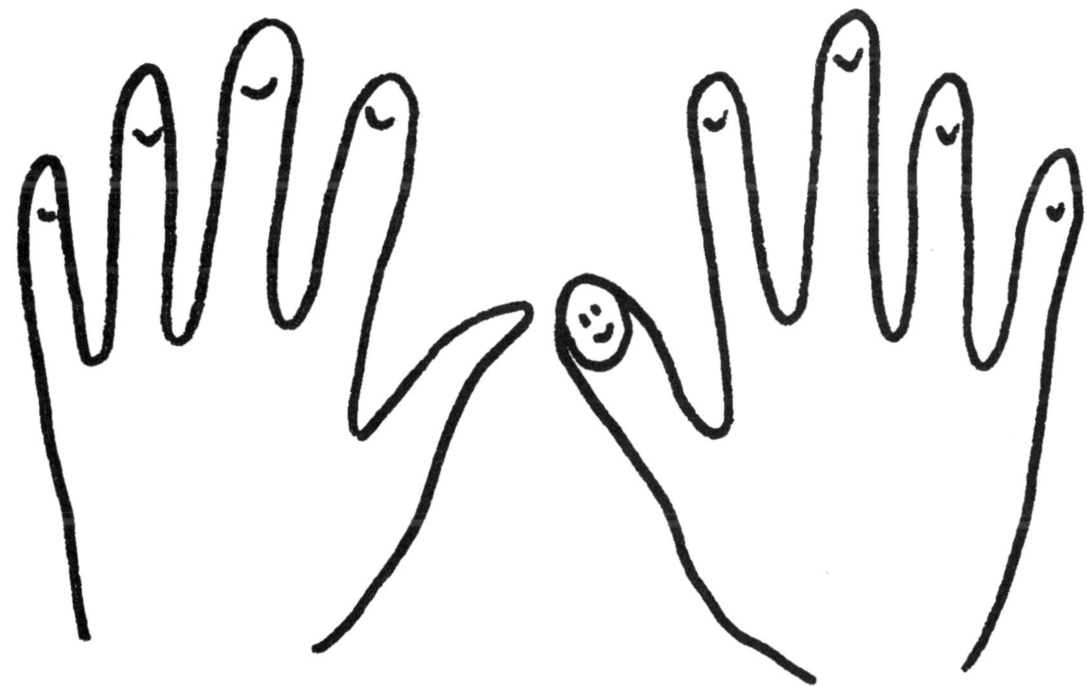

"We are not finished, what will happen to our story?" said the hands.

"CPU, Computer Brain, can wait forever. We can go to our piano lesson and come back, and CPU will still be waiting," said Tommy.

"That isn't fair. What if someone wants to play a game while we are gone?" said the other fingers.

"They can't; they will have to wait. We are not finished with our story," said Tommy.

Susie Software and Dizzy Disk Drive heard the hands talking.
Susie said, "We can help."
"How?" asked Tommy.

Susie said, "Sometimes I have games and programs on me, and sometimes I am blank. When I am a blank I can save things until you are ready to work on them again."

"How long can you save them?" asked Tommy.

"Forever — and you can even put a little more on and stop, and then a little more. I don't mind," said Susie.

"That sounds terrific. How do we do it?" asked Tommy.

"Use the menu," said Dizzy. "Remember — it's like a menu you use to order the food you want, only you order things like 'save' and 'print.'"

Mo Mouse slid to the Menu and pointed to SAVE; Monty Monitor said, "Type the name of your story and press Return." Dizzy Disk Drive spun Susie Software, and then the message "Your work has been saved" appeared.

"That was easy," said Tommy. "We'll be back!"

"We won't forget anything. Go to your piano lesson. When you come back, we can finish your story. You had a very good time, and we want to know how it ends," said Susie and Dizzy.

Lesson 3-1 Questions

1. How long can CPU wait for you to answer a question or finish working? (forever)
2. Who saves the information you are working on when you need to stop? (Susie Software and Dizzy Disk Drive)
3. What kind of disks does Susie Software use to save your work? (blank disks)
4. How long can Susie Software save information on her disks? (forever)
5. Can you add a little information at a time to a disk? (yes)
6. What is a food menu? (something to order the food you want)
7. What is a computer menu? (part of a program to order the game or activity you want)
8. How do you get your information from Susie? (open menu and choose by numbers or arrows)
9. How do you know your work has been saved for you? (The message "Your work has been saved" may be printed on the screen.)
10. Why do we need to save information? (so other people can use the computer, and we can continue where we left off later)

Inside Story

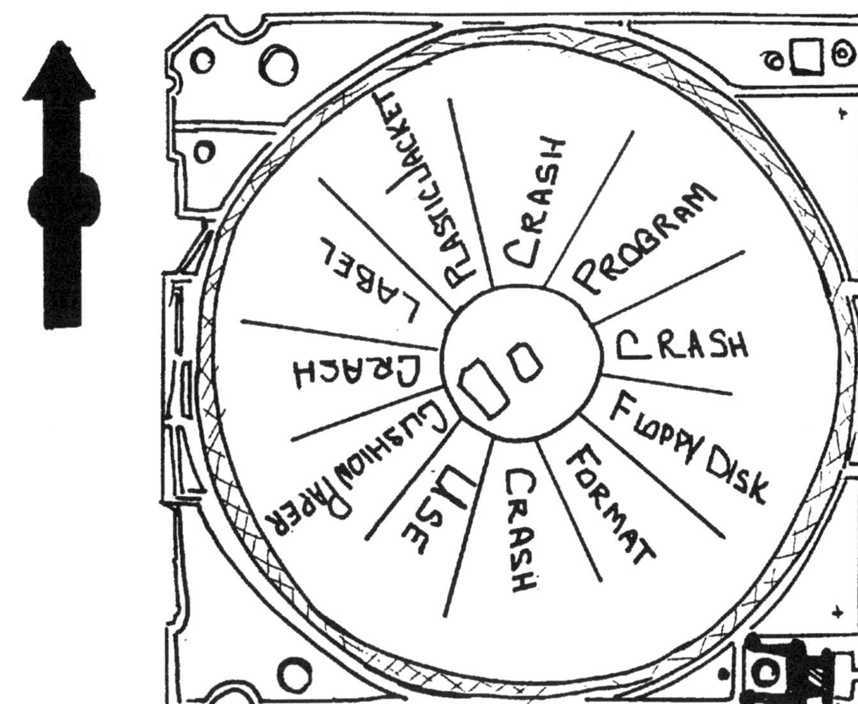

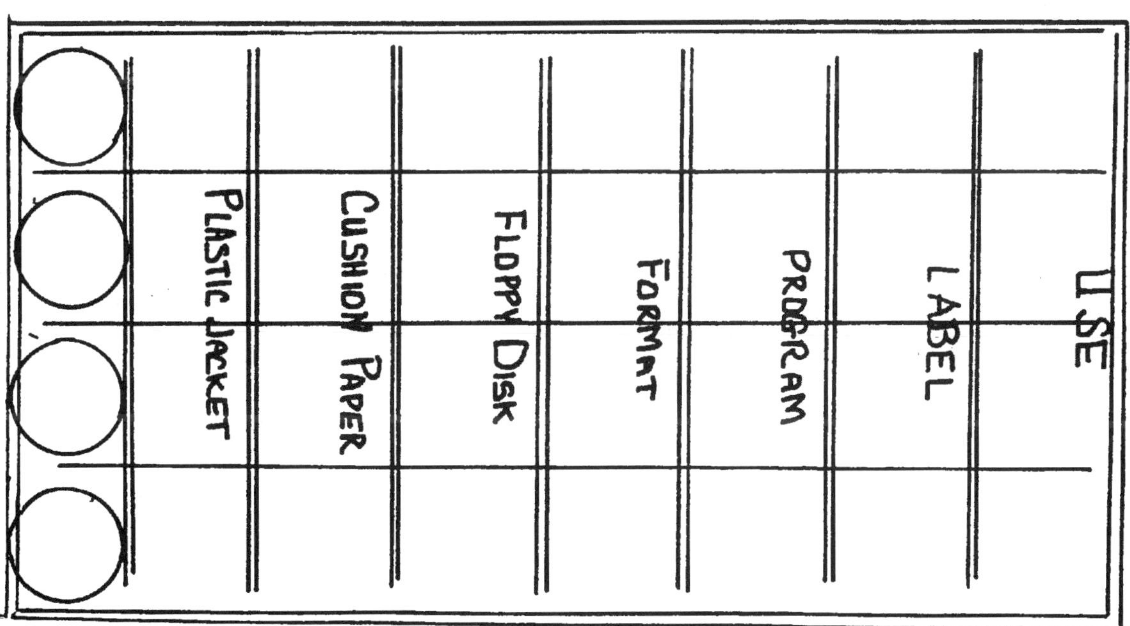

LESSON 3-2 SUSIE SOFTWARE GETS SICK

To the Teacher

Susie Software is feeling sick. Something has happened to her. She was left out in the sun, a goldfish splashed water on her, a pencil wrote too hard on her, and there are fingerprints and jelly smears on her. Tommy Thumb decides to make a list of rules to help Susie. Libby Label also has ideas to help Susie. The rules are to keep bad things away from Susie because she is allergic to them. Correct handling of software is taught.

New words in this lesson: jacket

I. Objectives

- Understand the correct handling of software.
- Grasp reasons why food, drink, dirty hands, and heat are bad for computer disks.

II. Instructional Input and Learning Activities

- Make overhead transparencies for each page of the story.
- Place the transparency on the stage of the overhead projector and cover the portion of the page you are not using.
- Read the story to the children.

III. Check for Understanding

Use the review questions at the end of the story to test for story comprehension. Cover the questions as you read the last page of the story. Answers are in parentheses.

IV. Guided Practice

The "Build-O" game reviews computer parts.

Materials—Build-O board, one die, and five different-colored markers for each player in a "bank." Students roll the die. They must roll the numbers in sequence — one first, two second, and so on. The number code for the computer pieces is on the game board. Students try to collect all five parts. If at any time they roll a six, they must return the last marker earned to the "bank."

V. Independent Practice and Application Using the Computer

Play a software game that reinforces the lesson.

LESSON 3-2 SUSIE SOFTWARE GETS SICK

One day Susie wasn't feeling well. She went to her mirror and looked at herself.

Tommy Thumb saw Susie.

"What is wrong?" Tommy asked.

Susie said, "I don't know."

Tommy was worried. He said, "Let me look at you. My dad is a doctor."

Susie said, "OK." She wanted to feel better.

Tommy looked and looked at Susie. He said, "Let me ask you some questions. When did you first start feeling bad?"

"It was right after I took off my jacket. I was lying on a table in the bright sunlight. I was getting really hot when Splash, the goldfish in the bowl next to me, flipped his tail and water hit me in the face. Then Felt-Tip Pen's friend Pencil started scratching all over me. He made me bend over in pain. He was really bad!"

"That is bad," said Tommy.

Tommy looked carefully at Susie. She had big fingerprints on her. He said "It is not bad enough that you have fingerprints on you; the finger- prints have jelly marks. You also have puddles of water on your face."

"What can I do?" asked Susie.

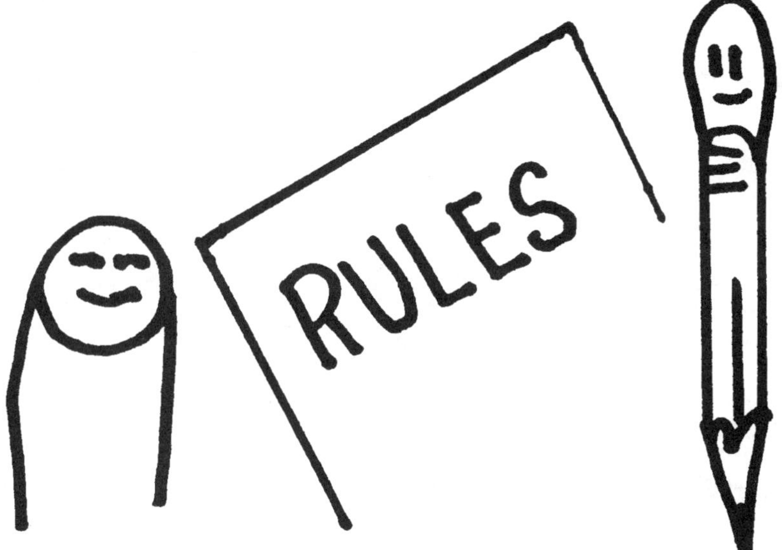

First Tommy said, "We need to put up RULES so this does not happen again."

He picked up a big piece of paper and called Pencil.

Tommy said "Look at Susie. You are one reason she feels so bad."

"What do you mean?" asked Pencil.

"You made marks on Susie that made her bend over in pain. Heat hurt her and so did water," said Tommy.

"What about you and your friends?" said Pencil. I see fingerprints and jelly stains. That comes from you and your friends."

"We have all treated Susie badly," said Tommy. "From now on, when Susie takes off her jacket, we will have to be more careful." Susie wears a paper or plastic jacket to protect her when she is not working.

Tommy said, "From now on RULE ONE is Be Careful With Susie. I will make the the rest of the fingers stay where they belong. They need to touch only enough to put Susie into Dizzy Disk Drive."

"RULES TWO and THREE are No Food or Drinks — or Fishbowls — around Susie. I think she is allergic to them."

Susie started feeling better when she heard her friends talking about how they were going to take care of her.

Pencil said, "Let's make the sign and put it by Computer Brain."

And that is what they did.

The sign said . . .

DON'T PUT SUSIE SOFTWARE IN THE SUN, OR NEAR WATER.
NO FOOD OR DRINKS NEAR SUSIE SOFTWARE.
DON'T BEND SUSIE SOFTWARE.
NO FINGERPRINTS ON SUSIE SOFTWARE.

HOLD SUSIE SOFTWARE VERY CAREFULLY.

ALWAYS PUT SUSIE'S JACKET ON HER WHEN SHE IS NOT BEING USED.

Why? Because Susie is allergic.

Lesson 3-2 Questions

1. What are some things that make software "sick?" (sun, water, pencils, bending, fingerprints, food)
2. Where did the water come from that splashed on Susie? (goldfish bowl)
3. What kind of food was on her? (jelly)
4. What did Pencil suggest the parts do to help Susie? (make a sign with the rules and put it by Computer Brain)
5. What were rules 1, 2, and 3? (be careful, no food or drink, no fish-bowls)
6. What does Susie wear to protect her when she is not being used? (jacket)
7. What is Susie's jacket usually made of? (paper or plastic)
8. How should you hold Susie? (carefully, with Tommy Thumb on label)
9. How much should you touch Susie? (only enough to put her in Dizzy Disk Drive and back in her jacket)
10. What happens if Susie gets sick? (The program will not be useable.)

Name ______________________________

Build-O

Build Your Computer

- Roll die 1=Disk Drive 2=CPU 3=Monitor 4=Keyboard 5=Mouse 6=RETURN LAST PIECE EARNED.

Must collect pieces in number order. 1=first, 2=second, etc.

First player with all five parts WINS!

LESSON 3-3 LIBBY LABEL MEETS SUSIE SOFTWARE

To the Teacher

One day Susie feels different. She has lost the paper that describes her software job. All of her sisters have the same problem. Libby Label gets the job of sticking with Susie as a close friend. CPU is happy because without labels, each disk must be loaded into his memory to find the job that each performs. Formatting is compared to bathing and brushing teeth to get ready for the day.

New words in this lesson: format label

I. Objectives

- Describe the need for labels on software.
- Understand that formatting makes disks ready for storage and use.

II. Instructional Input and Learning Activities

- Make overhead transparencies for each page of the story.
- Place the transparency on the stage of the overhead projector and cover the portion of the page you are not using.
- Read the story to the children.

III. Check for Understanding

Use the review questions at the end of the story to test for story comprehension. Cover the questions as you read the last page of the story. Answers are in parentheses.

IV. Guided Practice

The "Labels" work sheet teaches students that containers and wrappings usually provide an indication by pictures or words of what might be inside the container.

Duplicate the work sheet for students and instruct them to draw a line that connects the picture of an object with the picture of its container. The answer sheet follows the work sheet.

V. Independent Practice and Application Using the Computer

Play a software game that reinforces the lesson.

LESSON 3-3 LIBBY LABEL MEETS SUSIE SOFTWARE

Susie Software felt cold, so she put her jacket on. Her mother had always said every good little software needs a fine jacket to keep safe and protected from dirt and other bad things.

Susie held her jacket close to her body. She always kept it on when she wasn't making CPU, Computer Brain, work.

She had a real job that kept her head spinning. She never knew when CPU would want to play a game, or write a letter, or draw a picture. She and her sisters had to be ready to give the information to CPU.

Sometimes Computer Brain would say, "I have something important and I need someone to SAVE it for me." Susie would spin around in circles and put the information on herself.

Susie had little sisters and big sisters. All of them could play games or save things for Computer Brain.

Computer Brain was like a father; he took good care of Susie and her sisters. If one of them was blank, Computer Brain would make her like the others; he would FORMAT her.

FORMATTING is like taking a bath and brushing your teeth. That gets you ready for your day. Formatting gets disks ready for their day — to do what anyone wants them to do.

One day Susie felt different. She had her jacket on but something was missing.

She looked at herself in the mirror and saw the piece of paper that said SUSIE PICTURE MAKER SOFTWARE was gone.

Where could it be? Then she looked at two of her sisters. Their papers were gone, too. "What has happened to us?" they asked.

Susie said, "I don't know. Without our papers no one can tell who is picture maker, or game player, or letter writer."

Just then Computer Brain called and said, "I need to write a letter."

He looked at Susie and her sisters and said, "I can't tell who is who and I am in a hurry. How can I find out which one is Letter Writer?"

"You can guess," said Susie, "Or each of us can go to Dizzy Disk Drive to find out."

"I don't have a lot of time," said CPU. "Tell me who is Letter Writer."

Susie laughed, "I don't know. Let me spin around." Susie jumped and spun around in Dizzy Disk Drive. Pretty soon the words Picture Maker were on Monty Monitor's face.

"That isn't right," said CPU. I am in a HURRY."

"Our papers are missing," said Susie. "That is the easiest way to know who is who. I am going to get Felt-Tip Pen to write on a new paper and glue it on so I don't forget."

"HURRY UP," said CPU.

Susie whistled loudly and Felt-Tip Pen came. "What can I do?" asked Felt-Tip.

"Write Susie's name on her paper," said CPU.

Felt-Tip said, "OK, but how is that going to stay on Susie? She lost her other paper."

"I can help," said a small voice. It was Libby Label. Libby said, "I heard that Susie keeps losing her papers. I am a paper with a sticky back. If you write on me and stick me on Susie, I'll stay forever."

"That sounds like a good idea," said Susie. "I do a good job of remembering what CPU writes on me, and now I can just look at my . . . my . . ."

"Label," said Libby.

"Right," said Susie. "Label."

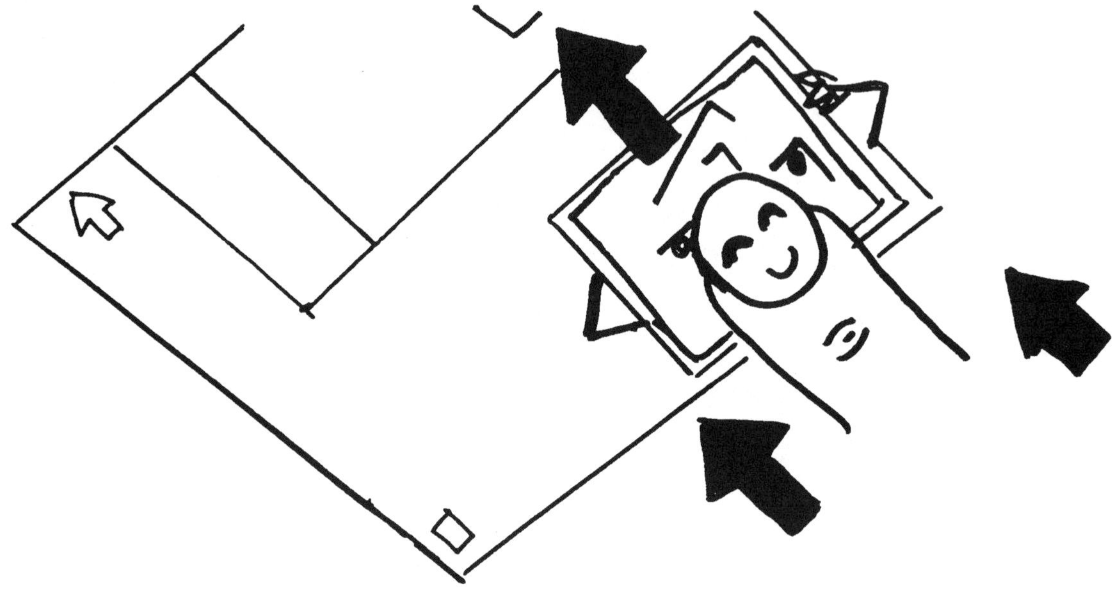

Libby Label said, "I'd really like to be a close friend. I can do something else. When you go into Dizzy Disk Drive, I will be on top to say This Way. I will also say Thumb on Label. I like thumbs and this will help to be sure you are handled without getting hurt."

"Very good idea," said Susie.

So Libby Label attached herself to Susie and her sisters. When Computer Brain wanted to write a letter he knew who was Letter Writer just by looking at her label.

Computer Brain was happy because he was always in a HURRY!

Lesson 3-3 Questions

1. Why does Susie need a jacket? (to keep safe and protected)
2. Protected from what? (dirt and other bad things)
3. What is formatting? (It gets disks ready to do what anyone wants them to do.)
4. What was Susie's problem? (She lost the paper with the program name.)
5. Can you tell what programs are on a disk without a label? (no)
6. How can you find out what is on a disk if there isn't a label? (spin the disk in Dizzy Disk Drive)
7. What kind of writing tool should be used on labels? (felt-tip pens)
8. Why are labels used? (to name programs on the disk permanently)
9. What is another use for a label? (to tell you which way the disk goes into Dizzy Disk Drive)
10. Can you write the label name on the jacket instead of the disk? (Yes, but it might get lost.)

Name ______________________________

Labels

Puppy All Gone
Wings for Feet
Fresh
Moo Juice
Big Bubble
I see

GUM

Labels (Answers)

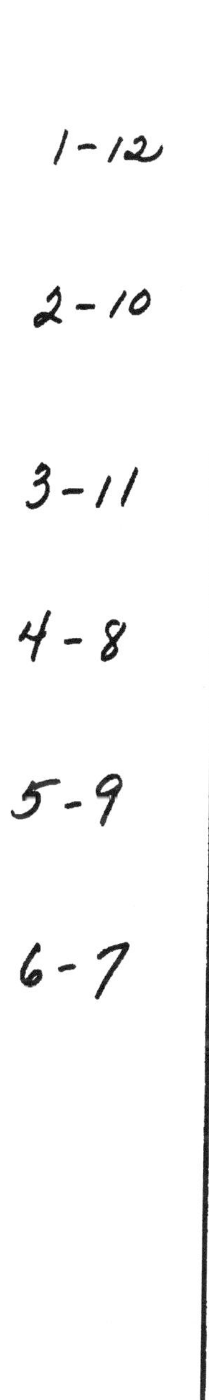

LESSON 3-4 LOAD THE SOFTWARE

To the Teacher

Susie Software and her friends, CD-ROM and Hard Drive, are very important. She tells CPU that humans have eyes, ears, hands, and mouths to input information. CPU agrees that Susie and her friends fill his memory in a way similar to the way that humans input information. Susie says they give CPU so much information that it is like loading a truck. CPU agrees that "load" is a better word. He asks Susie to load his memory so that he can learn about the eyes, ears, hands, and mouths of humans.

New words in this lesson: load backup copy CD-ROM

I. Objectives

- Understand that software, hard drives, and CD-ROMs as ways to input computer information.
- Compare computer input with the human senses for inputting and retrieving information.

II. Instructional Input and Learning Activities

- Make overhead transparencies for each page of the story.
- Place the transparency on the stage of the overhead projector and cover the portion of the page you are not using.
- Read the story to the children.

III. Check for Understanding

Use the review questions at the end of the story to test for story comprehension. Cover the questions as you read the last page of the story. Answers are in parentheses.

IV. Guided Practice

The "Sense-O" game lets the students use their "input devices" (senses) to guess items. They see that inputting data to humans is not as easy as inputting to a computer.

Materials—box with sensory items such as a lemon, a rock, salt, cotton, a disk, or any others you think would be interesting. Divide the class into teams; one person will be eyes, one ears, and so on. Place an item in the box. One person is chosen to sense the box item, using that particular sense, and then writes down his or her guess. Students will soon realize that items cannot be guessed by one sense only. Many experiments might be needed to guess a simple item like a pencil, or a spoon. The first person should be the sense of hearing, then smell, and so on. Hearing = 4 points, smell (second) = 3 points, touch (third) = 2 points, sight (fourth) = 1 point. Taste is eliminated because of toxic danger. The first team to twenty points is the winner.

V. Independent Practice and Application Using the Computer

Play a software game that reinforces the lesson.

LESSON 3-4 LOAD THE SOFTWARE

Susie Software is very important. She has the programs you will want to use. Programs can be games, or stories, or other things.

Susie and her companions, CD-ROM and Hard Drive, help you to do the things you want to do with Computer Brain. Whenever you want to play a game, your computer has to have that game in its memory.

If you want to put something in your memory you can use your eyes to see it;

your ears to hear it;

your nose to smell it;

your mouth to taste it;

or your fingers to touch it.

Computers don't have eyes, ears, noses, mouths, or fingers, so how does your computer get information?

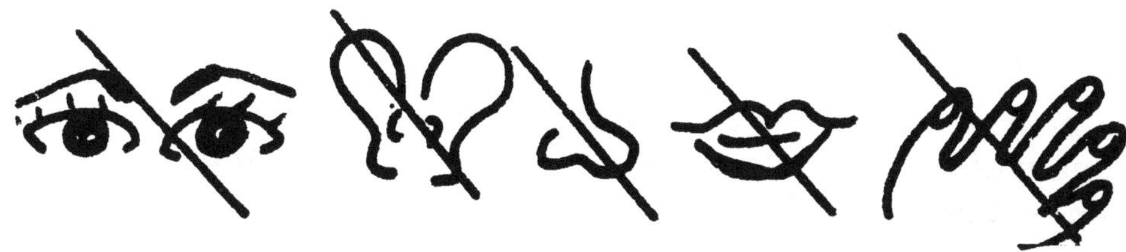

Computers can come from the factory with some programs already on Hard Drive. The factory doesn't know what each person will want to use. You may want dinosaurs, while someone else wants dolls.

In Computer Land, Susie Software sat on her shelf waiting to be needed. Susie usually sits on her edge so she won't get bent or damaged. She sits out of the sunlight and away from water and food. They can hurt her, too.

Susie just waited and waited for Dizzy Disk Drive to spin her around so she could give her information to Computer Brain. CD-ROM might also spin around to give information to Computer Brain.

Computer Brain said, "I can remember lots of things with the help of Hard Drive, CD-ROM, and Susie. They really fill my memory."

"We fill it, all right," said Susie. "We load your memory to the top."

"That's right," said Computer Brain. "You really load me up with information."

"Let's just say 'We load you up,'" said Susie. "It sounds more important."

Computer Brain agreed. "Load is a good word for all the information you give me. You can give me a dictionary,

or a football game,

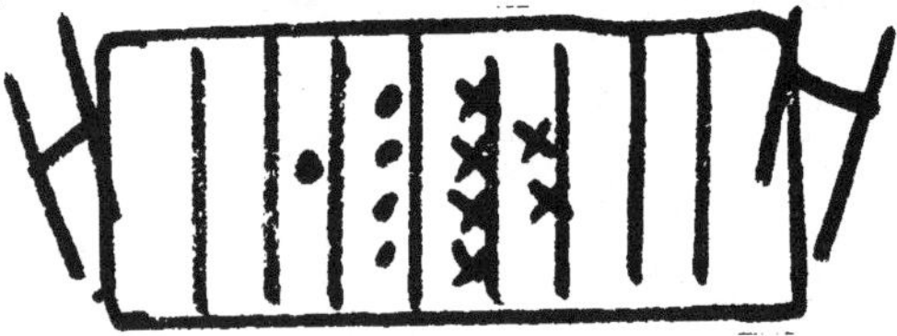

or an entire set of encyclopedias.

That is a lot of information — a real load for anyone," said Computer Brain.

"I wouldn't want to carry all that information in real books," said Dizzy Disk Drive.

Susie said, "I'm little but mighty."

"I thought I wouldn't be needed when Hard Drive moved into Computer Brain," said Susie, "But then I learned that Hard Drive needed a BACKUP COPY."

"What's does backup mean?" asked Dizzy.

"It means that I give information to Hard Drive, but if he gets overloaded, or breaks down, he will have to get the information from me again," said Susie.

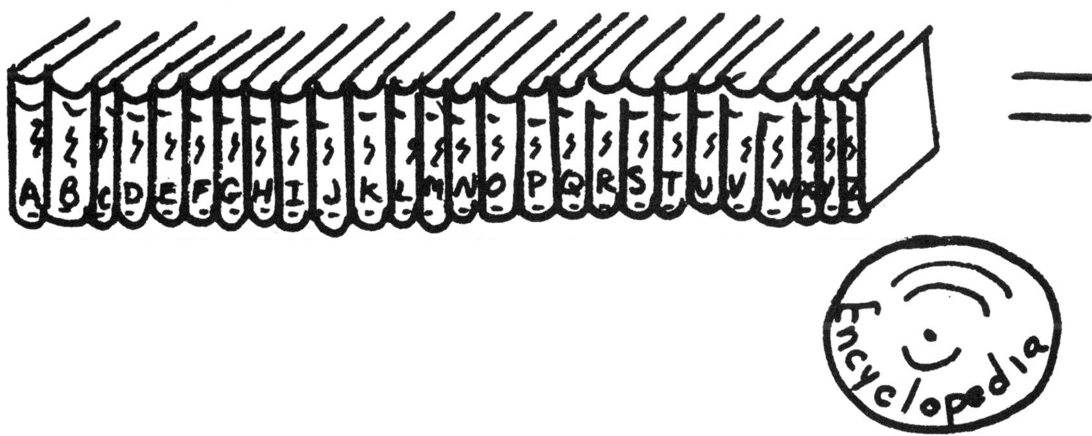

"I couldn't do it without you," said Computer Brain. "Let's load up the encyclopedia. I want to find out about eyes, ears, noses, mouths, and fingers. I hear they are important for loading information into boys and girls."

Lesson 3-4 Questions

1. Why is Susie Software important? (She has the programs we want to use.)
2. What are programs? (games, stories, and other computer activities)
3. Who helps Susie fill Computer Brain's memory? (CD-ROM and Hard Drive)
4. What do you use to put information into your brain? (eyes, ears, nose, mouth, hands)
5. How does a computer get information? (factory — chips, hard drive; you — disks)
6. How should Susie sit while she is waiting for CPU? (on her edge on a safe shelf, away from things that hurt her)
7. Why? (to avoid damage by falling, getting bent, sunlight, food, water)
8. How does Susie help Hard Drive? (backs up and saves special information)
9. What is another name for "fill" that is used with computer memory? (load)
10. Will computers come from the factory with all the programs you will ever want? (no)

LESSON 3-5 CD-ROM – GETTING BETTER EVERY DAY

To the Teacher

Susie Software and CPU talk about the old days. Susie is reminded that even with CD-ROM and Hard Drive around, she is still needed. CD-ROM tells Susie how they are alike and how they are different. Susie remembers that her mother had told her there would always be changes, and that change was good. Susie knows she isn't being replaced; she has just joined a bigger team — or is it the other way around? She also knows that the computer is one big family, and that it is always changing and always getting better.

New words in this lesson: There are no new words.

I. Objectives

- Compare the different kinds of storage devices.
- Comprehend the sizes and functions of computers — past and present.

II. Instructional Input and Learning Activities

- Make overhead transparencies for each page of the story.
- Place the transparency on the stage of the overhead projector and cover the portion of the page you are not using.
- Read the story to the children.

III. Check for Understanding

Use the review questions at the end of the story to test for story comprehension. Cover the questions as you read the last page of the story. Answers are in parentheses.

IV. Guided Practice

The "Same but Different" work sheet is designed to help students learn that objects do not always have to be the same to be able to accomplish the same task.

Duplicate the work sheet for students and instruct them to draw a line to pictures of objects that look different but can accomplish the same task. The answer sheet follows the work sheet.

V. Independent Practice and Application Using the Computer

Play a software game that reinforces the lesson.

LESSON 3-5 CD-ROM – GETTING BETTER EVERY DAY

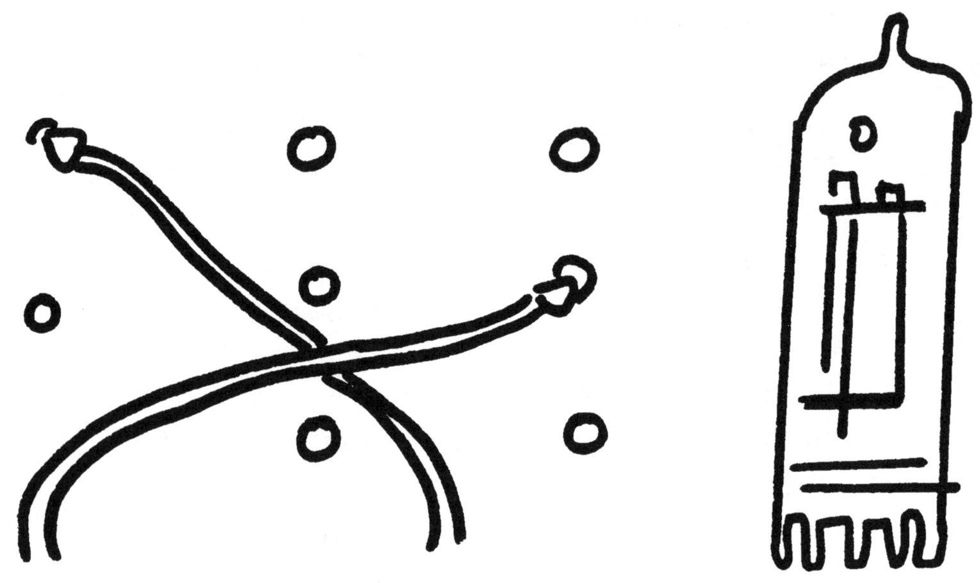

Susie Software has lived in Computer Land for a long time. Before Susie came along, if you wanted to do different things with your computer you had to change wire plugs from one hole to another.

Computers really didn't do the things that you are interested in. They did not play games, or write stories, or teach anything.

When Susie was born, it was super. She could keep the games and other programs on her disks and use them whenever she wanted.

Susie started out very big, about the size of your computer screen, because computers were very big also. As Susie noticed that computers were getting smaller and smaller, she got smaller and smaller, too. She has shrunk so that some disks are the size of your shirt pocket.

One strange thing is that, even though she has shrunk in size, she can remember more and more.

Susie was talking to Computer Brain, better known as CPU. She said, "Remember when you were as big as a room, and so hot that you burned out bulbs every five minutes?"

CPU said, "I remember. I like the way I am now. I can be so tiny that people can carry me on their wrists. I have shrunk in size, but not in brain power. My brain has gotten a whole lot bigger."

Susie said, "You have some changes besides your size."

CPU looked around. "Yes," he said. "Isn't that wonderful?"

"Sometimes I think you don't need me as much as you used too," said Susie, sadly.

CPU tried to think before he talked. He didn't want to hurt Susie's feelings. She was right. Her friends, CD-ROM and Hard Drive, were sometimes taking over for Susie, and she knew that.

CPU said, "It really does help to have CD-ROM and Hard Drive with us."

Susie said, "I know that, but I just need to know that I'm still important to you."

"Hard Drive and CD-ROM Drive are important to me, but so are you," said CPU.

"Boo hoo, boo hoo. I just don't feel needed anymore." Susie started crying.

"Why don't we talk to them before you get so upset?" said CPU.

Hard Drive spoke first. He said, "I am round like you, and I can remember programs like you, Susie. Don't you remember when you wanted CPU to have me?"

"No, no, no. You don't need me anymore," said Susie.

"That is not true," said Hard Drive. "You are on the outside of CPU. You give me your information and I keep it inside. You are there in case I forget my programs, or they get changed by accident. You are a BACKUP, and that is very important. I can't remember every program you know, so there is no way you could ever be replaced."

CPU said, "You are also needed to SAVE information for me outside of me. That is really important."

Susie felt a little better. "What about CD-ROM?" she asked.

CD-ROM said, "I'm just a shiny sister of yours, without a jacket. I sit right next to you, and can be used like you, and I have more memory than you, but you can do one thing I can't."

"What's that?" asked Susie.

"You can SAVE. I can't. All of my information comes from the factory. Your information can come from another computer," said CD-ROM.

CPU said, "I still need you. Your jobs may change a little. You have a big shiny sister who can give me programs but not SAVE them. And you have an inside brother who can work with the information you give him, but would never have enough room for all the software you have."

Susie remembered that her mother had told her a long time ago that there would always be changes, and that change was good. It was good to have her sister and brother as companions to help her with the programs that made CPU the exciting fellow he was.

Susie wasn't going to be replaced; she had just joined a bigger team — or was it the other way around? It was Susie's team, and Hard Drive and CD-ROM had joined her — to make CPU work better and faster.

Yes, that is the way she liked to think about it. She was the Big Sister. She still had to BACK UP her little sister and brother. Isn't that what all sisters and brothers do?

The computer family is one big family. It is always changing and always getting better.

Lesson 3-5 Questions

1. If you wanted to change programs before Susie came along, how did you do it? (moved wires and plugs)
2. Is Susie always the same size? (no — keeps getting smaller)
3. Is her memory getting smaller also? (no, bigger)
4. Who were Susie's little sister and brother? (CD-ROM and Hard Drive)
5. Where is Hard Drive located? (inside CPU's case)
6. What does Susie do? (new programs, backs up Hard Drive, and saves work)
7. Can CD-ROM and Susie do all the same things? (No. CD-ROM can't save work.)
8. Can Hard Drive remember every program? (no)
9. Can you save information on the hard drive? (yes)
10. Who has more memory — Susie or CD-ROM? (CD-ROM)

Name ______________________________

Same but Different

Same but Different (Answers)

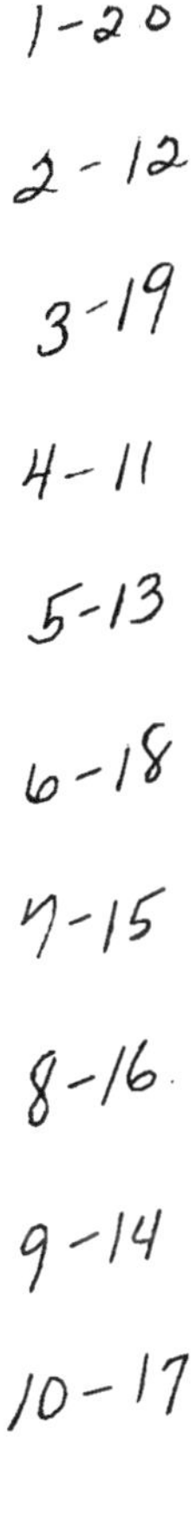

LESSON 3-6 RYAN AND THE MAGIC WINDOW

To the Teacher

Ryan learns that his computer's Windows program can make it very easy to use and enjoy software. All he needs to do is point and click his mouse to play games, write stories, draw pictures, and do thousands of other things without leaving his computer.

New words in this lesson: scroll bar

I. Objectives

- Identify the purpose of windows on computers.
- Understand the function of windows software.
- Realize that windows make computer activity easy.

II. Instructional Input and Learning Activities

- Make overhead transparencies for each page of the story.
- Place the transparency on the stage of the overhead projector and cover the portion of the page you are not using.
- Read the story to the children.

III. Check for Understanding

Use the review questions at the end of the story to test for story comprehension. Cover the questions as you read the last page of the story. Answers are in parentheses.

IV. Guided Practice

The object of the "Describe-O" game is to develop visualization skills. Students take turns trying to guess a secret object that is clearly visible to all. There is no penalty for a wrong guess, and the correct guess receives points. Decide on a point value and reduce it each time a new clue is added. Five points for the first clue make a good starting value. Keep track of the students' names and points earned on the board. The student with the most points is the winner. This is a good game for describing computer functions as well as objects in the classroom.

Example: Start with one clue; give as many as five.

1. I am looking at something that is small.
2. I am looking at something that is connected by wires.
3. I am looking at something that has movable parts.
4. I am looking at something that helps you use your computer.
5. I am looking at something that you point, click, and drag.

If it took five clues for the correct guess, the student receives one point.

V. Independent Practice and Application Using the Computer

Play a software game that reinforces the lesson.

LESSON 3-6 RYAN AND THE MAGIC WINDOW

Ryan was looking out the computer room window. He said, "You can see so many different things to do when you look through a window."

Ms. Barbara said, "That is true for computer 'windows' too."

There aren't any windows on a computer," Ryan said.

"Yes there are," said Ms. Barbara. "The computer windows are almost like magic. Monty Monitor's screen is a window to everything your computer can do. It is like a magic window, because you are able to do so many different things."

"A window in a Windows program is a rectangle on your screen that shows many different kinds of word information and pictures, or icons. Windows have names — titles of programs, of what you are going to do. You just point to a program and double-click the mouse button."

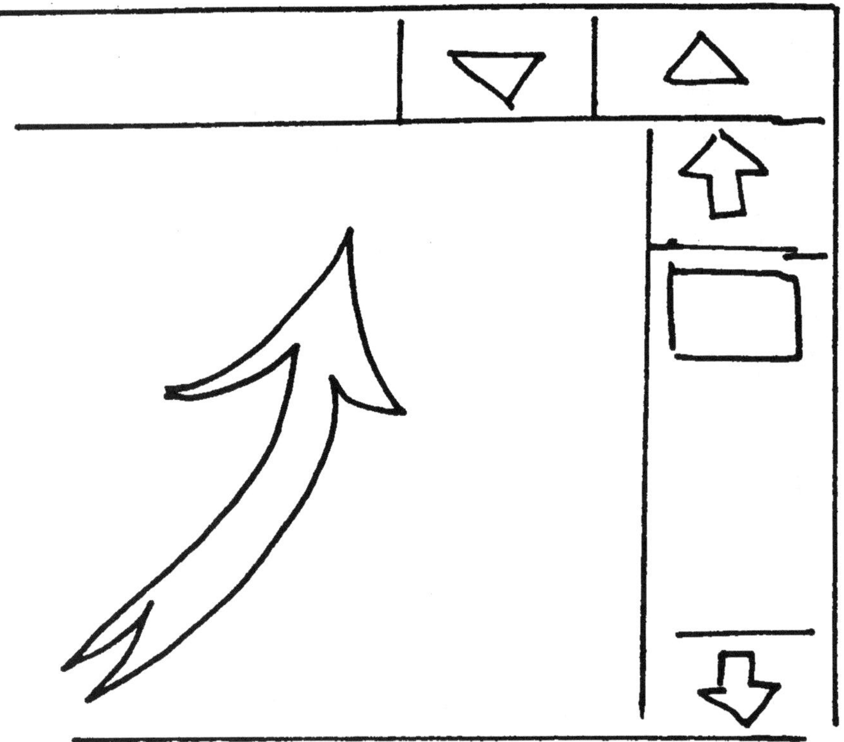

"Windows can show parts of a picture or story and you can use the side arrows to see the entire picture with something called a SCROLL BAR. The scroll bar moves with your mouse arrow to see the whole picture."

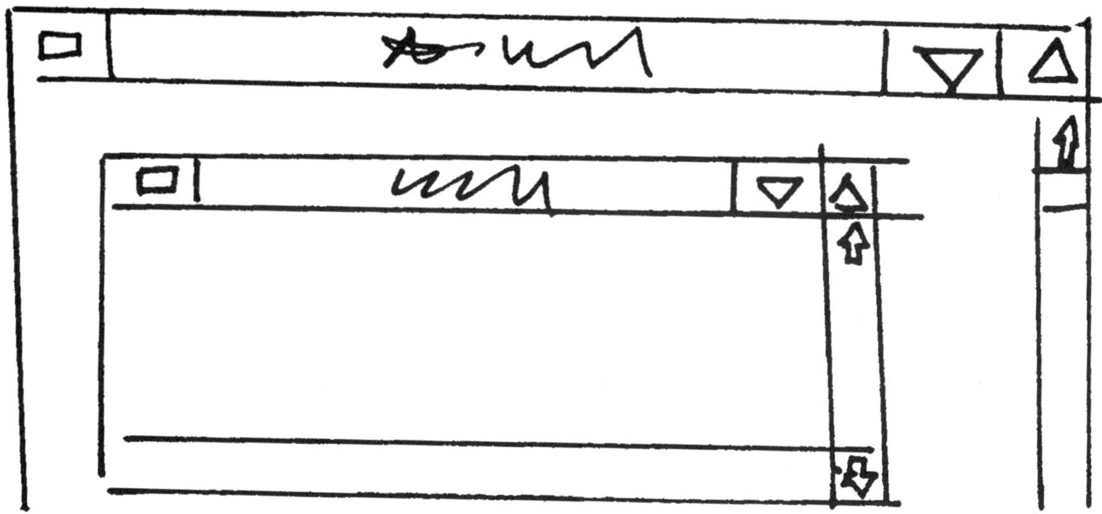

"Windows can stack smaller information windows on top of one another."

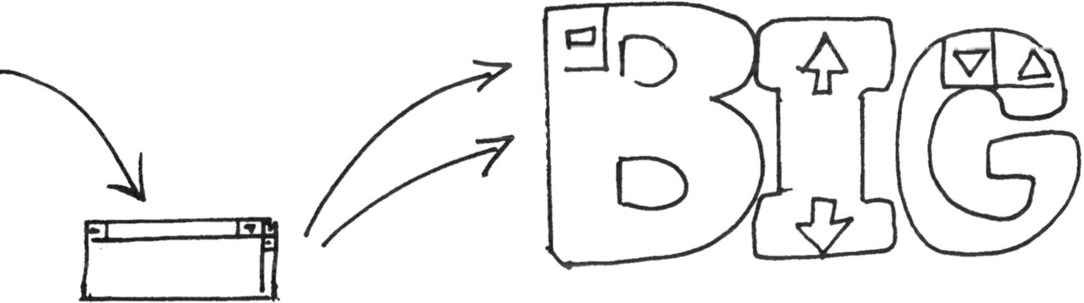

"Windows can grow smaller or bigger. They can open and close."

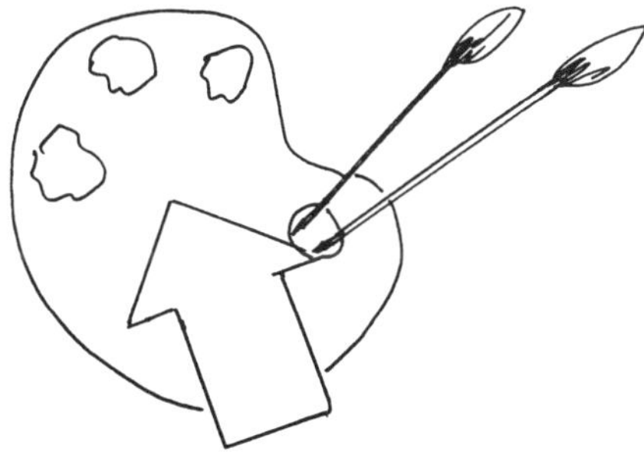

"Windows show icons, or pictures, to take you to games and other activities in your computer's memory. Hundreds of different things to do are right at the touch of your mouse finger—like magic. All you have to do is point and double-click the program you want to play, then enjoy it."

"You can see so many different things to do when you look through a window—a house window or a computer window. I don't need magic. All I need is a Windows program and my mouse finger. Let's do it," said Ryan.

Lesson 3-6 Questions

1. What is Ryan's "magic window?" (the screen of his monitor)
2. Why is it magic? (because he can see so many different things on it)
3. What is a "window"? (a rectangle on your screen that shows different kinds of information — words and pictures)
4. How do you see a picture or words that are larger than the monitor screen? (use the side arrows with the scroll bar)
5. How does the scroll bar move? (with your mouse arrow)
6. How do you scroll? (use the side arrow)
7. How do you work from a large field of information to a smaller one? (open and stack windows on top of one another)
8. What part of the computer is used to open, close, scroll, and choose information? (mouse button)
9. How do you use the mouse to select window information? (point to a program and double-click)
10. What does Ryan need to play and enjoy? (a Windows program and his mouse finger)

Glossary

alt key—used with another key to perform a specific task.

arrow keys—keyboard buttons which move the cursor up, down, left, or right without leaving marks.

back up copy—saving of computer work on a disk, hard drive, or paper to protect against information loss.

binary—the two-number code of ones and zeros.

caps lock—key which changes lower case letters to upper case. It does not affect the number keys.

CD-ROM—compact disk—read only memory—a laser disk with programs for the computer. It does not save your personal computer information.

centipede—a plastic carrier for a chip to connect it to the mother board or any other board in the computer.

characters—the symbols on the letter and number keys.

chip—a thin piece of silicon that contains the components of an electronic circuit.

click—one of the three things a mouse does. Clicking is the same as pressing the return key.

comma—a character used to separate a series of words or numbers.

computer—an electronic device, made up of several components that can be instructed to store, process, and manipulate data at very fast speeds.

control key—used with another key to perform a specific task.

CPU—central processing unit—the computer's brain.

cursor—the blinking square or I—bar that marks the exact position the computer is accessing.

data base—an organized collection of one or more files of information in a format of fields and records.

delete—remove information.

digital—information in binary units of 1=on, and 0=off.

disk drive—part of the computer system that reads and writes data and computer instructions on magnetic disks.

dot-matrix—least expensive printer. It uses a pattern of tiny dots to form images.

drag—one of the three things a mouse does. Drag lets you hold the button down and carry a picture or object or information from one place to another.

electricity—power used to run computers, lights, television.

enter key—like return key, tells the computer to work.

escape key—enables you to exit software programs.

format—make disks compatible with computer to receive information.

function keys—let you perform specific tasks quickly.

golden rule—"Do unto others as you would have them do unto you"—gentle treatment of computers.

hard copy—permanent paper copy of computer produced material.

hard drive—disk with high capacity, inside a computer used to store programs and information.

hardware—all of the parts of a computer you can see or touch.

highlighted—emphasis given to an object or word by giving the object a different look from the surrounding objects.

home row—the placement of fingers on the keyboard to be able to type quickly. The letters are asdfghjkl.

inkjet—a low-priced printer that forms images with a print head that sprays ink on the page through tiny holes.

icons—graphic objects representing options or actions to be performed.

input—data entered into a computer.

integrated circuits—a complete circuit on a chip.

Internet—a computer network made up of smaller networks that offer various services like sending letters and information all over the world.

jacket—protective covering for a computer disk made of paper or plastic.

keyboard—input device for a computer; looks like typewriter keys.

label—sticky paper on a disk that tells the name of the program.

laser—a high quality printer that uses a laser beam to form images on the page.

librarian—person who arranges and stores books for human use.

load—the act of inputting information into a computer.

main menu—the screen of a software program that displays your choices.

maze—a network of paths, some with dead ends, to confuse and bewilder.

memory—the place in a computer system where data and programs are stored temporarily.

microscope—a device to see very small objects.

microwave—a device to cook food really fast.

modem—a device for computers to communicate around the world using telephone lines.

monitor—the part of the computer that lets you see what the computer is doing.

mouse—a device used to input information by pointing, clicking, and dragging the button.

notebook—a portable all-in-one computer resembling a large book when closed.

numerical keypad—a grouping of the number keys for fast input of numerical information.

output—printed or otherwise displayed information that is the finished product of a computer.

point—one of the three things the mouse does—lets you select and manipulate information by denoting where you are.

printer—a device to make a hard copy of the computer's work on track paper or single sheets.

process—perform operations on data.

program—step-by-step instructions that tell a computer how to perform a task or solve a problem.

QWERTY—the line of letters in the top row of the most widely used keyboard—computer or typewriter.

rectangle—a four sided shape with the opposite sides the same length and four ninety degree angles.

return key—like enter key, used to tell the computer to work.

save—store computer information either to a disk or hard drive.

scroll bar—a mouse-activated part of a windows program used to see parts of the information outside of the present viewing area.

shift key—the button which changes lower case letters to upper case, and numbers to symbols.

signals—electronic pulses of information.

silicon—component of common sand, second most abundant element on earth. Used to make computer chips.

soft copy—information on a computer screen or disk.

software—directions for a computer. Also called a program.

space bar—moves the cursor right, divides words.

special keys—have duties other than printing letters, numbers or symbols—escape, shift, tab, enter, return.

splash screen—title of the software on the monitor, comparable to the title page of a book.

switch—a device to change electronic machines from on to off or vice versa.

supermarket checker—person who uses computerized scanning equipment.

symbol—something chosen to represent something else.

tower—a case shape of a computer that sits on the floor instead of the table.

track paper—connected pages of computer paper with holes at the sides to grab cogs and move the paper through the printer.

transistor—semiconductors used to open and close an electronic circuit.

vacuum tube—electronic bulbs, resembling light bulbs, without air used to power early computers—were not reliable.

versatile—capable of changing.

windows—areas on a computer screen to access programs by mouse.

world wide web—computer sites around the world sharing pictures, video and sound communication links and other computer sites by highlighted (hypertext) words.

x-ray—a means of producing a photographic image of the internal structures of the human body.